PACIFIC
VICTORY

PACIFIC VICTORY

TARAWA TO OKINAWA 1943–1945

FOREWORD BY BRIG-GEN E.H. SIMMONS USMC (RET)

DERRICK WRIGHT

First published in 2005
This edition published in 2010

The History Press
The Mill, Brimscombe Port
Stroud, Gloucestershire, GL5 2QG
www.thehistorypress.co.uk

British Library Cataloguing in Publication Data.
A catalogue record for this book is available from the British Library.

ISBN 978 0 7524 5813 7

Typesetting and origination by The History Press
Printed in India by Replika Press Pvt. Ltd.
Manufacturing managed by Jellyfish Print Solutions Ltd

CONTENTS

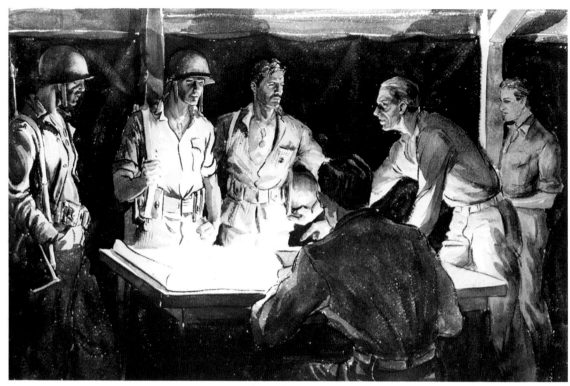

Final Instructions at Guadalcanal, a painting by Col Donald L. Dickson. (USMC Art Collection)

A flame-thrower in action in the Bougainville jungle, April 1944. (National Archives)

FOREWORD

In *Pacific Victory* Derrick Wright demonstrates once again his facility for compressing vast amounts of information into a short coherent narrative, in this case the Second World War as it was fought in the Pacific Ocean Area. As a centerline for this, Wright has chosen to follow the progress of Adm Chester Nimitz's advance across the Central Pacific, a strategic counteroffensive that had been contemplated in contingency planning for the long-foreseen war with Japan and as set down in the not-so-secret US War Plan Orange.

It would be an essentially naval war with the Army and what was still at first the Army Air Corps playing supporting roles. A subset to this planning was the work of the US Marine Corps, which, with minuscule budgets, drew up paper solutions to the amphibious assault of fortified positions, based largely on lessons learned from the failure of the British at Gallipoli in 1915. All of this was war-gamed at the Naval War College in Newport, Rhode Island. Complementary studies went on at Marine Corps Schools in Quantico, Virginia. A few Fleet exercises squeezed out of slender operating budgets gave a practical but limited testing of tentative doctrine.

The results, when war came, were remarkably prophetic. As a sop to the Army, Plan Orange promised a reinforcement of the Philippines, but the admirals in their heart-of-hearts doubted that the Japanese could be stopped short of Hawaii. It is said that the only unforeseen surprise was the emergence of the aircraft carrier as the dominant capital ship, supplanting the heavy gunned battleship.

As peg points along the line of advance, Wright has chosen the amphibious assaults of Tarawa, the Marshalls, the Marianas, Peleliu, Iwo Jima and Okinawa. Wright's writing is studded with statistics and tables, but he gets past these with illuminating anecdotal passages that bring the fighting down to the foxhole and gun-tub level. These human touches lubricate Wright's fast-paced writing style. The surviving combatants who fought these battles are now very old men – the writer of these remarks is one of them – and they are dying off rapidly. Those who remain and their sons and grandsons will find their deeds, in a world that now seems lesser in valor, are still remembered in reminders such as *Pacific Victory*.

Edwin Howard Simmons
Brigadier General, US Marine Corps (Ret)
Director Emeritus, Marine Corps History

ACKNOWLEDGEMENTS

As with my previous books on the war in the Pacific, I have received generous help from many veterans of the battles, and I would particularly like to express my gratitude to the following: Col Charles Waterhouse USMC (ret.), for permission to reproduce some of his outstanding paintings from his book *Marines and Others*. The late Tom Lea and the US Army Center for Military History, for permission to use some of Lea's paintings and drawings. The Navy Art Collection, Washington DC, for the use of drawings by Kerr Eby. The USMC Art Collection, for the use of some of the pictures from their collection. Mr Taro Kuribayashi, for supplying photographs and unique information about his father, Gen Tadamichi Kuribayashi.

For the use of wartime and contemporary photographs of the Pacific battlefields I am indebted to Charles Owen, Robert Riebe, Eric Mailander, David Green and Thomas Climie. For other valuable information and their generous cooperation, Peter Walker, John Lane, Bert Clayton, Oliver Sweetland, Charles Owen, Thomas Climie, Robert Riebe, Dale Worley, Gen Paul Tibbets, Robert Singer and Gen James R. Jones. The wartime photographs are reproduced by courtesy of the National Archives, Washington DC, the US Marine Corps, the USMC University Archives, Quantico, the US Navy, the US Army, the US Air Force or as individually credited in the text.

Opposite: A Marine falling after being hit by shrapnel.
(USMC)

CHRONOLOGY OF THE PACIFIC WAR

1933	Japanese troops occupy northern China.
1934	Japan denounces the Washington Naval Treaties of 1922 and 1930.
1937	Japan begins all-out war with China.
1939	The USA denounces its trade pact with Japan.

1940

| September | Germany, Italy and Japan sign the Tripartite Pact; the Japanese occupy parts of French Indo-China; the USA imposes a steel embargo on Japan. |

1941

8 March	Lend-Lease Act is passed by the US Senate.
27 June	Japan declares the 'Greater East Asia Co-Prosperity Sphere'.
7 December	Japan attacks Pearl Harbor; the USA declares war on Japan.
8 December	Japan attacks the Philippines, Hong Kong, Malaya and Wake Island.
10 December	Sinking of HMS *Prince of Wales* and HMS *Repulse* off the east coast of Malaya.
11 December	Germany and Italy declare war on the USA.
24 December	Japan occupies Wake Island.
25 December	Hong Kong surrenders to Japanese forces.
31 December	Japanese troops advance on Manila, the capital of the Philippines.

1942

16 January	Japanese troops cross the Burmese border.
15 February	Gen Percival surrenders Singapore to Lt-Gen Yamashita.
12 March	Gen MacArthur is evacuated from the Philippines.
18 April	Doolittle Raid on Japan.
30 April	Japanese forces complete conquest of central Burma.
6 May	All US forces in the Philippines surrender.
7–8 May	Naval Battle of the Coral Sea; both sides lose one carrier; Japanese troops are prevented from landing at Port Moresby.
4–7 June	Naval Battle of Midway, the turning point of the Pacific War.
7 June	Japanese troops invade the Aleutian Islands.
7 August	US Marines land on Guadalcanal in the Solomon Islands.
17 August	US Marine Raiders attack Makin in the Gilbert Islands.
24 August	Naval battles off the Eastern Solomons.
11 October	Naval battles off Cape Esperance, Guadalcanal.
26 October	Naval Battle of Santa Cruz; the aircraft carrier USS *Hornet* is sunk by Japanese carrier aircraft.
15 November	A Japanese transport convoy is destroyed off Guadalcanal.
30 November	Naval Battle of Tassafaronga.

18 December — US and Australian troops engage in a fierce battle with Japanese forces in Papua New Guinea.

1943

4 January — Japanese evacuation of Guadalcanal gets under way.

11 January — President Roosevelt requests a war budget of $100,000,000,000.

1 February — All Japanese troops are evacuated from Guadalcanal.

2–5 March — Naval Battle of the Bismarck Sea; a Japanese transport convoy is sunk off Lae.

17 March — Japanese forces attack Arakan in Burma.

18 April — Adm Yamamoto shot down and killed by US fighters over Bougainville.

20 June — Japanese forces launch major attack in New Guinea.

30 June — 'Operation Cartwheel', an amphibious attack against Japanese positions in the Solomon Islands.

1 July — US forces capture Viru Harbor and consolidate positions in New Guinea.

24 August — Quadrant Conference in Quebec.

25 August — Adm Mountbatten appointed Supreme Commander, South-East Asia.

28 August — Japanese troops evacuate New Georgia and other Solomon Islands to consolidate positions on Bougainville and New Britain.

5 September — US and Australian forces land east of Lae in New Guinea.

11 September — Allies capture Salamaua in New Guinea.

15 September — Allies capture Lae.

6 October — US Marines land on Kolombangara, New Georgia.

20–23 November — Battle of Tarawa.

25 December — US Marine units land in New Britain.

29 December — Marines capture Cape Gloucester airfield.

1944

31 January–
5 February — US invasion of the Marshall Islands.

4 February — Japanese forces launch an offensive at Arakan in Burma.

18 February — Task Force 58 attack Truk; 400,000 tons of shipping is sunk and 270 aircraft are destroyed.

21 February — Gen Tojo is appointed Chief of Staff of the Japanese Army.

29 February — US troops land on Admiralty Islands.

8 March — Japanese forces begin drive on Imphal – 'Operation U-Go'.

9 March — Japanese forces go on the offensive in Bougainville.

16 March — Japanese forces cross the Chidwin river and advance towards Kohima along the road from Imphal.

29 March — Siege of Imphal; US task forces attack in the Caroline Islands.

5 April — British forces in Kohima surrounded.

22 April — US forces land in Hollandia, New Guinea.

17 May — US forces land on Wadke Island, New Guinea.

27 May — US Marines attack Biak.

3 June — End of the Battle of Kohima.

15 June — US forces invade Saipan in the Marianas; island secured on 13 July.

19–20 June — Naval Battle of the Philippines Sea (Turkey Shoot) – 250 Japanese aircraft destroyed.

21 July — Invasion of Guam in the Marianas; island secured on 8 August.

24 July — Invasion of Tinian in the Marianas; island secured on 1 August.

25–7 July — Task Force 58 attack the Palau Islands.

31 August — Task Force 58 attack the Bonin Islands.

15 September — Battle of Peleliu; island secured on 12 October.

17 September — US troops invade Angaur; island secured on 23 October.

10–11 October	Task forces raid Formosa, Ryukyus and Luzon.
20 October	US landings on Leyte, the start of the invasion of the Philippines.
23–6 October	Naval Battle of Leyte Gulf – Japanese forces lose 4 aircraft carriers, 3 battleships, 10 cruisers, 11 destroyers; US lose 1 light carrier, 2 escort carriers, 3 destroyers, 2 submarines.
25 November	First B29 'Superfortress' bombing raid on the Japanese mainland from the Marianas.
26–7 December	Major Japanese counter-attacks on Leyte.

1945

1 January	US Army starts mopping-up operations on Leyte.
6 January	Task forces attack in Lingayen Gulf; major kamikaze attacks.
23 January	US 6th Army approach Clark Field on Luzon.
1 February	US 6th Army drive towards Manila, the capital of the Philippines.
13 February	British 14th Army cross the Irrawaddy river, south of Mandalay.
16 February	Task Force 58 raid Tokyo and Yokohama with over 1,000 carrier planes.
19 February	Battle of Iwo Jima; island secured on 26 March.
24 February	US forces control most of Manila.
8 March	US troops land on Mindanao in the southern Philippines.
10 March	Fire raid on Tokyo by B29s; Japanese casualties are in excess of 80,000.
13 March	British 14th Army cut the escape route for Japanese forces from Mandalay.
19 March	Japanese forces are driven out of Mandalay.

29 March	US Navy bombards Okinawa.
1 April	Start of Battle of Okinawa; island secured on 22 June.
6 April	Start of mass kamikaze attacks on US fleet off Okinawa.
7 April	Japanese super battleship *Yamato* sunk.
12 April	Death of President Roosevelt; Harry S. Truman is sworn in.
10 May	British 14th Army link up with forces from Arakan cutting off all Japanese forces west of the Irrawaddy.
14 May	B29 bombing raids on Japan continue.
19 May	End of Japanese resistance on Luzon.
25 May	Chiefs of Staff draw up plans for the invasion of the Japanese mainland.
10 June	Australian forces invade Borneo.
1 July	Australian forces invade Balikpapan.
10 July	Task Force 30 launch a 1,000-aircraft raid on Tokyo from its carriers.
16 July	First Atomic bomb successfully tested at Los Alamos in New Mexico.
18 July	US carrier planes sink the battleship *Nagato* in Tokyo Bay.
2 August	B29 bombers drop 6,600 tons of incendiaries on five Japanese cities.
6 August	Atomic bomb dropped on Hiroshima; 80,000 dead and 80,000 injured.
9 August	Second atom bomb dropped on Nagasaki; 40,000 dead and 60,000 injured.
13 August	US carriers launch a 1,600-plane attack on Tokyo.
14 August	Japan agrees to an unconditional surrender.
16–28 August	Japanese forces surrender in Manila, Java, Manchuria and Rangoon.
2 September	Surrender document signed aboard the battleship USS *Missouri* in Tokyo Bay.

INTRODUCTION

A NEW SUN RISING

Japan's emergence as a major military and political power in the Pacific began in the middle of the nineteenth century, after hundreds of years of self-imposed feudalism. The arrival of Commodore Perry's 'black ships' in Tokyo Bay in 1853, bringing offers of trade with the West, led to the signing of the Treaty of Kanagawa in 1854 and the establishment of a US consulate in Tokyo. By 1858, most of Japan's major ports were open to Western trade. With the deposition of the shoguns, the warlords who had virtually controlled the country for centuries, imperial power was restored under the Emperor Meiji. However, real control was maintained by a political and military clique interposed between the Emperor and the Diet, the Japanese parliament, a system that was to continue until the end of the war in 1945.

Japan rapidly adopted the industrial and military skills of the West, and, armed with a belief that they had a divine right to rule in eastern Asia, Japanese forces embarked upon a programme of expansion. Under the Emperor Taisho, a short, fierce war in 1895 against the Chinese gave them control of Korea, Formosa and the Liatung Peninsula on the Yellow Sea coast, and in 1904, forgoing a declaration of war, they attacked Russian shipping at Inchon and Port Arthur. In the ensuing Russo–Japanese War the Japanese were victorious on land in Korea and Manchuria; and, more significantly, at sea in the great naval Battle of Tsushima in May 1905, when most of the Russian Fleet was destroyed for negligible Japanese losses.

It was at this time that the USA began to emerge as a significant power in the Pacific; and the acquisition of the Philippine Islands and Guam in the Marianas, as part of the spoils of the Spanish–American War of 1898, sowed the seeds of distrust between the two powers. Japan's alliance with the Western Powers in the First World War was rewarded at the 1919 Treaty of Versailles with the trusteeship of the former German possessions in the Marshall and Caroline Islands, and Saipan and Tinian in the Marianas, all of which were to become vital parts of Japan's outer defence perimeter in 1941. The Washington Naval Treaty of 1921–2 attempted to control the size of US, British and Japanese Fleets in the Pacific, but the larger tonnage allowed to the USA and Britain because of their Atlantic commitments was seen as a humiliation, and Japan renounced the treaty in 1934. The Wall Street Crash of 1929 and the

MONGOLIA

MANCHURIA

CHINA

TIBET

INDIA

KOREA

SEA OF JAPAN

J

OKINAWA

IWO JIM

FORMOSA

BURMA

HONG KONG

FRENCH INDOCHINA

SIAM

LUZON

PHILIPPINE
ISLANDS

SOUTH CHINA SEA

MINDANAO

MALAYA

SUMATRA

BORNEO

CELEBES

JAVA

SOUTH-EAST ASIA
COMMAND

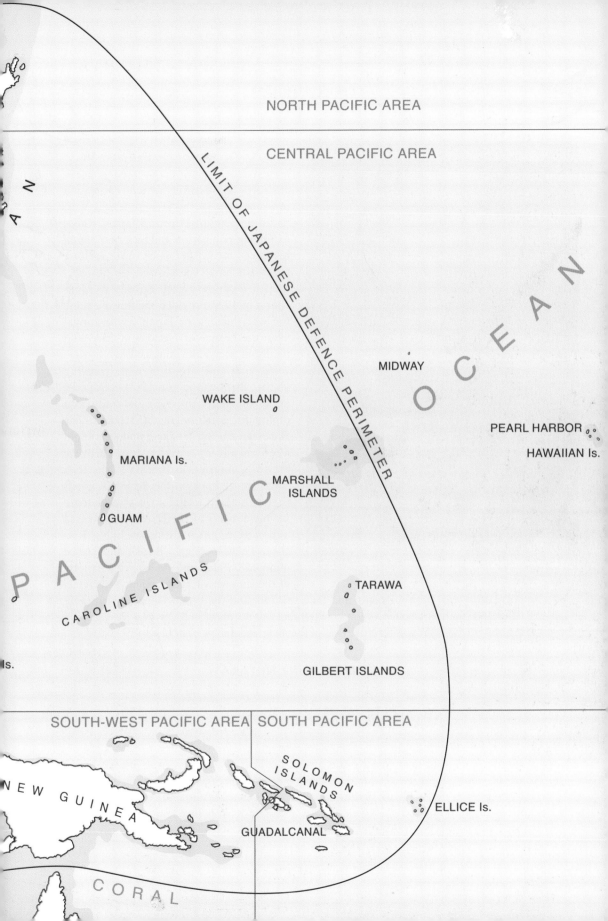

NORTH PACIFIC AREA

CENTRAL PACIFIC AREA

LIMIT OF JAPANESE DEFENCE PERIMETER

PACIFIC OCEAN

MIDWAY

WAKE ISLAND

PEARL HARBOR

HAWAIIAN Is.

MARIANA Is.

MARSHALL ISLANDS

GUAM

TARAWA

CAROLINE ISLANDS

GILBERT ISLANDS

Is.

SOUTH-WEST PACIFIC AREA   SOUTH PACIFIC AREA

NEW GUINEA

SOLOMON ISLANDS

ELLICE Is.

GUADALCANAL

CORAL

Emperor Hirohito, the Japanese Head of State and Supreme Commander of all the Armed Forces. (Real War Photos)

ensuing depression, which continued until the start of the Second World War, had a devastating effect on Japan, whose exploding population and lack of material resources forced her once more to look towards China. The blowing-up of a section of Japanese-owned railway in Manchuria in 1931 provided the flimsy excuse for war, leading to Japan's withdrawal from the League of Nations in 1933 and to all-out war with China in 1937.

Viewing the situation with growing alarm, Britain and the USA conducted an escalating campaign of trade and diplomatic sanctions against Japan. The American ban on Japanese immigration in 1924 had already soured relations between the two countries. In June 1938 the USA placed restrictions on the export of goods that would be useful in war and froze Japanese assets in the USA and increased aid to Nationalist China's Chiang Kai-shek. The Americans, British and Dutch imposed an embargo on strategic exports in the summer of 1941. Japan had signed the Tripartite Pact with Germany and Italy in 1940, and the Russo-Japanese Neutrality Pact of 1941 with the Soviet Union ensured that her northern borders were safe, leaving her free to being what was to prove one of the most unequal wars in history.

'CLIMB MOUNT NIITAKA'

'What did you think about Pearl Harbor? I never thought about anything except my duty and my work.'

(Capt Tadashi Kojo)

That the USA was surprised by the attack on Pearl Harbor is probably the most startling fact of the entire war. It was widely recognised by the US Government that the only country in the Pacific with the capability of attacking them, and the only one with any reason for doing so, was Japan; for decades the US Navy had carried out its Pacific exercises in accordance with 'Plan Orange', a thinly disguised code for war with Japan. Questions and conspiracy theories abound as to whether Roosevelt and Churchill knew in advance about the forthcoming attack and allowed it to happen to ensure the USA's entry into the war; what cannot be questioned is that cryptanalysts from the USA, Britain and Australia had already broken parts of the Japanese diplomatic codes charting the rapid breakdown of relations between Japan and the US, and that the main Japanese naval cipher, JN25, had been compromised as early as 1932. Whatever the political ramifications, the fact remains that at 6 a.m. on 7 December 1941 a wave of 183 Japanese aircraft attacked the US Pacific Fleet at anchor in Pearl Harbor, and that an hour later a second wave of 170 aircraft arrived to complete the devastation.

The Pearl Harbor attack was the brainchild of Fleet Adm Isoroku Yamamoto, who had been appointed Commander of the Combined Fleet in 1939. A veteran of the great naval Battle of Tsushima in 1905, he had spent a number of years in America in the 1920s and was an advocate of naval air power. Yamamoto had been influenced to some extent by the spectacular success of the Royal Navy's Fleet Air Arm at Taranto in 1940, when a few obsolete biplane torpedo bombers had sunk or disabled a large proportion of the Italian Fleet, and he was convinced that carrier-launched attacks were destined to play a vital part in future operations. The 1st Air Fleet, composed of Japan's 6 largest carriers and accompanied by 2 battle-cruisers, 9 destroyers, 3 submarines and a train of tankers and supply ships, had assembled in the anchorage

Adm Isoroku Yamamoto. Yamamoto tried to deal a
knockout blow to the United States by planning and
executing the Pearl Harbor attack in December 1941.
(National Archives)

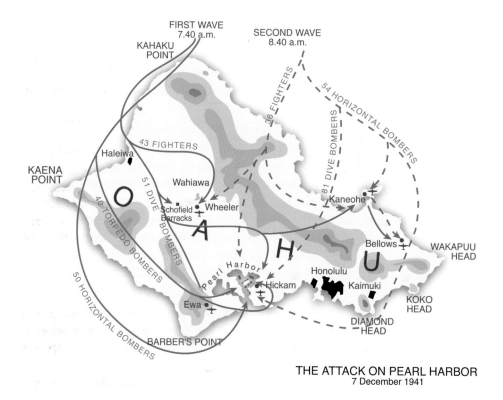

THE ATTACK ON PEARL HARBOR
7 December 1941

of Etorofu in the Kurile Islands in northern Japan. Commanded by Vice-Adm Chuichi Nagumo, the fleet sailed to a point some 275 miles north of Oahu and awaited the coded message for the attack – 'Climb Mount Niitaka'.

Assembled around Ford Island in the centre of Pearl Harbor were 70 warships of the US Pacific Fleet: 8 battleships, 2 heavy cruisers, 6 light cruisers, 29 destroyers, 5 submarines and 24 auxiliaries; there were no torpedo nets, no barrage balloons, no facilities for smokescreens, and the bulk of the ammunition was locked away. Most of the officers and enlisted men were anticipating a quiet Sunday after the regular Saturday evening shore leave, but their hopes were soon shattered. Working to tactics that they had rehearsed for months, the torpedo and dive-bombers swooped on 'Battleship Row' and the barracks and airfields on Oahu, achieving total surprise.

The damage sustained by US forces was huge: 5 battleships and 3 destroyers sunk; 3 battleships and 2 cruisers badly damaged; 200 Army and Navy aircraft destroyed and 3,478 personnel killed or wounded. Yamamoto had hoped to wipe out most of the US Navy carrier force in the attack, but his intelligence was obviously at fault: the *Yorktown* was in the Atlantic, the *Saratoga* was undergoing repairs in San Diego, and the *Enterprise* and the *Lexington* were returning from Midway and Wake Island after delivering aircraft to Marine units. Lt-Cdr Mitsuo Fuchida, operational leader of the attack, urged Nagumo to send in a third wave of aircraft to destroy the tank farms and engineering shops which stood untouched, but the Admiral's timidity prevailed and an opportunity to neutralise Pearl Harbor completely was lost. Had these facilities been destroyed, the remains of the Pacific Fleet would probably have had to retire to the US West Coast. Nevertheless, Yamamoto's huge gamble had paid off and his faith in naval air power had been vindicated. The Japanese were amazed at the scale of their victory; the bulk of the US Pacific Fleet had been put out of action for the loss of twenty-nine Japanese aircraft and fifty-five aircrew.

The news of the attack was greeted with horror throughout the USA, and President Roosevelt's speech marking the 'date that will live in infamy' was a prelude to the declaration of war against Japan on 8 December 1941. Germany's and Italy's declarations of war against America on the 11th marked the turning point of the global conflict. The USA's isolationist stance was over; victory over the Axis, though the struggle would be long and costly, was guaranteed; and Adm Yamamoto's prediction that 'we have wakened a sleeping giant' was to prove tragically prophetic.

THE JAPANESE OCTOPUS

Pearl Harbor marked the beginning of a series of disasters for the Allies that would continue until the end of 1943. Even as Nagumo's carrier planes were returning from Oahu, troops of Lt-Gen Tomoyuki Yamashita's 25th Army were being transported

The aftermath of Pearl Harbor. The USS *Maryland* towers over the upturned hull of the USS *Oklahoma*. (National Archives)

A scene of devastation at Naval Air Station, Pearl Harbor, 7 December 1941. (National Archives)

to Singora, Patani and Kota Bharu in northern Malaya; Japanese bombers were destroying the RAF's few planes at Hong Kong and troops were crossing the colony's borders; and Lt-Gen Masaharu Homma's 14th Army was occupying the northern islands of the Philippines prior to an all-out invasion. Already, two of the edicts laid out in Japan's 'Greater East Asia Co-Prosperity Sphere' were being fulfilled: the domination of the whole of the western Pacific and the expulsion of the Western imperialist powers. With the Imperial Japanese Navy now in control of most of the Pacific, there was little chance of intervention by the Allies; and, although the resources available to the Japanese for their attacks on Malaya, Burma and the Dutch East Indies were limited as the majority of Japan's fifty-one infantry divisions were spread between China, Manchuria, Korea and the Russian border, speedy and fluent advances through jungle territories that complacent Allied generals had considered impassable allowed the Army to fulfil its timetable of 50 days for the capture of the Philippines, 100 days for Malaya and 150 days for the Dutch East Indies.

'A GREAT DISASTER FOR BRITISH ARMS'

Japan's attack on the Malayan Peninsula preceded the attack on Pearl Harbor by thirty minutes, with amphibious landings at Kota Bharu and on the north-east coast in the early hours of 8 December (7th, Pearl Harbor time), which were rapidly followed by landings at Patani, Singora and at Bangkok in Siam. These operations involved two armies: the 15th, who were to occupy Siam and advance into Burma to capture Rangoon, and the 25th, who would advance through the Malayan Peninsula to Singapore, the great British naval base. Before the war it had been planned for the RAF to have 22 squadrons with 336 aircraft situated throughout the Malayan Peninsula, which would be capable of destroying any invasion fleet and dominating the sky. In fact, by December 1941 they had in place only 13 squadrons with 158 aircraft, many of them obsolete, and the Japanese, with superior-quality aircraft flying from bases in Indo-China and Siam, were able to systematically destroy the British airfields and overwhelm the outdated aircraft. Despite valiant Allied attempts to secure a line across the peninsula, Lt-Gen Yamashita's Army repeatedly forced the British and Commonwealth troops to retreat by landing behind their lines, and the campaign deteriorated into a hopeless rearguard action all the way to Singapore.

On 8 December, Vice-Adm Sir Thomas Phillips, CIC British Far Eastern Fleet, was informed of Japanese landings in northern Malaya. Phillips assembled 'Z Force', including HMS *Prince of Wales*, a new 35,000-ton battleship, HMS *Repulse*, an older 32,000-ton battlecruiser, and four destroyers, and headed northward to intercept the Japanese transports in the Gulf of Siam. Phillips requested air reconnaissance for 9 December and fighter cover for the 10th, but what remained of the RAF was desperately trying to halt the multiple Japanese assaults; most of the airfields were under constant attack and the requests could not be guaranteed.

For twenty-four hours 'Z Force' was shielded by heavy cloud and rain, but on the 9th the weather cleared long enough for enemy reconnaissance planes to locate them, so Phillips turned about and headed back for Singapore. How-ever, fresh reports were received indicating a landing at Kuantan and as this lay just a little off his return route he decided to investigate. The report proved to be false, but 'Z Force' had been spotted by a Japanese submarine and at 3.40 a.m. on 10 December aircraft of the 22nd Air Flotilla based in Indo-China were alerted. Shortly after 11.00 a.m. at approximately sixty miles east of Kuantan, eighty bombers and torpedo planes sighted 'Z Force' and the attack began. In a little over two hours both the *Prince of Wales* and the *Repulse* had been sunk with the loss of nearly a thousand men, including Adm Phillips and Capt Tennant of the *Repulse*.

In the 1920s Brig-Gen 'Billy' Mitchell of the US Army had controversially presented the view that US Navy ships, particularly battleships, were highly vulnerable to attacks from the air – a view that he pressed so vigorously that he was court-martialled and suspended from the Army. His predictions were to be tragically realised at Pearl Harbor and in the Gulf of Siam. By 31 January, the Japanese had occupied the whole of the mainland, and the island of Singapore seemed frighteningly vulnerable. On the night of 8–9 February, elements of the 5th and 18th Divisions

A Japanese infantryman, the backbone of the Japanese Army, in M1938 field dress. (National Archives)

landed on the west coast and late on the 9th the Imperial Guards Division attacked near the Johore Bharu causeway. The collapse of British resistance in Singapore was now only a question of time, and on 15 February Lt-Gen Arthur Percival surrendered his command to Lt-Gen Yamashita.

In the greatest military defeat in the history of the British Army, 138,708 service personnel surrendered to a Japanese force half that size and would go on to endure nearly four years of brutal captivity from which one-third were never to return.

The whole campaign reflected the complacency and incompetence of those who had planned the defence of the Malayan Peninsula in general and the island of Singapore in particular. Responsibility lay not only with the hapless Percival, but with the British Government's failure to provide modern aircraft and armour in sufficient quantities and in time, and above all in the arrogant and stupid underestimation of the Japanese. Gen Sir Henry Pownall, Gen Wavell's Chief of Staff, summed up the situation well. 'It is a great disaster for British arms, one of the worst in history. From the beginning to the end of this campaign we have been outmatched by better soldiers.'

'I SHALL RETURN'

'Plan Orange', America's pre-war strategic plan for war with Japan, saw the Philippines as the most important outpost in the western Pacific. In the event of war, the garrison was expected to hold out until the arrival of the Pacific Fleet and reinforcements, but events at Pearl Harbor and Japan's ability to land upwards of 100,000 troops from Formosa and the Palau Islands meant that the Philippines were doomed from the start. On 8 December, Gen Douglas MacArthur, who had been Military Adviser to the Philippines government since 1936, was recalled from retirement and given command of all forces on the islands, now designated US Army Force in the Far East (USAFFE). News of the attack on Pearl Harbor was received at 2.30 a.m. in Manila, the Philippines' capital city, the delay being due to the five time zones and 5,000 miles separating the two locations, although it must be said that MacArthur did hear the news on the radio.

Earlier in 1941, MacArthur had convinced Gen Marshall, the US Army Chief of Staff, that he could hold the Philippines if he had sufficient air power, as he did not expect any Japanese attack before 1942. As a result, more than a hundred fighters and thirty-five of the new B17 'Flying Fortress' bombers were sent to the islands. In addition, the Asiatic Fleet under Adm Thomas Hart had been increased to 3 cruisers, 13 destroyers, 6 gunboats, 6 motor torpedo boats and 29 submarines; and MacArthur also had under his command a total of 31,000 troops, including Philippine Scouts (Filipino troops in the regular US Army).

The Japanese started their attack with raids on the airfields at Clark Field and Iba, and were amazed to find most of the Far Eastern Air Force on the ground. Chaos had reigned after the news of Pearl Harbor, and Gen Lewis Brereton, the Air Force Commander, had been unable to get MacArthur to make any firm decisions – at first

GENERAL HOMMA SECURES LUZON

he had ordered his B17s south to Del Monte on Mindanao, but the order was not carried out. Brereton had asked permission to send them out on a bombing raid to Formosa to attack the Japanese airfields, but this had been denied; instead they went out on patrol (without bombs). At 10.45 a.m., MacArthur finally gave permission for the bombing raid and the B17s returned to Clark Field to bomb-up and refuel, and it was at this time that the Japanese attack began. From the north, 108 bombers escorted by 84 fighters swooped in and wreaked havoc among the neatly lined-up rows of B17s and their fighter escorts. Clark Field was reduced to rubble and almost all of the aircraft were destroyed together with the adjoining hangars and barracks. A simultaneous attack at Iba Field to the west caught the P40 fighters of the 3rd Pursuit Squadron circling to land and short of fuel, and all but two of them were shot down. In two hours, the Japanese had destroyed 17 B17s, 56 P40s and 30 other aircraft, for the loss of 7 of their own planes. The Far East Air Force had ceased to exist and from then until the final capitulation at Corregidor the US forces were virtually devoid of air cover.

Sensing the desperate situation that was developing in the Philippines, the US Navy Department ordered Adm Hart to pull out his ships – he sent nine of his destroyers and one cruiser to Borneo and two cruisers to the southern Philippines. Following the occupation of a few northern islands and the landing of a detachment at Aparri on the northern coast of Luzon, Lt-Gen Homma's 14th Army executed a classic pincer movement, landing the 48th Division at Lingayen Bay in the north-east on 22 December and the 16th Division at Lamon Bay in the south-west on the 24th. MacArthur requested reinforcements and more aircraft, but Washington had now accepted that the Philippines would have to be written off, and the General was on his own. MacArthur transferred his HQ to the tiny island of Corregidor at the entrance to Manila Bay as his troops, under Lt-Gen Jonathan Mayhew Wainwright, fought a hopeless rearguard action down the Bataan Peninsula. With diminishing supplies of ammunition and food and the added burden of thousands of Filipino civilians to support, Wainwright bravely fought on. On 22 February, Roosevelt ordered MacArthur to leave the Philippines for Australia to assume command of the newly created South West Pacific Theatre, and on 11 March he left Corregidor by PT boat for Mindanao, from where he was flown to Australia.

On 9 April, all resistance on the Bataan Peninsula ceased and Wainwright transferred his HQ to Corregidor, where the garrison surrendered on 6 May. The US and Filipino prisoners from Bataan and Corregidor now endured a 65-mile march to Camp O'Donnell. In what became infamously known as the Bataan Death March, the already starving prisoners were given no food or water and anyone breaking ranks risked death. More than 5,000 were to die on the march and only 9,300 survived until the end of the war, among them Lt-Gen Wainwright, whose emaciated figure at the Japanese surrender aboard the USS *Missouri*, along with his equally skeletal British counterpart Lt-Gen Percival, added a poignant presence.

MacArthur arrived in Australia vowing 'I shall return', and he redeemed his vow when his army retook the Philippines in 1945 after conducting a brilliant series of leaps across New Guinea and the Dutch East Indies. After the war, he was to oversee the rebuilding of Japan, and he later took charge of Allied forces during the Korean conflict, being eventually removed from command by President Harry Truman for refusing to obey orders. A vain, conceited and arrogant man, the title 'American Caesar' conferred on him by the author William Manchester was not inappropriate. However, his brilliant progress through New Guinea to Morotai, and his seemingly

Gen Douglas MacArthur. On 11 March 1942, shortly before
the fall of the Philippines, he was evacuated to Australia,
pledging, 'I shall return'. (National Archives)

instinctive ability to strike the enemy where and when it would do most damage, places him alongside Adm Chester Nimitz as one of the great commanders of the Pacific War. Nevertheless, his defence of the Philippines was seriously flawed: by allowing his air force to be destroyed on the ground and by not withdrawing to the Bataan Peninsula sooner, he must bear much of the responsibility for the debacle.

A GALLANT GARRISON

Two small but important islands were next on the Japanese list: Guam and Wake Island. Guam was a lost cause from the start. Flanked by the enemy-held islands of Saipan and Tinian, it was overwhelmed in two days; but there was to be a very different outcome to the invasion of Wake Island. Lying halfway between Guam and Pearl Harbor and some 600 miles north of Kwajalein in the Marshall Islands, Wake was actually an atoll of three islands around a lagoon, which had been designated for development as a submarine base and airstrip by the US Navy before the war. Defended by 13 officers and 365 Marines, the island also housed a considerable number of civilian workers engaged in preparing the defences. These defences consisted principally of six 5in naval guns in three batteries, three batteries of anti-aircraft guns and a number of obsolete 'Wildcat' fighters. Following three days of air raids from Kwajalein, the main invasion force arrived on 11 December, consisting of 3 light cruisers and 6 destroyers plus transports carrying 450 Special Naval Landing Force troops, all under the command of Vice-Adm Shigeyoshi Inoue.

As the Japanese ships came within range, the 5in guns opened up, damaging the light cruiser *Yubari*, sinking the destroyer *Hayate*, and damaging three other ships. Four of the US aircraft that had survived the earlier bombing raids now pursued the retreating ships, sinking the destroyer *Kisaragi* and damaging a light cruiser and two other vessels. In one short engagement the Japanese had lost over 400 sailors and airmen, an overwhelming but short-lived victory for the US forces.

As in the Philippines, confusion and indecision reigned. Adm Husband E. Kimmel, CIC of the Pacific Fleet, ordered Task Force 14 under Rear-Adm Jack Fletcher to Wake Island. But Kimmel was relieved shortly afterwards as a result of his performance at Pearl Harbor, and his temporary replacement, Vice-Adm William S. Pye, was reluctant to send a task force to Wake without direct orders from Washington; being more concerned with preserving what little remained of the Pacific Fleet, he ordered the return of Fletcher's force.

It was now just a matter of time before Wake succumbed: air raids had continued incessantly since the first assault; the Marines had no aircraft left; and ammunition, food and morale were diminishing. On the 23rd, the Japanese began landing troops at various points on the island and the garrison bowed to the inevitable. In all, the Japanese had lost over 800 dead and 300 wounded for 120 American dead. Of the 1,146 civilian workers on Wake at the time of the invasion, 70 died and 12 were wounded. Apart from 100 civilians who stayed behind on Wake, the others and remaining Marines, sailors and soldiers spent the rest of the war in POW camps. As a result of US air raids on the island in October 1943, the Japanese commander, Rear-Adm Sakaibara, had the civilian contractors executed, fearing an imminent US invasion. He was later hanged as a war criminal. The defence of Wake Island, and the fighting spirit of its defenders, was the one bright spot in a scene of gloom for the Allies in the Pacific.

THE ROAD TO MANDALAY

Having secured the northern end of the Malay Peninsula, the Japanese were free to attack Burma. The 15th Army under Lt-Gen Shojiro Iida had occupied Bangkok, the Siamese capital, on 8 December, and troops moving from the south took Victoria Point, Mergui and Tavoy in rapid succession, securing three important airfields en route. The main attack, which came from Raheng inside Siam, was directed at Moulmein; simultaneously, heavy air raids were mounted against Rangoon in which 3,000 civilians were killed. Though heavy losses inflicted on the Japanese Air Force by RAF fighters called a temporary halt to the raids, there was little overall opposition to the Japanese. The British CIC, Lt-Gen Hutton, had just taken up his post after years of deskbound appointments at home, and the only troops available were the 46th Brigade of the 17th Division, the 16th Indian Brigade and the 2nd Burma Brigade – few of these men were trained in jungle fighting and most of the best officers had been transferred to North Africa. By 26 January, Moulmein was under heavy attack and on the 31st it succumbed. Reinforcements were trickling into Rangoon, but it was becoming obvious that the city would have to be evacuated soon if there was not to be a repeat of the Singapore debacle. Gen Sir Harold Alexander, who had replaced Hutton on 5 March, ordered the evacuation on 7 March and the demolition of any equipment that could be useful to the Japanese. Successes elsewhere in South-East Asia allowed the Japanese to bolster their forces in Burma by 2 divisions, 2 tank regiments and over 200 aircraft, and as the British and Commonwealth armies moved into central Burma it was clear that the writing was on the wall. Emulating the campaign in Malaya in a series of retreats, hampered by the monsoon and appalling jungle conditions, the British retreated for 1,000 miles to the borders of India.

Vast amounts of equipment had been destroyed and 13,000 men had been lost, most of them as prisoners. The Burma Road from Lashio into China, the last land route by which Britain and the USA could send supplies to Chiang Kai-shek and the Chinese Nationalist Army was lost. Christmas 1941 was not a time for celebration: Hong Kong fell on Christmas Day and the Japanese had effectively taken control of Malaya, the Philippines and Burma. The way was now clear for the occupation of the Dutch East Indies and its huge oilfields.

THE EAST INDIES FALL

The Japanese planned a three-pronged attack on the Dutch East Indies: the western force, sailing from French Indo-China, was to head for Sumatra to capture Palembang and then move into Java; the central force, coming from the Palau Islands, would take the oilfields of Borneo and move south to join up with the western force; and the eastern force, also from the Palaus, would take the Celebes, Ambon and Timor. In overall command was Lt-Gen Imamura of the 16th Army, which was supported by units of the Special Naval Landing Force, around 450 aircraft and a naval force of 2 battleships and numerous smaller vessels under Vice-Adm Nobutake Kondo. The campaign went with astonishing ease; Sumatra suffered heavy air raids from Malaya and, although Allied air forces were able to cause some damage to the western-force troop convoys, the Japanese were able to land 3,000 troops on the Sumatra coast while paratroopers seized the main airfield and oil installations. The central force rapidly occupied Tarakan, Balikpapan and Bandjarmasin in Borneo, and by 10 February the whole island was in Japanese hands; on the same day, ground troops and paratroopers captured Menado in the Celebes and within three days they had occupied the whole island.

Japanese domination in the air had prevented Allied naval forces from playing any significant part in the defence of the East Indies, but a 'Combined Striking Force' of Dutch, British and American vessels had been assembled under Dutch Rear-Adm Karel Doorman, and on 19 February it clashed with a Japanese force in the Lombok Straits off eastern Bali. Two enemy destroyers and a transport were damaged for the loss of one Dutch destroyer, but the invasion of Bali was in no way interrupted. Another

Japanese paratroopers being dropped over the Dutch East Indies. (IWM HU2767)

battle followed on 26 February, when Doorman's ships sailed out of Surabaya on the north Java coast to intercept the invaders. The ensuing action in the Java Sea was a total disaster for the Allies, with the loss of two Dutch cruisers and two destroyers, heavy damage to the British cruiser HMS *Exeter* and the death of Rear-Adm Doorman. The Japanese had expected to occupy the Dutch East Indies in about six months – it took them only three, and the coveted oil resources were secure.

CLEARING THE INDIAN OCEAN

With the occupation of Burma now a certainty, Britain realised that there was a significant threat to the island of Ceylon, a vital link in the defence of India and an importance source of rubber following the fall of Malaya. A Japanese occupation of the island was unthinkable; it would alter the whole balance of power in the Middle and Near East. Six brigades of troops, desperately needed elsewhere, were rushed to the island and an Eastern Fleet of 5 battleships, 3 aircraft carriers, 7 cruisers and 14 destroyers, all under Adm Sir James Somerville, was assembled. The fleet looked impressive on paper, but there were serious deficiencies: four of the battleships were old, of First World War vintage, and therefore vulnerable to air attack; and one of the carriers, HMS *Hermes*, was small and carried only a few obsolete aircraft.

In fact, the Japanese had no intention of attacking Ceylon, but they saw the Eastern Fleet as a threat to their troop convoys, which were using Rangoon as their principal port of entry into Burma to supply the 15th Army. As a result Vice-Adm Nagumo's 1st Air Fleet, under the control of Vice-Adm Kondo, sailed to the Indian Ocean to intercept Somerville, and simultaneously Vice-Adm Jisaburo Ozawa led a force of 1 light carrier, 7 cruisers and 11 destroyers into the Bay of Bengal to attack merchant shipping.

Somerville split his force into two groups – the fast (the battleship HMS *Warspite* and the carriers HMS *Indomitable* and HMS *Formidable*) and the slow (four old battleships and the *Hermes*) – and patrolled south of Ceylon. But after two days there was no sign of the enemy so he detached *Hermes* to Trincomalee and two cruisers, HMS *Cornwall* and HMS *Dorsetshire*, to Columbo, and the rest of the fleet retired to a base in the Maldives. On 5 April, the Japanese fleet was spotted by reconnaissance aircraft, and Somerville immediately left the Maldives hoping to engage them; but he was over 600 miles to the west, and Japanese carrier planes caught the *Cornwall* and *Dorsetshire* and sunk both of them within twenty minutes. Somerville was now warily keeping to the south-east of Ceylon and did not make contact with Nagumo's ships, which had turned their attention to Trincomalee. They bombed the port and sank HMS *Hermes* and a destroyer before joining up with Ozawa's roving force, which had sunk 23 merchant ships totalling 112,000 tons.

The Indian Ocean episode only proved that the Royal Navy's old and semi-obsolete ships were no match for the fast Japanese carriers with their modern aircraft and experienced pilots. The Eastern Fleet was soon disbanded, leaving the Imperial Navy virtually masters of the sea.

THE DOOLITTLE RAID

President Roosevelt was very concerned about the effect on the American public of the seemingly endless string of disasters in the Pacific, and demanded some kind of morale-booster – the result was a bold and imaginative raid on the Japanese capital, Tokyo. The idea originated with Capt Francis Low, a member of Adm Ernest Joseph King's staff, who suggested that twin-engined bombers might be able to take off from the deck of an aircraft carrier. The idea was developed by Capt Donald Duncan, King's air-operations officer, and tests were carried out off the coast of Virginia with B25 'Mitchell' bombers taking off from the new carrier USS *Hornet*. Once it was established that the B25s could clear the deck (with room to spare), plans for the raid got under way in earnest.

The raid would have to be a joint Navy–Army affair. A specially created task force of two carriers with cruiser escort would get the Army flyers to within 500 miles of the Japanese coast; and after the raid the B25s would fly on to China and land at airfields under the control of Chiang Kai-shek's Nationalist Forces. The whole operation was risky and would depend on skill and outstanding leadership.

The ideal leader was already available. Lt-Col James Doolittle had an outstanding record, the holder of dozens of aviation trophies and records, the first man to fly an 'outside' loop, and the first pilot to take off, fly a course and land without seeing the ground. He was full of enthusiasm and within a month had organised and trained the crews of the sixteen B25s required for the raid.

The new task force (TF16), under Adm William Frederick Jr ('Bull') Halsey, left San Francisco on 2 April 1942. On the 18th, by which time they were within 700 miles of Japan, they were located by two enemy ships and the element of surprise was lost. The bombers were immediately dispatched, but the premature departure meant that they would have an extra 200 miles to add to their overall trip. Flying at low level, the bombers attacked targets in Tokyo, Kobe and Nagoya and then flew on to China. Many ran out of fuel and, due to incompetence and misunderstandings on the part of the Chinese, the airfield at Chuchow was in total darkness. Despite many crash landings and diversions (one crew ended up in Vladivostok in Russia!), seventy-one of the eighty crew members survived.

The damage caused by the raid was negligible, but the effect on US morale was huge and the Japanese, fearing further attacks, moved four fighter groups back to the homeland. The Chinese were to pay a fearful price for the raid when the Japanese killed over 250,000 people in reprisal, one of the worst atrocities of the war.

STALEMATE IN THE CORAL SEA

Having secured the Dutch East Indies, the Japanese now turned their attention to the east and to Port Moresby in Papua New Guinea, vital to the Allies for the security of Australia. US cryptanalysts had intercepted some of the Japanese naval code JN25 and were aware of the threat to Port Moresby; the Navy had therefore assembled a task force based on the carriers *Yorktown* and *Lexington*, with an additional Australian cruiser squadron, all under the command of Rear-Adm Frank Jack Fletcher. Hearing of a landing at Tulagi north of Guadalcanal in the Solomon Islands, Fletcher headed north to intercept it, but found that the covering naval force had already left. He then sailed to the eastern tip of New Guinea, hoping to catch the invasion convoy heading for Port Moresby, while his aircraft searched the Coral Sea for enemy carriers.

Unknown to Fletcher, a separate enemy task force under Vice-Adm Takeo Takagi had entered the Coral Sea on 5 May and was only 70 miles to his north-east. On the morning of 7 May, reconnaissance planes from both task forces reported seeing fleet carriers; both were wrong. Fletcher's planes had sighted the light carrier *Shoho*, part of the retiring escort from the Tulagi force; and Takagi's planes had sighted a destroyer and a tanker which Fletcher had detached from his main force. Carrier planes were immediately dispatched by both sides, and the *Shoho*, the destroyer (USS *Sims*) and the tanker (*Neosho*) were all sunk.

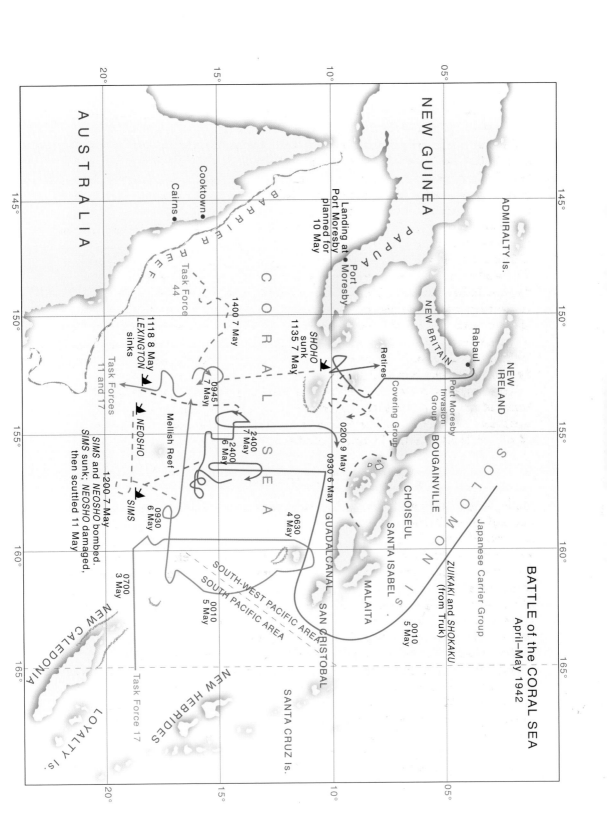

BATTLE of the CORAL SEA
April–May 1942

NEW GUINEA

PAPUA

AUSTRALIA

Cooktown
Cairns

GREAT BARRIER REEF

Task Force 44

1400
7 May

Landing at Port Moresby planned for 10 May

Port Moresby

CORAL SEA

SHOHO
sunk
1135 7 May

Retires

0945
7 May

2400
7 May

2400
6 May

0200 9 May

0930 6 May

Covering Group

1118 8 May
LEXINGTON
sinks

Task Forces
11 and 17

NEOSHO

Mellish Reef

SIMS

0930
6 May

1200 7 May
SIMS and NEOSHO bombed.
SIMS sunk; NEOSHO damaged,
then scuttled 11 May

0630
4 May

0010
5 May

GUADALCANAL

SAN CRISTOBAL

SANTA ISABEL

MALAITA

CHOISEUL

BOUGAINVILLE

SOLOMON IS

NEW BRITAIN

NEW IRELAND

Rabaul

ADMIRALTY Is.

Port Moresby
Invasion Group

Japanese Carrier Group

ZUIKAKU and SHOKAKU
(from Truk)

0010
5 May

SOUTH-WEST PACIFIC AREA
SOUTH PACIFIC AREA

0700
3 May

0010
5 May

NEW HEBRIDES

SANTA CRUZ Is.

Task Force 17

NEW CALEDONIA

LOYALTY Is.

With its fires out of control, the USS *Lexington* (CV-2) explodes and sinks in the Coral Sea. (US Navy)

An escorting destroyer picks up survivors from the doomed *Lexington*. (US Navy)

Both task forces were now aware of each other and on 8 May began mounting air strikes. The Japanese carrier *Shokaku* received three hits on her flight deck and withdrew, and seventy Japanese planes attacked the *Lexington*, causing extensive damage with bombs and torpedoes; the *Yorktown* was also damaged. By late afternoon the *Lexington* was in flames as fuel lines ruptured; the crew abandoned ship and a destroyer sank her with torpedoes. Casualties had been heavy: the Japanese lost an aircraft carrier and the use of another; 77 aircraft had been shot down and 1,074 personnel killed. US forces had lost a precious fleet carrier, and damage had been sustained to another; 66 planes were lost and 543 sailors killed.

The battle was the first in naval history to be conducted by carrier aircraft alone, without either fleet coming within sight of each other. The Japanese achieved a tactical victory but suffered a strategic defeat; the Port Moresby invasion had to be called off as Adm Shigeyoshi, Takagi's superior, regarded the depleted Japanese force as insufficient to cover the invasion.

DECISIONS, DECISIONS

Like Hitler in Europe, the Japanese were stunned by their own success. In the space of five months they had overrun Hong Kong, Malaya, Burma, Siam, Guam, Wake, the Philippines and the Dutch East Indies, and had all but swept the Allies from the Pacific Ocean. The big question was what to do next. The options were many: to the west lay Ceylon, the gateway to India, but with the Army already stretched to breaking point the military were reluctant to embark on yet another campaign; to the south lay Australia, where the Allies were already building a command structure under Gen MacArthur. In March, the 41st Division of the US Army was already on its way to Sydney, and two Australian divisions were being recalled from the Middle East.

So seriously did the Japanese regard the threat to their southern perimeter that on 19 February 1942 they bombed the town of Darwin on the Australian north-west coast, sinking 11 ships in the harbour and causing over 500 casualties. Some members of the Japanese General Staff called for the invasion of northern Australia, but the Army again argued that the troops were not available; others suggested that New Caledonia, Fiji and Samoa, all to the north of New Zealand, were vulnerable and that their occupation would sever the communications link between Australia and the USA. Adm Yamamoto was to provide the answer to the problem. He had earlier suggested that if Midway, a tiny atoll north-west of Hawaii, was attacked, the US Pacific Fleet would be obliged to come to its defence. The Imperial Navy with its overwhelming strength, would then finish the job that they had begun at Pearl Harbor and leave the Hawaiian Islands open to attack. The General Staff were a little wary, and considered Yamamoto's deadline of June as somewhat premature; but the Doolittle Raid on Tokyo settled the matter, and on 5 May 1942 Adm Nagano, Chief of the Navy General Staff, gave the go-ahead for the operation. On 31 December 1941, following the Pearl Harbor debacle, Adm Chester W. Nimitz had been appointed Commander in Chief of

Adm Chester Nimitz was appointed Commander in Chief, Pacific Fleet after the debacle at Pearl Harbor. He eventually commanded the largest naval and marine force in history. (US Navy)

the Pacific Fleet. The choice was an inspired one. A quiet and studious man, he had a brilliant mind and an outstanding ability to coordinate the abilities of his staff. He was later to oversee the island-hopping campaign across the Pacific which would bring the Americans to the very shores of Japan; but his expertise would be tested to the limit in the forthcoming battle to decide the fate of Midway.

CATASTROPHE AT MIDWAY

Adm Yamamoto was not unduly troubled by the failure of the Navy to land troops at Port Moresby. He had been informed that both the *Lexington* and the *Yorktown* had been sunk in the Coral Sea, and he felt that now was the time to deliver the knockout blow to the seriously weakened Pacific Fleet.

As with most of Japan's naval operations during the war, the plan devised by the Navy General Staff was needlessly complex. The 1st Carrier Striking Force, under Adm Nagumo, based on the carriers *Hiryu*, *Soryu*, *Kaga* and *Akagi*, along with two battleships and three cruisers, would attack the atoll of Midway, north-west of Hawaii, and pave the way for an invasion by troops from the Midway Invasion Force under Vice-Adm Kondo. Simultaneously, a North Aleutian Force under Vice-Adm Kakuji Kakuta, built around the carriers *Ryujo* and *Junyo*, would attack the Aleutian Islands to the north as part of a diversionary operation. Backing up the whole operation would be the Main Force under Yamamoto, flying his flag in the 72,000-ton super-battleship *Yamato*, including 6 other battleships, 3 light carriers, 2 light cruisers and 12 destroyers. To further complicate the operation, a force of sixteen submarines was to scout ahead of Nagumo's force and a minesweeper group would operate to the south, arriving via Saipan and Wake. Yamamoto felt that the threat to Midway, an important Marine base and submarine refuelling facility, would make Nimitz deploy what was left of the Pacific Fleet; the overwhelming power of the Imperial Japanese Navy would then force a decisive battle in which the remains of the US Navy would be utterly destroyed.

For Yamamoto's plan to work it was essential that he had the element of surprise; but as early as March 1942, US Naval Intelligence cryptanalysts were aware that something big was brewing, though still uncertain what or where. The letters 'AF' kept showing up in Japanese signals, and Nimitz's brilliant code-breaker, Cdr Joseph J. Rochefort, devised a scheme to identify the location. By sending a message via a low-grade cipher which he knew the Japanese could break, he indicated that Midway was

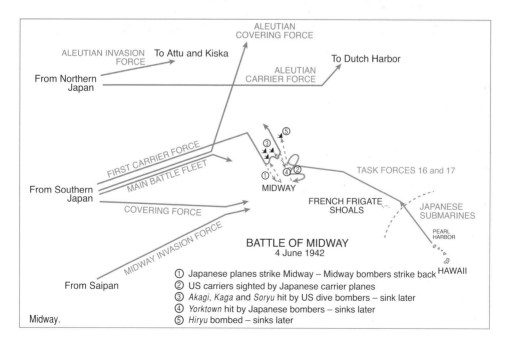

BATTLE OF MIDWAY
4 June 1942

① Japanese planes strike Midway – Midway bombers strike back
② US carriers sighted by Japanese carrier planes
③ *Akagi*, *Kaga* and *Soryu* hit by US dive bombers – sink later
④ *Yorktown* hit by Japanese bombers – sinks later
⑤ *Hiryu* bombed – sinks later

Midway.

short of fresh water due to a breakdown of the water-filtration plant. The Japanese duly intercepted the message and reported to HQ and the fleet that 'AF is short of water'. Rochefort, an accomplished and eccentric officer who spent most of his time attired in slippers and a smoking-jacket, had unlocked the mystery that had been puzzling US Intelligence for months, and Nimitz, backing him all the way, confirmed his own outstanding leadership by committing his three remaining carriers to the battle. The *Yorktown*, contrary to Yamamoto's belief, had not been sunk in the Coral Sea and, though badly damaged, had limped back to Pearl Harbor. Once there, repairs initially calculated as needing three weeks were carried out in three days thanks to the superhuman efforts of the dock workers, many of whom were still working on the ship when she sailed for Midway.

Two task forces were assembled. TF17, under Rear-Adm Fletcher, based on the *Yorktown*, along with 2 cruisers and 6 destroyers; and TF16, under Vice-Adm Raymond Ames Spruance, with the carriers *Enterprise* and *Hornet*, 6 cruisers and 9 destroyers (TF16 should have been commanded by Adm 'Bull' Halsey, but he was confined to hospital with a severe case of dermatitis).

The first strike in the battle was by Nagumo against Midway itself, with 108 aircraft causing serious damage and shooting down 17 Marine planes. The Midway force retaliated by sending ten torpedo bombers to attack Nagumo's fleet, but only three returned, having inflicted little damage (mainly the fault of US torpedoes, which were ineffectual for at least the first two years of the war). The leader of the attack on Midway, Lt Joichi Tomonaga, urged Nagumo to mount a second strike and the Admiral ordered the planes already on deck to have their torpedoes removed and replaced with bombs. While this was in hand, a Japanese reconnaissance plane reported sighting a US force with at least one carrier 240 miles north of Midway. The normally cautious Nagumo now began to panic: should he attack the carriers or mount another attack on Midway? Further ineffectual attacks from Midway by dive-bombers, high-altitude B17s and lumbering, obsolete 'Vindicator' bombers only added to the confusion, and he reversed his original decision and ordered the torpedoes to be replaced.

Meanwhile, Spruance had assembled 67 'Dauntless' dive-bombers, 29 'Devastator' torpedo bombers and 20 Wildcat fighters in the skies above TF16. They headed for Nagumo's force, but when they arrived he had altered course and they had to disperse in various directions to look for him. Two torpedo squadrons succeeded in locating the Japanese force at 9.30 a.m. and they attacked immediately. All were shot down; only one crew member, Ens George Gay, survived. Minutes later, two more torpedo squadrons arrived, one from the *Enterprise* and one from Fletcher's TF17, but again they were decimated, with only three of the twenty-six aircraft surviving. Assuming that the American attacks were over, some of Nagumo's four carriers began to recover their 'Zero' fighters, while the others, their decks full of refuelled and rearmed 'Vals' and 'Kates', prepared for the attack on the US task forces. Suddenly, thirty-six 'Dauntless' dive-bombers from *Enterprise* and *Yorktown* appeared as if from nowhere. With little fighter support and their decks crowded with aircraft, bombs and

Originally designed as a battlecruiser, the Japanese carrier *Kaga* took part in the Pearl Harbor operation, but was sunk at Midway on 4 June 1942. (RMAS Collection)

torpedoes hastily discarded during the chaotic changeovers, the carriers were literally sitting ducks; the American pilots could hardly believe their luck.

First to go was *Akagi*, with a bomb squarely in the hangar near to the torpedo store and another on the deck amid the rows of aircraft. The ship was soon a mass of flames, Nagumo transferred his flag to the cruiser *Nagara*, and *Akagi* sank at 7.15 p.m. *Kaga* was hit four times, with bombs exploding among the parked aircraft on the flight deck; though she remained afloat for some hours, she soon became a raging inferno, and was finally dispatched by a US submarine. *Soryu* took three direct hits which caused massive fires below deck, which in turn ignited the fuel storage tanks in the stern, which exploded and blew the ship in two. Only *Hiryu* survived the attack; she was sailing some miles to the north-east and had escaped the attention of the 'Dauntless' pilots.

Determined to salvage something from the fiasco, Nagumo launched a strike by forty-six bombers from the *Hiryu*, whose pilots followed a number of the aircraft returning to the *Yorktown*. Although suffering heavy losses from anti-aircraft fire and fighters, the near-suicidal Japanese pilots scored three hits on the carrier, which was critically impaired. Frantic damage control kept *Yorktown* afloat for two days, and she was taken under tow by the minesweeper USS *Vireo*, only to be sunk by the Japanese submarine I-168. A retaliatory strike from Spruance's carriers damaged the *Hiryu* to such an extent that Japanese destroyers had to sink her on 5 June.

Yamamoto's Main Force was 800 miles to the north-west of Midway, and he ordered the two carriers of the North Aleutian Force and the remains of Nagumo's 1st Carrier Striking Force to join him in pursuit of TFs 16 and 17. But Spruance had prudently withdrawn to the east and, with Kakuta's carriers unlikely to reach Midway before 8 June, Yamamoto bowed to the inevitable and abandoned the operation.

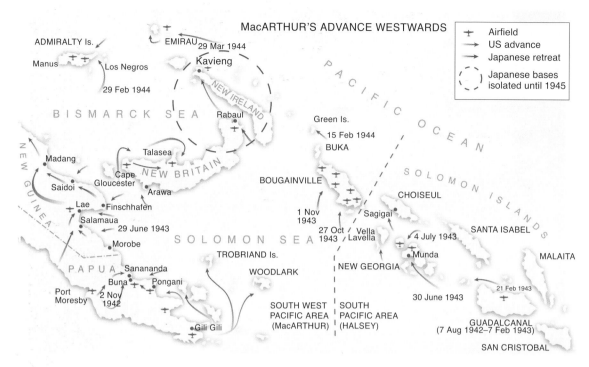

MacARTHUR'S ADVANCE WESTWARDS

+	Airfield
→	US advance
→	Japanese retreat
⌐⌐⌐	Japanese bases isolated until 1945

ADMIRALTY Is.

Manus

Los Negros

29 Feb 1944

EMIRAU 29 Mar 1944

Kavieng

NEW IRELAND

B I S M A R C K   S E A

P A C I F I C   O C E A N

Rabaul

Green Is.

15 Feb 1944

BUKA

Talasea

Madang

NEW BRITAIN

S O L O M O N   I S L A N D S

Cape
Gloucester

Saidoi

Arawa

BOUGAINVILLE

CHOISEUL

N
E
W

Lae

Finschhafen

1 Nov
1943

Sagigai

Salamaua

29 June 1943

27 Oct
1943

Vella
Lavella

4 July 1943

SANTA ISABEL

G
U
I
N
E
A

Morobe

S O L O M O N   S E A

Munda

MALAITA

PAPUA

Sanananda

TROBRIAND Is.

NEW GEORGIA

Buna

Pongani

WOODLARK

Port
Moresby

2 Nov
1942

30 June 1943

21 Feb 1943

Gili Gili

SOUTH WEST
PACIFIC AREA
(MacARTHUR)

SOUTH
PACIFIC AREA
(HALSEY)

GUADALCANAL
(7 Aug 1942–7 Feb 1943)

SAN CRISTOBAL

Water-filled Foxhole, one of Col Waterhouse's
outstanding depictions of war in the jungle.
(Charles Waterhouse)

Bougainville Landing, one of the brilliant paintings by Col Charles Waterhouse, former official artist to the US Marine Corps. (Charles Waterhouse)

ON THE OFFENSIVE

Midway was a massive blow for the Imperial Japanese Navy; one from which it never fully recovered. It would have taken years to replace the four fleet carriers that had been lost, and there were virtually no replacements for the hundreds of experienced aircrews who had died. It is little wonder that after the battle the balance of power in the Pacific began to shift.

The Japanese now occupied a massive swathe of the western Pacific from Burma in the west to the Dutch East Indies, New Guinea and the Solomons in the south and the Gilberts and Marshall Islands in the east. The Army had neither the men nor resources for further conquests and the Navy was seriously weakened; the emphasis was now on consolidating the outer defence perimeter. Thwarted in their attempts to land troops at Port Moresby by sea, the Japanese opened a campaign from Buna on the north coast of New Guinea in an attempt to cross the formidable Owen Stanley mountain range by the Kokoda Trail. This was eventually to fail in the face of strong opposition from Australian and US ground and air forces, while to the east, in an attempt to threaten the supply route between the USA and Australia, troops were landed on the island of Guadalcanal in the Solomon Islands. On 7 August 1942, a 19,000-strong force from the 1st Division of the United States Marine Corps (USMC),

Four Japanese Mitsubishi G4M 'Betty' bombers run the gauntlet of anti-aircraft fire in an ultra-low attack on US transports off Guadalcanal. (USMC)

Japanese bombers attack Henderson Field on Guadalcanal. (Marine Corps University Archives)

US ground crew and Seabees examine a shot-up 'Corsair' fighter after it has returned from an attack on Rabaul. (Marine Corps University Archives)

under Gen Alexander Vandegrift, landed at Lunga Point on the north of the island and occupied the airfield that the Japanese were constructing – renamed Henderson Field, it was to play a vital role in the ensuing battle for the island, which continued until the Japanese were finally driven out in February 1943.

With the eastern Solomons secure and an ever-increasing supply of men and materials flowing from a rejuvenated economy, the USA was now in a position to go on the offensive. As 1942 drew to a close, the joint Chiefs of Staff decided upon their major operations in the Pacific for the coming year: in the south an advance across the Solomons and New Guinea to secure the important base at Rabaul; in the central Pacific the elimination of the base at Truk (often referred to as the 'Gibraltar of the Pacific') and the occupation of strategically important islands in the Carolines and the Marianas; and in the north the reoccupation of the Japanese-held islands of Attu and Kiska in the Aleutians. The campaign in the Aleutians was a relatively minor affair and the islands were back in US hands by August; the two remaining operations – MacArthur's westward thrust through the Solomons, New Guinea and the Dutch East Indies, which would eventually facilitate his return to the Philippines and enable him to fulfil his pledge to return; and Nimitz's advance across the central Pacific (the 'island hopping' campaign) – would constitute two giant pincers that would tear out the heart of the Japanese war machine. It is with this latter operation that we are concerned. It started in dramatic and violent fashion at a tiny atoll in the Gilbert Islands called Tarawa.

ONE

TARAWA

THE TURNING OF THE TIDE

With men and materials flowing at an ever-increasing rate from an invigorated US war machine, the Allies were at last in a position to go on the offensive. Midway had removed the threat to the Hawaiian Islands, and MacArthur's victories in New Guinea and the Solomons ensured the security of Australia and the vital supply lines from America. The Navy's depleted carrier force was being rapidly reinforced with the new 'Essex' class carrier, capable of operating over eighty aircraft, and US shipbuilders were turning out battleships, cruisers and other vessels at an astonishing rate. As MacArthur continued his thrust westward towards his ultimate goal, a victorious return to the Philippines, Adm Ernest King, Chief of Naval Operations, pressed for an advance through the islands and atolls of the central Pacific; 'island hopping' through the Gilberts, Marshall Islands and Carolines towards the Japanese mainland, occupying those islands that were of strategic importance and isolating those that were of no military value or were geographically unsuitable for amphibious operations.

At the Casablanca Conference in January 1943, Adm King and Gen George Marshall, Army Chief of Staff, persuaded the Combined Chiefs to agree to a series of operations against the Gilbert Islands and the Japanese-mandated Marshalls and Carolines; this was confirmed in May at the Trident Conference in Washington. Originally it was intended that the Marshall Islands would be the starting point for the campaign, but the threat of a massive retaliation from the Japanese naval base at Truk persuaded Nimitz and Spruance to go for the less risky option of the Gilberts.

In August 1942, a Marine Raider battalion had attacked the island of Makin in the northern Gilberts, and, though the raid had achieved little, the propaganda value had been immense and had raised the USA's flagging morale. But the Japanese saw the raid as a precursor to an all-out assault on the Gilberts and immediately set about reinforcing Tarawa, the largest atoll in the islands.

Lying some 2,500 miles south-west of Hawaii and 1,300 miles south-east of Truk, Tarawa was the most southerly point in Japan's outer defence ring and was in a key position along the vital lifeline from the United States to the south Pacific. The Gilbert Islands had been under British jurisdiction before the war, and US forces had access to up-to-date information about the islands, something that was not available to them for the Marshalls. At a meeting in Hawaii in September 1943, 'Operation Galvanic' – the invasion of Tarawa, Makin and the tiny island of Apamama – was formulated, and the 'island hopping' campaign was up and running.

'OPERATION GALVANIC'

'The question of landing in the face of an enemy is the
most complicated and difficult of the war.'

(Gen Sir Ian Hamilton (Gallipoli Diary))

Mounting an amphibious assault against a heavily defended island is fraught with huge problems under the best of conditions. At this stage of the war nobody knew if such a dangerous and complex undertaking could succeed, and at what cost. US forces had only limited experience of amphibious warfare, unlike the Japanese, who at that time were probably the world's leading exponents; but a start had to be made somewhere and Tarawa was to be the testing ground.

The Marines for the operation, the 5th Marine Amphibian Corps (VMAC), were under the overall command of Lt-Gen Holland M. Smith, a volatile officer whose initials 'H.M.' were adapted to 'Howlin' Mad' by his men, a name that stuck for

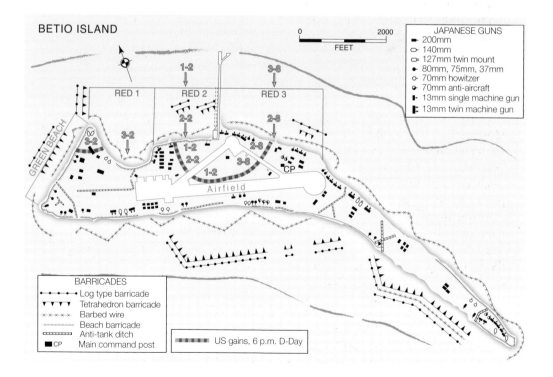

Betio Island. (Author)

the rest of his career. The assault on Betio (pronounced 'Bay-sho'), the largest island
of Tarawa Atoll and the site of the only airfield in the Gilberts, was allocated
to the 2nd Marine Division under its commander, Maj-Gen Julian C. Smith, while
the occupation of the more northerly Makin went to the Army's 27th Division under
yet another Smith, Maj-Gen Ralph C. Smith. Getting the Marines and soldiers to
the Gilberts was the responsibility of the commander of Task Force 24,
Rear-Adm Richmond Kelly Turner – 'Terrible Turner' to one and all. The most experienced American in the art of amphibious warfare, he had overseen and organised
the landing on Guadalcanal in 1942 and was later to oversee the assaults on the
Marshalls, Marianas, Iwo Jima and Okinawa.

The defence of the Gilberts came under the joint jurisdiction of the CIC South-
East Asia, Vice-Adm Kusaka, and the CIC 2nd Fleet, Vice-Adm Kondo; but once
'Operation Galvanic' got under way the islands were virtually written off. In
September 1943, Rear-Adm Keiji Shibasaki was appointed as commander on Betio,
and an impressive programme was put in hand to make the island one of the most
heavily defended outposts of the Japanese perimeter.

The first obstacle that the Marines would encounter was a natural one, a shelflike
reef that extended between 800yd and 1,200yd offshore, to which the Japanese added
further hazards in the shape of log barricades, barbed wire, and pyramid-shaped
concrete tetrahedrons. At the shoreline a barricade of logs, 3ft to 5ft high, was constructed around most of the island's perimeter, behind which were machine-gun and
rifle emplacements. Anti-tank ditches were dug at various strategic positions on the

south shore and to the east and west of the airfield. At various points around the island were coastal-defence guns ranging in calibre from 205mm to 80mm; dual-purpose anti-aircraft guns between 127mm and 70mm and over thirty other artillery pieces from 75mm pack howitzers, 37mm light field guns, heavy 13mm machine-guns and an assortment of mortars (see map on p. 31). In the centre of the island the airfield, with its 4,000ft runway dominated the landscape, and the Admiral's command post, a reinforced concrete structure measuring 60ft × 40ft × 25ft high, stood a short distance inland from the short Burns-Philp pier. The 111th Construction Unit under Lt Murakami had performed a brilliant job in turning Betio into what was probably, yard for yard, the most heavily defended position in the world at that time – indeed Adm Shibasaki boasted, 'the Americans could not take Tarawa with a million men in a hundred years'.

PLANNING

The US force was divided into two groups. The northern group (Task Force 52), with the Army's 165th Regimental Combat Team (RCT) of the 27th Division, had the task of securing Makin. Vice-Adm Richmond Kelly Turner, accompanied by Holland Smith, was in command. In his mind was the possibility of a major Japanese retaliation from Truk. If this happened, he wanted the most powerful naval force and the top commanders available in the north.

The southern group (Task Force 53), was under Rear-Adm Harry Hill. 'Handsome Harry', as he was known, would support the Marines of the 2nd Division in their assault on Betio. Maj-Gen Julian Smith had taken command of the 2nd Division in May 1943 while they were recuperating in New Zealand after fighting alongside the 1st Division on Guadalcanal. They were in poor condition; there were over 13,000 confirmed cases of malaria alone, and a large number of replacements were being shipped out from America. The division consisted of three infantry regiments – the 2nd, 6th and 8th Marines – together with a regiment of artillery (the 10th), a tank battalion and an amphibious tractor battalion. The Engineers, the Pioneers and the Naval Construction Battalion ('Seabees') were grouped with the 18th Marines. The elements of the United States Navy accompanying the VMAC could only be described as awesome (the rate at which the shipyards of America replenished the Navy after Pearl Harbor is one of the unsung epics of the war). Harry Hill's Task Force 53 consisted of 3 battleships, 2 heavy cruisers, 3 light cruisers, 9 destroyers, 13 attack transports and, to supply air cover, 3 aircraft carriers.

The Gilberts had been under British control since 1915, and the Marines were able to draw on the experience of a number of expatriates, whom they labelled the 'Foreign Legion'. The maps and charts of the area dated from the turn of the century, and intelligence was based more on aerial photographs, along with surveys made of the islands by the submarine USS *Nautilus*. A vital factor in the invasion was going to be the depth of water around Betio on D-Day, which was set for 20 November. The 'Foreign Legion' offered various opinions about the tides, but one dissonant voice, that of Frank

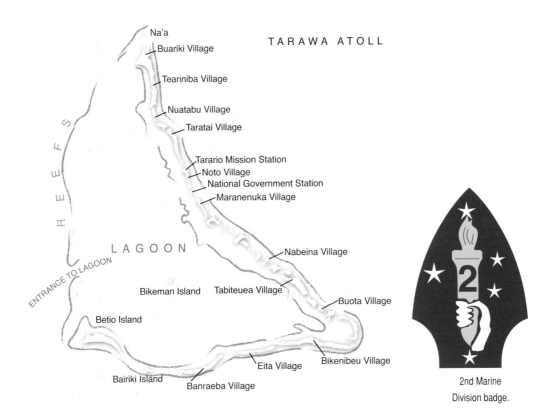

2nd Marine
Division badge.

Holland, was adamant that the water would be too low on that day. Holland had spent fifteen years in the islands and had made a hobby of studying the tides; he was appalled at the Marine's choice of D-Day and declared that there would be a 'dodging tide' – an extra-low tide – on 20 November.

There were to be two ways of transporting the Marines from the troopships to the shore. The first three waves of 1,500 men were to go in amphibious tractors (Amtracs), so the depth of water was theoretically irrelevant; but the remainder would come ashore in Higgins Boats (Landing Craft, Vehicle, Personnel, or LCVP), shallow-draught 36ft-long boats with wide ramps which drew only 3–4ft of water when loaded. If Frank Holland's predictions were correct, the Higgins Boats would ground on the reef and the Marines would have no option but to wait for returning Amtracs or wade to the shore.

A careful study of aerial photographs had convinced Col David M. Shoup, the Divisional Planning Officer, that the Marines should attack from the lagoon side of the island. Three landing beaches had been designated: 'Red 1', a deep cove stretching from the north-west tip of the island for around 500yd – here the 3rd Battalion of the 2nd Marines (3–2), under Maj John Schoettel, would land; 'Red 2', from the edge of the cove to the long pier, was assigned to the 2nd Battalion of the 2nd Marines (2–2), under Lt-Col Herbert R. Amey; and 'Red 3', from the edge of the pier to a point in line with the end of the main runway was allocated to the 2nd Battalion of the 8th Marines (2–8), under Maj Henry P. 'Jim' Crowe (see map on p. 31). The western end of the island was designated 'Green Beach' and the southern shores as 'Black 1' and 'Black 2', but no landings were planned here for D-Day. Most of the Marines had no idea of what they were going to be up against; the constitution of Japanese forces was pretty much a mystery to all but the senior ranks, and rumours had it that they would be fighting their opposite number – 'Imperial Marines'. No such unit existed, but they were not far from the truth.

THE JAPANESE SPECIAL NAVAL LANDING FORCES

The Special Naval Landing Forces (SNLF), the 'Rikusentai', could trace their origins back to the earliest days of the Imperial Japanese Navy. Initially developed as small infantry units attached to naval ships, they gradually developed into larger units of highly trained amphibious infantry. In the early years of the war, SNLF units were used as shock troops for the invasion of Wake Island, where 450 troops overwhelmed the small Marine garrison, and in 1941 a force of 5,000 landed on Guam. They were also the first reinforced units to land on Guadalcanal, and they offered fierce resistance to the 1st Marine Division's landings on Tulagi and Gavutu.

By 1942, there were some 50,000 Rikusentai based at various locations throughout the Pacific, and their experience of amphibious warfare gave them an expertise that no other country possessed. A typical unit was commanded by a navy captain and had three rifle companies supplemented by anti-aircraft, coastal-defence, field-artillery and anti-boat units. At Tarawa, the USMC would face the 3rd Special Base Force (formerly known as the 6th Yokosata Special Naval Landing Force), the 7th Sasebo Special Naval Landing Force, the 111th Pioneers and the 4th Construction Unit – over 4,850 troops in total. The SNLF were elite troops specially trained in the use of a wide variety of weapons and all imbued with the spirit of 'bushido' – death before dishonour. They were to distinguish themselves at Tarawa; after 76 hours of savage fighting, 4,690 lay dead and only 17 wounded Japanese surrendered. A mere 146 prisoners were listed at the end of the battle – almost all conscripted Korean labourers.

'IN LANDING OPERATIONS RETREAT IS IMPOSSIBLE' (LT GEN GEORGE S. PATTON JR)

The battle had a deceptively quiet start. The huge invasion fleet of transports, battle-ships and carriers lay off the coast of Betio in the pre-dawn darkness of 20 November, but it was so quiet that some doubted whether there were any Japanese on the island. 'Try as I might, I never got over the feeling that the Japs had pulled out of Tarawa – not until the first bullet whizzed by my ear,' said war correspondent Robert Sherrod.

By 3.00 a.m., the transports had assembled in their formations and the Marines began disembarking into the Amtracs and Higgins Boats, a difficult task for a 'Leatherneck' burdened with up to 100lb of equipment, some with extra items such as radios, mortars, ammunition and stripped-down machine-guns. Many eyes on many ships were watching Betio, and at 4.40 a.m. all heads turned as a single red star shell rocketed from the centre of the island – any doubts about a Japanese presence were gone.

Shortly after 5.00 a.m., Harry Hill's flagship, the USS *Maryland*, launched her Kingfisher spotter plane, and the Japanese, seeing the flash from the catapult, opened up with one of their 8in guns at Temakin Point. The shells overshot the battleship and, in response, the US ships opened up with their 16in and 8in guns, which began pounding the enemy positions. The salvos from the *Maryland*'s massive guns made the old ship shudder; dust spurted from every crevice, crumbling insulation showered down, lights went out, and the massive vibrations caused the radios to malfunction. This loss of communications was to prove a serious problem throughout the battle and later resulted in the practice of adapting transport ships, bristling with antennae, as the communications centres for future invasion fleets.

Around 5.40 a.m. the bombardment ceased: Harry Hill had learned that a strong current was carrying the transports southward. They were not only straying into the warships' field of fire; they were drifting within range of the enemy guns. The repositioning of the transports and their landing craft not only delayed the operation; it gave Adm Shibasaki time to move men and equipment from the southern shore to the lagoon side of Betio, where it was now obvious that the landings were going to be made. An air strike from the carriers *Essex*, *Bunker Hill* and *Independence* had been arranged, but the planes were conspicuous by their absence. Hill could not contact the carriers because of his radio problems, and he was just about to resume his bombardment when they finally arrived. The 'Dauntless' and 'Avenger' bombers, and 'Hellcat' fighters, plastered the island for seven minutes (the plans had called for much longer), and Harry Hill then mounted his main bombardment of the island. For an hour and twenty minutes three battleships and four cruisers raked the island from end to end; great gouts or sand and coral erupted into the air, palm trees were ripped from the ground, ammunition dumps exploded and a great pall of smoke from a fuel dump added to the shroud of dust that hung over Betio.

Spectacular as it was, the greatest pre-invasion bombardment of the war thus far failed in its main objective of destroying the enemy defences. Many shells were fired from close offshore and, with a low trajectory, simply bounced off the island and into the sea beyond; others missed the island altogether. Nor did it eliminate the garrison; the Japanese simply retired to their well-prepared bunkers and dugouts and sat out the storm.

It was a long haul for the landing craft. After leaving the transports they had a 3½-mile slog to the line of departure just inside the lagoon, and another 6,500yd to the beaches. By the time they landed, some of the Marines would have been afloat for nearly six hours. Lt-Cdr Robert MacPherson, the observer in the Kingfisher spotter

Down the Net, Kerr Eby's depiction of 2nd Marine Division personnel climbing down to their landing craft on D-Day. (US Navy Art Collection)

plane, had a dramatic view of the bombardment but was becoming concerned about the slow progress of the landing craft, which were also being tracked on the radar of the minesweeper *Pursuit*. As reports filtered through to Harry Hill, he realised that he had no choice but to delay H-Hour, the time at which the landing craft were to hit the beaches, by an hour until 9.00 a.m.

Braving anti-aircraft fire, MacPherson's plane dived in low to have a look at the reef. What he saw filled him with horror: instead of the 4 or 5ft of water that had been expected, the sea was so low in places that long stretches of coral were drying in the sun. He knew that the Amtracs would grind over the reef, but the fourth, fifth and sixth waves of Higgins Boats were inevitably going to run aground hundreds of yards out. Frank Holland's predictions were going to haunt a lot of people before the end of the day.

HORROR AT THE REEF

As the Amtracs and Higgins Boats left the point of departure, a lone boat surged ahead of them. Lt William Hawkins and his Scout Sniper Platoon were heading for the end of the long pier; their task was to clear from it any Japanese troops who could fire on the waves of landing craft that would shortly be passing on either side. Landing at the Y-shaped seaplane dock at the seaward end, Hawkins and his men silenced a machine-gun and then proceeded to shoot, grenade and flame-throw their way down the quarter-mile-long pier, clearing snipers from small barges moored alongside it and silencing another machine-gun nest on a platform under the trestles.

The lines of landing craft were now on their final approach. As Ralph Butler of 3–2 recalled, 'After what seemed like hours of milling about we were in proper alignment and proceeding shoreward. We were in high spirits. There was even a sense of adventure. I don't recall how far from shore we were when all hell let loose: explosions, detonations, bodies slumping and bloody, and as we crunched to a halt somebody yelling, "Get the hell out of here fast."'

As the rows of Amtracs entered the cove on 'Red Beach 1', heavy machine-guns and artillery opened up from ahead and from both sides. Within minutes, Amtracs were burning as their unarmoured fuel tanks exploded; others spun as their drivers fell dead or wounded; and some just disappeared in a ball of flame as they were blown apart by artillery at almost point-blank range. The pattern of landings planned for 'Red 1' had disintegrated as the drivers took the line of least resistance and headed as far away from the enemy fire as possible.

The heaviest fire appeared to be coming from the eastern side of the cove between 'Red 1' and 'Red 2', and consequently more and more craft were veering to the west. Ralph Butler observed that 'Fire was also coming from a half-sunken freighter in the lagoon. We were getting raked with fire from all directions. People would attempt to return fire but if exposed would be killed immediately.' The old inter-island steamer *Niminoa*, which had run aground in 1941 about 100yd west of the end of the pier, now sheltered at least one machine-gun and many snipers. She was finally blasted by gunfire from the offshore fleet after an attack by carrier planes proved to be unsuccessful.

Maj Michael Ryan, CO of Company L of 3–2, had made an arduous trip ashore, having waded in from the reef. In the absence of his battalion commander, Maj Schoettel, who was still out in the lagoon with the fourth wave, he began gathering up anyone that he could find and attempted to make a coherent force of them. Things were obviously not going to plan. As the Amtracs braved the shredding fire from their left and front, the majority veered to the right and ended up near to the junctions of 'Red 1' and 'Green Beach', where they were rounded up by Maj Ryan.

Out in the cove the situation was much grimmer as the second and third waves of Higgins Boats approached the reef. Pfc Bob Libby, from the 81mm Mortar Platoon of 3–2, was in the third wave:

Across the Reef, Col Waterhouse's vivid image of Marines wading in against murderous enemy fire. (Charles Waterhouse)

About 500yd out the boat rammed into the reef and everyone was ordered over the side. I leaped out and went into water over my head as I missed the actual reef due to the boat being held up against it. Now that the boat was empty it drifted over the reef and began to float shoreward. I pushed myself up and attempted to keep the boat between me and the heavy fire coming from shore as long as possible. Machine-gun fire kept skipping off the surface and a movement from one side to another helped allow for this, but there was no predicting where the next mortar round would land. Everywhere there were knocked-out tractors burning fiercely, men falling all around me, bodies and parts of bodies floating everywhere in the pink water. The sound of screaming shells passed overhead. The unmistakable crack of rifle fire zipped around our ears. The screams of the wounded were almost lost in the cacophony of sound. Every step was a life or death situation. How anyone reached that shore is still a mystery to me. Half an hour elapsed before I put foot on dry land. Along with a few other survivors

A Marine surveys the devastation on the beaches. (USMC)

I dashed for the wooden sea wall, totally exhausted. One Marine raised himself up to look over, just in time to have an anti-tank shell glance off the front of his helmet. He did a flying backward somersault, but apart from a headache there was not a thing wrong with him.

The next landing was on 'Red 3' at 9.17 a.m. The destroyers USS *Ringgold* and *Dashiel* had come as close to shore as possible and had maintained a constant barrage of 5in shells all along the landing beaches. But Maj 'Jim' Crowe's men were still hammered from the shore. Crowe, the only one of the three assault-battalion commanders to reach the shore on D-Day, had to wade in when his Higgins Boat ground to a halt; he took cover behind an Amtrac that had almost reached the shore but was knocked flat when it hit a mine. Seventeen of Crowe's Amtracs ended up at the far west of the beach near the pier, and two of them found a gap in the sea wall and advanced inland for about 100yd to the north-east taxiway of the airfield. But as soon as the Marines disembarked, the Japanese began filtering back between them and the shore, and they had no option but to withdraw before being cut off.

Company F of 2–8 on the left managed to reach the short Burns-Philp wharf in the centre of 'Red 3', and consolidated their position. Correspondent Robert Sherrod came ashore with the fifth wave: 'I felt that something was wrong. There were very few boats on the beachhead and they were all amphibious tractors. There were no Higgins Boats and there should have been by now.'

On 'Red Beach 2', Lt-Col Amey's 2–2 were the last of the initial wave of assault battalions to reach the shore, and the defenders had plenty of time to prepare themselves. F Company were supposed to land on the left and E Company on the right, with G Company in support. But in face of the murderous fire from beyond the sea wall, which ran the length of the landing beach, the Navy coxswains were putting their craft ashore wherever they could find a space; some even ended up on 'Red 1'.

As the Amtracs crunched to a halt, the Marines made a record-breaking sprint for the sea wall, the only cover available; ironically, the first ashore were the lucky ones. Huddled behind every available foot of cover, they were horrified to see the next waves clambering out of their Higgins Boats, which were already grinding to a standstill on the reef, then splashing and wading to the shore amid a hail of artillery, mortar and machine-gun fire. Lt-Col Amey was only 200yd from the shore when the Amtrac carrying his HQ Group became entangled in a barbed-wire barricade. Amey ordered everyone over the side, and they sheltered alongside the motionless Amtrac to escape the heavy fire. Moving inshore, they crawled until they reached shallow water, where Amey stood up and shouted, 'Come on, these bastards can't stop us.' He was hit in the chest by a burst of fire and was killed instantly.

Meanwhile, Col David Shoup and his Regimental Landing Team HQ Group had managed to get ashore after encountering heavy resistance. He received a shrapnel wound in the leg and, after clearing a low-lying air-raid shelter of its occupants, his group set up their HQ and attempted to get in touch with Maj-Gen Julian Smith

Tarawa, a painting by Sergeant Tom Lovell. Wading ashore from the reef and the long pier accounted for most of the Marine casualties at Tarawa. (Tom Lovell/USMC Art Collection)

Behind the Sea Wall. Those lucky enough to survive the struggle ashore took shelter behind the wooden sea wall before going on to face a fanatical enemy. (Charles Waterhouse)

aboard the USS *Maryland*; but Smith was still suffering serious communications problems, and only intermittent signals were being received.

Once he had become established in his shelter, Shoup began to assess the situation. Most of the manpack radios were inoperable after being submerged in seawater, so runners were sent to his left and right to try to make contact with the company commanders. Many never returned, but slowly news began to filter through. Crowe appeared to be in the best shape. Some of his men were near the airfield taxiway and to the east some were nearly 200yd inland. Lt-Col Walter Jordan, an officer from the 4th Division who had come ashore as an observer, had taken over when Amey was killed; he was instructed to maintain command. Shoup was also aware that there were troops on 'Red Beach 1', but as yet he could not make contact with them and did not know of Maj Ryan's gallant rallying of the stragglers at the end of the beach. Shoup had already committed his reserves, the 1st Battalion 2nd Marines under Maj Wood Kyle, with instructions to land on 'Red Beach 2' and attempt to work their way westward to link up with 'Red 1'. Kyle had great difficulty in rounding up enough Amtracs, and, when he finally headed for the beach, the enemy fire was so heavy and accurate that most of the craft veered off to the west onto 'Red 1', where they joined up with Ryan's rapidly growing squad. Julian Smith was becoming very concerned. Despite the lack of information from Betio, he could see that the landings were faltering. The 6th Marines were still aboard the transports and could not be deployed without V Corps' authority. He was left with only two battalions in reserve, the 1st and 3rd of the 8th Marines.

At 10.18 a.m., he sent 3–8 under Maj Robert H. Ruud to the line of departure, so that they could be available if Shoup needed them. He also radioed Holland Smith with the Northern Task Force to tell him that he was committing one team from the reserves. Holland Smith viewed this news with some anxiety, as he knew that it was not usual to send in reserves this early in a battle. Aboard the cruiser USS *Indianapolis*, Vice-Adm Spruance was also worried at the progress of the battle. The naval bombardment had not crushed the enemy as expected. From what little information he had received it was clear that the landings were chaotic and the tides had obviously been miscalculated; all the ingredients for a disaster were at hand.

SLAUGHTER IN THE AFTERNOON

Around 11.30 a.m., Shoup ordered Maj Ruud and his 3–8 Marines to leave the line of departure and land on 'Red 3' to support Crowe. There were no Amtracs available; it was back to the Higgins Boats again. Even before they reached the reef, the artillery shells and mortars were causing havoc and, as the boats hit the coral and the ramps came down, the Marines fled their floating coffins and ran straight into murderous fire from the entrenched Japanese positions. 'This is as far as I go,' yelled one coxswain, and the Marines rushed forward into 15ft of water. Many drowned before they could disentangle themselves from their equipment. Overhead in his Kingfisher,

Marines come ashore alongside the pier
on D-Day. (USMC)

Lt-Cdr MacPherson watched the Marines' agony: 'The water never seemed clear of tiny men, their rifles over their heads, slowly wading beachward – I wanted to cry.'

Seeing the slaughter from out in the lagoon, Maj Ruud took the courageous decision to order back the fourth wave. Shortly afterwards, much to Ruud's relief, Col Elmer Hall, the Regimental CO, sent the order, 'Land no more troops until directed'. The persistent radio failures led to even more confusion at command level. Some 1,500 Marines held tenuous footholds on the western point of 'Red 1' and on either side of the long pier on 'Red 2' and 'Red 3'. Julian Smith had only one reserve unit, Maj Robert Hays's 1–8, and he placed them at the point of departure to be available to Shoup. At 1.30 p.m., he radioed Holland Smith asking for the 6th Marines to be turned over to him, adding the ominous rider, 'Issue in doubt'. At 2.30 p.m., he received permission to release the 6th Marines. He then felt free to commit Hays's 1–8 to the battle, and asked Shoup where he wanted them. The message was never received. Getting no reply, Smith sent them to the eastern end of the island with instructions to work their way westward to link up with Shoup. Again the message never got through, and 1–8 spent the rest of the day and the following night in their boats, awaiting orders.

Seven waterproofed Sherman tanks had weaved their way ashore on 'Red 3': four of them went to Crowe and the other three were placed at Shoup's disposal on 'Red 2'. The commander of the Tank Battalion, Col Alexander B. Swenceski, had been severely wounded when his Amtrac received a direct hit. He crawled to a pile of bodies lying on a reef, climbed to the top and flopped down totally exhausted; he was found alive twenty hours later.

At the western end of 'Red Beach 1', Maj Ryan found himself in charge of a bizarre group. He had the remains of three rifle companies, one machine-gun platoon, an assortment of Amtrac drivers, heavy-weapons men (minus weapons), engineers, corpsmen and signals men, and now he was joined by around a hundred men from

Maj Kyle's 1–2. Ryan had originally decided that his best option was to try to advance along 'Green Beach', but being short of heavy weapons, and with little ammunition and evening approaching, he opted for creating a defence perimeter around the ground that he already held. As Bob Libby recalled, 'I was one of the remnants that Maj Ryan gathered. We set up a good defence perimeter that night, and we knew the sods were all around us.' As the day wore on, some people became aware of a sickly smell that pervaded the air. Betio is only 80 miles north of the equator, and the sun had been beating down all day creating furnace-like temperatures; the dead floating in the lagoon and lying on the beaches were beginning to stink.

It was sometime during the afternoon of D-Day that an event of huge significance occurred that was arguably to change the whole course of the battle. For reasons that have never been properly established, Adm Shibisaki and his staff decided to move

Evening on D-Day. The beaches are strewn with the bodies of Marines killed while wading in from the offshore reef. (USMC)

Evening on D-Day. The grim business of identifying the dead gets under way. (USMC)

from their concrete command bunker to another location somewhere on the south side of the island (it has been suggested that he was moving so that his bunker could be used as a hospital, but this is uncertain). As he and his staff were waiting, a shell from either the USS *Ringgold* or the *Dashiel* exploded among them, killing the Admiral and his entire staff. During the following night it was expected that the Japanese would mount a large-scale counter-attack against the precarious US beachhead; the death of the Admiral and his top men explains why such an order was never given.

As the first day of battle drew to an end, the situation for US forces was indeed hazardous: Ryan and his men held an enclave on the north-west tip of the island about 250yd wide and 300yd long; on the combined 'Red 2' and 'Red 3' beaches the Marines held areas either side of the pier, and some elements had advanced as far as the main runway of the airfield (see Map on p. 50). Shoup expected a major Japanese counter-attack during the night (night attacks were a Japanese speciality). At 7.11 p.m. Maj-Gen Smith issued the rather optimistic order, 'Hold what you have. Develop contact between landing teams. Clear hostile machine-guns still holding out on beaches. Make provision to meet organised counter-attack.' The question to the fore in Shoup's mind was, could the Marines hold or would they be swept back into the sea?

No Man's Land: beyond the end of the log pier, Marines fight to dislodge Japanese defenders around the airfield, 22 November 1943. (USMC)

DAY TWO

Apart from sporadic machine-gun and rifle fire, there was no serious Japanese retaliation during the night. A few bombers arrived from the Marshall Islands but were driven off by heavy anti-aircraft fire after jettisoning their bombs. Viewed in retrospect, it is clear that the Japanese failure to mount a major counter-attack on the night of 20/21 November was their greatest mistake and cost them the battle; most of the enemy garrison were still alive, they had masses of ammunition and supplies and the US forces were in a very vulnerable position. On the USS *Maryland*, Julian Smith passed one of the worst nights of his life and declared that this was the crisis of the battle. A major counter-attack would almost certainly have driven the Marines back into the sea, whence they could only have been evacuated with appalling losses.

Maj Hays's 1–8 were still at the point of departure, having been cramped in their landing craft since mid-morning the previous day without food, drink or toilet facilities. They finally set out around 6.15 a.m., after being embarked for twenty hours, and ground to a halt on the reefs hundreds of yards short of 'Red 2'. The previous day's lessons had still not been learned and again the men waded ashore in the face of a vicious barrage of mortar, machine-gun and small-arms fire. Hays reported to Shoup around 8.00 a.m. Most of his battalion's equipment had been lost in the water and around 50 per cent of his men were dead, wounded or missing. It was only later in the day as the tide rose that heavier equipment such as 37mm anti-tank guns, jeeps, bulldozers and half-tracks could be brought ashore.

The stalemate had to be broken, and Shoup decided that his best prospect was to attempt to reach the far shore of Betio and split the Japanese garrison in two. The Marines of Maj Kyle's 1–2, who had advanced the previous day into the triangle formed by the airfield runways, were almost isolated from 'Red 2', and supplies and ammunition were running low. But after carrier planes laid on a concentrated attack against enemy positions on their flanks, they made the final 125yd dash across the main runway and reached the southern shore. Although their position was tenuous and they were receiving vicious counter-attacks from the enemy on their eastern flank, the Marines of 1–2 and 2–2 held their ground and late in the afternoon Col Jordan arrived to take command.

The most significant gains of the day, and probably the turning point of the whole battle, were about to occur on 'Green Beach', where Ryan and his assortment of Marines, bolstered by the addition of two Sherman tanks, were preparing to advance southward towards Temakin Point. During the night a naval gunfire spotter, Lt Green, had come ashore and linked up with two offshore destroyers. At 10.00 a.m., they opened up on the enemy emplacements all along the beach: 'The attack was well coordinated. In fact, the fire requested was so close to where we reported our front line that the naval ships would not respond to the request unless the Divisional Commander himself approved', recalled Ryan. Once the barrage was over, the Marines and the two Shermans stormed forward and in one short and brilliantly

The flame-thrower was a devastating weapon. The barely recognisable remains of Japanese defenders lie near the sea wall. (USMC University Archives)

The southern end of 'Green beach'. Concrete tetrahedrons can be seen in the foreground; further inland is one of the many tank traps. (US Navy)

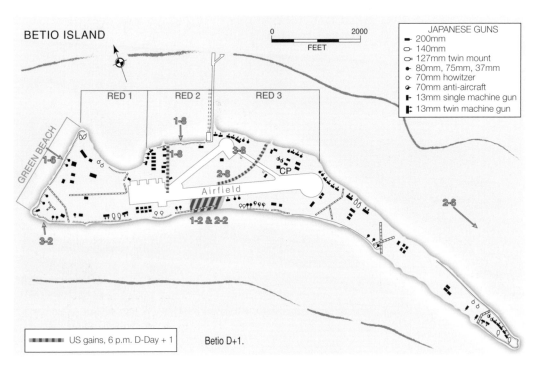

Betio D+1.

coordinated attack cleared the whole of 'Green Beach' as far as Temakin Point. The way was now open for the 6th Marines to make their much-delayed landing. Julian Smith was jubilant and declared it 'the most cheering news of D+1'.

At the tip of Temakin Point were two 8in Vickers guns, whose origin remained a mystery for years afterwards. They were constantly referred to as the 'Singapore' guns, as it was assumed that they had been part of Singapore's defences and that the Japanese had dismantled them and brought them to Tarawa. However, in 1974, after an examination of their identification numbers, it was confirmed by Vickers that they were part of an order supplied to Japan in 1905 during the Russo-Japanese War – almost a hundred years later the guns remain in position, pointing out across the vast reaches of the Pacific.

At 4.00 p.m., Shoup gave Julian Smith his assessment of the situation. Ryan and his men held 'Green Beach' to a depth of 100–150yd inland; on 'Red 2', elements of 1–8 held the beach as far as the junction with 'Red 1'; and on 'Red 3', the Marines were deployed as far as the Burns-Philp Wharf. Inland, 2–8 had advanced to the edge of the airfield's main runway; and on the south coast, elements of 1–2 and 2–2 held a 200yd enclave, with the enemy pressing on their east and west flanks. Shoup added, 'casualties many, percentage dead not known, combat efficiency – we are winning'. Julian Smith forwarded a copy of Shoup's report to Holland Smith, who was with the northern force. He is reported to have smiled at Kelly Turner for the first time in weeks.

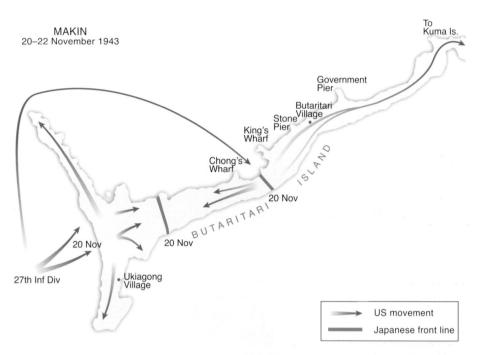

MAKIN
20–22 November 1943

To
Kuma Is.

Government
Pier

Butaritari
Village

Stone
Pier

King's
Wharf

Chong's
Wharf

20 Nov

BUTARITARI ISLAND

20 Nov

20 Nov

27th Inf Div

Ukiagong
Village

US movement

Japanese front line

Rows of 'Hellcats' warming up aboard USS *Yorktown*
during the Gilberts campaign. (National Archives)

During the afternoon of D+1, an observer on one of the ships in the lagoon reported seeing enemy troops swimming from the eastern tip of Betio to Bairiki, the next island in the chain; at low tide it was possible to swim or even wade across the coral that connected the many islands of the atoll. Lt-Col Raymond Murray's 2nd Battalion of the 6th Marines were diverted to Bairiki to block the escape route and to occupy the thirty or so other islands that constituted Tarawa Atoll. After a week-long trek from island to island, during which Murray's men fought a number of vicious engagements with the substantial Japanese forces who had either escaped from Betio or were members of the garrison occupying the remainder of the atoll, they reached the island of Na'a – the end of the line. Murray called in a bombardment of the island by Navy aircraft and destroyers; after a twenty-minute pounding his men made the final crossing and found nothing but torn-up buildings and bodies. Their mission complete, they retired to the island of Eita for rest and reorganisation.

TASK FORCE 50 AT MAKIN

The Northern Task Force was of similar size to that at Tarawa. But, with the possibility of a retaliation from the Japanese base at Truk, it also included Task Force 50–1 under Rear-Adm Charles Pownell, which comprised the fleet carriers *Lexington* and *Yorktown*, the light carrier *Cowpens*, three battleships and six destroyers. 'Baldy' Pownell's 50–1 was supplementary to the main components of the Makin force, Task Force 50–2, under Adm A.W. Radford. This was to operate in direct support of the operation and consisted of the fleet carrier *Enterprise* and the light carriers *Belleau Wood*, *Liscomb Bay* and *Monterey*, supported by the battleships *Pennsylvania*, *North Carolina* and *Indiana* and six destroyers. The plan at Makin was for two battalions of the Army's 165th Infantry Regiment from the 27th Division, under the command of Maj-Gen Ralph Smith, to attack the western end of the main island of Butaritari, while a third battalion landed in the centre of the six-mile-long island, between Chong's Wharf and King's Wharf (see map on p. 51).

Holland Smith was expecting a short, sharp engagement, as the Army force of over 6,500 soldiers would be attacking a garrison of around 800 men; but he was to be bitterly disappointed. In stark contrast to the Marines' experience at Betio, the Army units encountered virtually no opposition as they came ashore. The Japanese had dug in inland and they stayed there. The two battalions in the west soon secured the beaches and advanced rapidly inland, while the battalion that landed near Chong's Wharf reached the Japanese defence line and stopped. Living up to his nickname of 'Howlin' Mad', Smith came ashore and demanded to know what was going on. He found tanks standing idle and infantrymen firing indiscriminately; and when he confronted Ralph Smith, he was told that there was heavy fighting in the north. Commandeering a Jeep, he drove to the scene of the supposed battle and reported it as being 'as quiet as Wall Street on a Sunday'. The Makin fiasco was to have serious repercussions in relations between the Army and the Marine Corps later in the war.

The most serious casualties in the northern phase of the operation was sustained by the US Navy, with the sinking of the light carrier *Liscomb Bay*. The Japanese submarine I–175 had been lurking in the area for some time and, on the morning of 24 November, the *Liscomb Bay* turned north-west to launch aircraft, a move that brought her directly across the I–175's bow. The submarine captain unleashed three 'long-lance' torpedoes with horrific results. One struck the bomb-storage compartment, and every bomb exploded simultaneously, blowing off the stern of the carrier; the fuel-storage tanks caught fire, and there was a huge explosion that showered plating, debris and human flesh onto the battleship USS *New Mexico*, sailing a mile astern. The *Liscomb Bay* sank in 23 minutes with the loss of 644 lives, including Rear-Adm Henry Mullinex. The loss was more than ten times as great as that suffered by the Army on Makin. The I–175 escaped to Kwajalein in the Marshall Islands.

THE STRUGGLE FOR BETIO

Maj Ryan's victory gave Gen Smith an undefended beach on which to disembark the 1st Battalion of the 6th Marines under Maj William Jones, and they landed in rubber boats (LCRs) from the transport *Feland* around 7.00 p.m. on D+1. The choice of rubber boats was an unfortunate one, as many of them drifted away and had to be taken in tow by Higgins Boats, causing the landings to drag on until late evening. As a consequence, 1–6 stayed on the beach for the night. For the third day of the battle, Shoup and Col Merritt Edson, the Divisional Chief of Staff, who was now ashore, opted for a three-front attack. Jones's 1–6 were to pass through Ryan's men and attack eastward between the airfield and the sea; Maj Hays's 1–8 were to strike west from 'Red 2' to reduce the batteries of gun emplacements at the junction of 'Red 1' and 'Red 2'; and Col Elmer Hall, with 2–8 and 3–8, was to thrust eastward against positions inland from the Burns-Philp Wharf (see map on p. 54). In addition, the Marines of 3–6, who had been at the point of departure since 4.00 p.m. the previous day, were to finally land on 'Green Beach'.

Jones's 1–6 got under way at 8.00 a.m., but the narrowness of their front forced them to advance in column of companies spearheaded by three Stuart light tanks. Progress was surprisingly good, and they joined up with 1–2 in their enclave south of the airfield at 11.00 a.m., an indication of the weakening of the opposition. After a short stop, Jones continued eastward, supported by naval gunfire and strikes by carrier aircraft.

Meanwhile, Maj Hays and his 1–8 began their attempt to reduce the stronghold at the 'Red 1–2' junction, which had now been labelled 'The Pocket' by the Marines. Assisted by three Stuart tanks, and later by two half-tracks mounting 3in guns, he battled all day; but to little effect – 'The Pocket' was to be the last position on Betio to fall to the Marines.

Col Hall's composite 2–8 and 3–8 advancing from the Burns-Philp Wharf were hampered by a series of obstacles which included a steel pillbox, a log machine-gun emplacement and a large concrete bunker. A mortar barrage and a handy Sherman

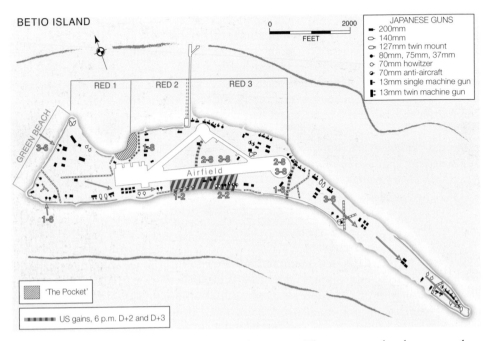

BETIO ISLAND

GREEN BEACH

RED 1   RED 2   RED 3

Airfield

JAPANESE GUNS
- 200mm
- 140mm
- 127mm twin mount
- 80mm, 75mm, 37mm
- 70mm howitzer
- 70mm anti-aircraft
- 13mm single machine gun
- 13mm twin machine gun

0   2000
FEET

'The Pocket'

US gains, 6 p.m. D+2 and D+3

tank disposed of the pillbox and the machine-gun. The concrete bunker proved to be a tougher nut to crack; and it was only after a concerted attack by engineers, flame-throwers and tanks, an operation in which Lt Alexander Bonnyman received a posthumous Medal of Honor, that the way was clear for Hall and his men to link up with Jones's 1–6 column near the end of the airfield.

The island of Betio had become a grotesque site, a moonscape of shredded palm trees and shell and bomb craters. The smell of death was everywhere: hundreds of bodies lay where they had fallen – burned, blasted and torn – and in the lagoon and on the beaches, the bodies of the Marines who had died during the initial landing still lay decomposing in the searing heat, while others bobbed in the water. Attempts were made to identify the bodies and a temporary burial site was established, but it was not until after the battle was over that a full assessment of the number of casualties could be made.

Japanese resistance was gradually weakening. Thousands had been killed and others, sensing defeat, were committing suicide. During the night, about 50 Rikusentai crept out of the undergrowth and attacked Maj Jones's men at the end of the airfield. At 3.00 a.m., a much larger 'banzai' attack developed, and a fierce mêlée, in which grenades, knives and bayonets were prominent, was finally dispersed when Jones called in the guns of the destroyers *Schroeder* and *Sigsbee* to blast the area east of the airfield and prevent reinforcements from moving forward. The morning revealed the extent of the carnage: over 320 Japanese lay dead – the banzai charge had failed. Jones's men suffered 173 casualties: 45 dead and the remainder wounded.

Dead Marines on the beaches. (USMC)

Near to a bunker constructed of logs and coral, the bodies of Japanese defenders litter the shore. (USMC)

MOPPING UP

All that now remained of the Japanese defences was the complex of bunkers and machine-gun nests at the junction of 'Red 1' and 'Red 2' – 'The Pocket' – and the eastern tail of the island beyond the airfield. Lt-Col Kenneth McLeod's 3–6 had arrived from 'Green Beach' and passed through Jones's 1–6 to assault the tail end of Betio. Destroyers and carrier planes pounded the area for half an hour before McLeod, supported by 2 Shermans and 7 Stuart tanks, advanced against a maze of blockhouses, dugouts, and log barriers in which over 500 Japanese were thought to be entrenched. Despite fanatical resistance, the Marines burned and blasted their way to Takarongo Point, killing over 470 of the enemy for the loss of only 9 killed and 25 wounded. At 1.00 p.m., a sweaty Marine swilled his face with seawater from the tip of Betio; the eastern end of the island was in US hands.

'The Pocket' had survived three days of pounding and was responsible for more casualties than any other Japanese position. Shoup ordered Hays's 1–8 to attack from the east, while Maj Schoettel, who had finally come ashore, swung 3–2 around the western end of the airfield and joined up with Hays to encircle the enemy; 75mm artillery pieces mounted on half-tracks pounded the complex from close range, and determined attacks by infantry with demolition charges and flame-throwers finally wore down the defenders. A few surrendered, many killed themselves, and by 1.00 p.m. the battle was over. Messages were flashed to Harry Hill, Holland Smith and Vice-Adm Spruance aboard the USS *Indianapolis*, and war correspondent Robert Sherrod observed, 'the smell of death was unbelievable. The ruptured and twisted bodies which exposed their rotting inner organs was inexpressibly repellant. A fire had reached six nearby Japanese bodies which sizzled and popped as the flames consumed their flesh. Two others are blown to a hundred pieces, a hand here, a head there, a hobnail boot further on.'

A range-finder at the rear of a Japanese gun emplacement, with the body of a dead Japanese soldier in the left foreground. (US Navy)

THE RECKONING

Tarawa had been a pioneering operation for the Marines, a baptism of fire. Many things had gone wrong, many lessons needed to be learned, and at CINCPAC headquarters on Hawaii the inquest started immediately. The next amphibious assault, on the Marshall Islands, was only two months away and the lessons learned at Tarawa needed to be implemented without delay. The use of warships as command centres was condemned by all; a chronic breakdown in sea-to-shore communications had hindered the progress of the battle throughout. There was also much criticism of the naval bombardment, massive as it was; the assumption that saturating the enemy with heavy gunfire would silence the defences had proved to be mythical (the Navy did not fully appreciate or accept this point, and the Marines, and Holland Smith in particular, remained critical of the naval support during the landings at Peleliu and Iwo Jima). The Amtrac came into its own at Tarawa and all future operations were to see increased numbers of better-armed and better-armoured versions to spearhead the assaults. Other items such as portable manpack radios needed improving, as did the coordination of air strikes from the offshore carriers.

The question of tides was a critical factor in the Tarawa landings. Despite warnings from experts, the planners had given priority to prearranged timetables, with the

'Corsair' fighters stationed on Tarawa after the battle. (IWM NYF41740)

SBD dive-bombers and J2F DUKW amphibians at Tarawa airfield in 1944. The graves in the foreground are those of Marines who fell in the struggle for the island. (National Archives)

Many Marines died of their wounds on the troopships returning them to Hawaii. They were buried at sea with full military honours. (National Archives)

COMMAND AND STAFF – 5TH AMPHIBIAN CORPS AND 2ND MARINE DIVISION

5th Amphibian Corps
Commanding General – Lt-Gen Holland M. Smith
Chief of Staff – Brig-Gen Graves B. Erskine

2nd Marine Division
Commanding General – Maj-Gen Julian C. Smith
Ass. Divisional Commander – Brig-Gen Leo D. Hermle
Chief of Staff – Col Merritt A. Edson

2nd Marine Regiment	6th Marine Regiment	8th Marine Regiment	10th Marine Regiment
Col David M. Shoup	Col Maurice G. Holmes	Col Elmer E. Hall	Brig-Gen Thomas E. Bourke
1st Battalion	1st Battalion	1st Battalion	1st Battalion
Maj Wood B. Kyle	Maj William K. Jones	Maj Lawrence C. Hays Jr	Lt-Col Presley M. Rixey
2nd Battalion	2nd Battalion	2nd Battalion	2nd Battalion
Lt-Col Herbert R. Amey	Lt-Col Raymond L. Murray	Maj Henry P. Crowe	Lt-Col George R.C. Shell
3rd Battalion	3rd Battalion	3rd Battalion	3rd Battalion
Maj John F. Schoettel	Lt-Col Kenneth F. McLeod	Maj Robert M. Ruud	Lt-Col Manly L. Curry
			4th Battalion
			Lt-Col Kenneth A. Jorgensen
			5th Battalion
			Maj Howard V. Hiett

2nd Amphibian Tractor Battalion   2nd Tank Battalion
Maj Henry C. Drewes   Lt-Col Alexander B. Swenceski

JAPANESE GARRISON

Gilbert Islands Garrison Force Headquarters (Betio)
Commander – Rear-Adm Keiji Shibasaki

3rd Special Base Force (formerly 6th Yokosuka Special Naval Landing Force)	1,122 men
7th Sasebo Special Naval Landing Force	1,497 men
111th Construction Unit	1,247 men
(Detached) 4th Fleet Construction Dept	970 men
Total	4,836 men

CASUALTIES ON TARAWA

USMC	Dead 990	Wounded 2,296	
Japanese	Dead 4,690	Prisoners 17	Prisoners (Korean) 29
US Navy	Dead 687 (USS *Liscomb Bay* 644, USS *Mississippi* (explosion in turret) 43)		

One of Kerr Eby's best-known images, *Ebb Tide*. (US Navy Art Collection)

result that scores of Higgins Boats grounded on the reef and the Marines were left with no alternative but to wade ashore against withering fire with the resultant heavy casualties. The Japanese had mounted an heroic defence of the island up to the time that Adm Shibasaki had been killed, when their command structure began to crumble. Had he lived to mount a counter-attack on the first night, the battle could have ended disastrously. The Medal of Honor, the USA's highest military decoration, was awarded to four combatants: Staff Sgt William Bordelon, for silencing enemy gun positions on the beach; Lt Alexander Bonnyman, for his part in neutralising an enemy blockhouse; 1Lt Deane Hawkins, for his part in clearing the long pier and suppressing enemy strong-points near the airfield; and Col David Shoup, for organising and directing operations throughout the battle despite his wounds. Shoup was the only recipient to live through the battle; the others were all killed in action. In view of his outstanding leadership and initiative on day one and his brilliant action in clearing 'Green Beach' on day two, it is surprising that Maj Michael Ryan was not also awarded the Medal of Honor. Tarawa shattered the myth, which had been perpetrated until then by Hollywood, of the Japanese fighting man as a myopic, buck-toothed midget. The American public soon realised, after seeing the newsreel pictures of Marine bodies floating in the lagoon, that the war was going to be long and bloody. But it also ended the catalogue of disasters that had beset the Allies in the Pacific after Pearl Harbor, and uplifted the spirits of the American people. From here on, the war would only be going one way.

Two

The Marshall Islands

'Operation Flintlock'

'Amphibious flexibility is the greatest strategic asset that a
sea power possesses.'

(Sir Basil Liddell-Hart)

Many hard lessons had been learned at Tarawa and the subsequent inquest into the battle had hopefully ironed out most of the problems. The landings in the Marshalls were to see the new techniques devised as a result of this inquest refined and improved to a remarkable degree. Scattered over an area of some 600 miles, the Marshall Islands form a necklace of tiny islands and atolls 620 miles north-west of the Gilberts which had been mandated to Japan after the First World War (see map on p. 62). The operation had originally been scheduled for 1 January 1944, but a shortage of troop transports forced Nimitz to postpone the invasion until the 31st.

There were differences of opinion as to where the initial landings should be made. Wotje, Maloelap, Kwajalein and Jaluit were all known to have airfields, and Spruance, Turner and 'Howlin' Mad' Smith all favoured Maloelap and Wotje for the start of 'Flintlock'. But Nimitz in this rare instance disagreed with them, insisting that Kwajalein Atoll in the heart of the Marshalls should be the main target and that the other atolls should be bypassed. The undefended atoll at Majuro, 300 miles south-east of Kwajalein, and the site of an excellent anchorage, would also be seized as an advanced naval base. The ground forces for the attack would be drawn from both the US Army and the United States Marine Corps (USMC). Adm Turner, commanding Task Force 51, would lead the Southern Attack Force (TF52), landing Maj-Gen C.H. Corlett's 7th Infantry Division of the US Army, which would take Kwajalein Island; while Rear-Adm Richard L. Connolly would land the Northern Attack Force (TF53), comprising the USMC's 4th Division under Maj-Gen Harry Schmidt, to secure the twin islands of Roi-Namur. Holland Smith would be in overall command of the 84,000-strong force and sail with Turner aboard the newly adapted command ship *Rocky Mount* (another of the recommendations after the Tarawa inquest). In addition to Turner's and Connolly's task forces, a third task force (TF58), under

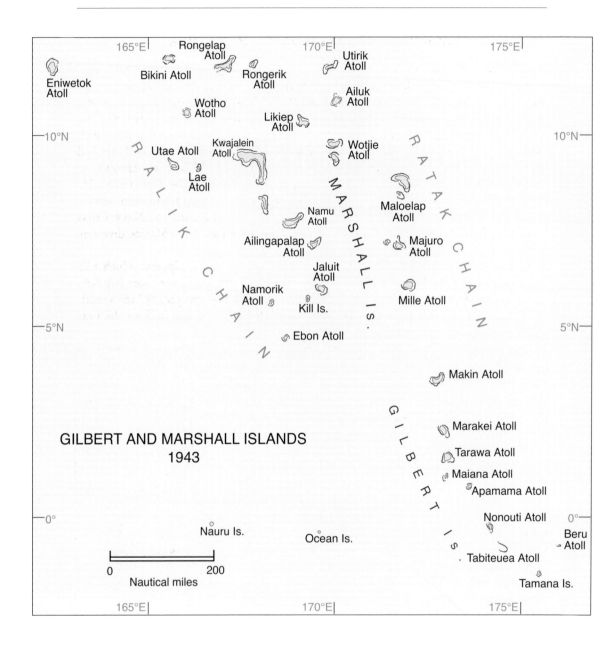

GILBERT AND MARSHALL ISLANDS
1943

Vice-Adm Marc Mitscher, comprising 6 fleet carriers, 6 escort carriers, 8 battleships and a host of cruisers, destroyers and submarines, would support the invasion forces; and land-based aircraft of VII Air Force, plus Navy and Marine aircraft, all based in the Gilbert and Ellice Islands, would pound the Japanese defences.

NORTHERN ATTACK FORCE – ROI-NAMUR

Kwajalein is the largest atoll in the world, 60 miles long and 20 miles wide and consisting of a series of 80 reefs and islets surrounding a huge lagoon of 800 square miles. The two main objectives were Kwajalein Island at the southern end of the atoll and the twin islands of Roi-Namur at the northern extremity (see map on p. 63). The invasion of Roi-Namur was assigned to the 4th Marine Division, which had recently been formed at Camp Pendleton in California and had arrived in the Marshalls after an arduous 4,300-mile trip from San Diego via Hawaii. In command was Maj-Gen Harry Schmidt, popularly known as 'The Dutchman'. He had entered the Marine Corps as a 2nd lieutenant in 1909 and had seen service in China, Mexico, Cuba and Nicaragua, where he was awarded the Navy Cross (second only to the Medal of Honor). He would later command the Marine divisions at Iwo Jima.

Kwajalein was the proving ground for the new tactics and equipment which had been devised as a result of the Tarawa battle: armoured amphibious tractors (LVT(A)s) fitted with 37mm cannons replaced the Amtracs which had spearheaded the assault on Betio; rocket-firing gunboats (LCI(G)s) supported the landings; and amphibious

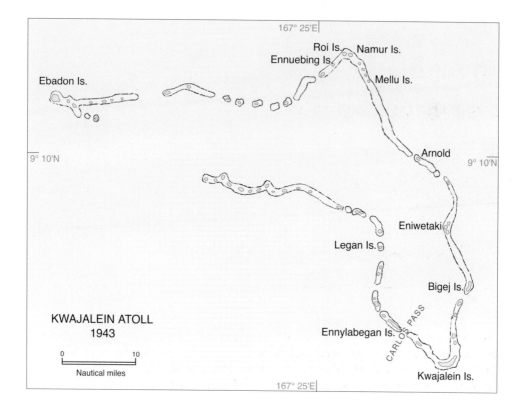

trucks (DUKWs), always referred to as 'Ducks', hauled supplies and ammunition ashore. A new tactical development was the occupation of small islets and islands close to the main objectives, used as artillery platforms to support the main landings.

For the Northern Attack Force, the islands of Mellu, Ennuebing, Ennugarret and Obella, all within artillery range of the Roi-Namur complex, were occupied by the 25th Marines, who brought in 75mm and 105mm howitzers. Despite some initial confusion, the artillery was in position by nightfall; all was now ready for the 23rd and 24th Marines to begin the assault on Roi-Namur the following day. D-Day brought some minor problems: rough seas and a continuation of the radio-communications difficulties that seemed to plague the Marines delayed the attack by an hour. Meanwhile, the naval bombardment thundered on all morning, and carrier-based planes, including Marine gunfire controllers, blasted the Roi-Namur airfield and defences. As the 23rd Marines headed for Roi and the 24th churned towards Namur, the Navy poured 6,000 tons of shells onto the island, leaving the defenders so stunned that they could only offer sporadic resistance.

Marines advance on Namur. (USMC)

The first assault waves approach the beach. Photograph taken from landing craft APA-34. (USMC)

Marines ponder their next move among the chaos of 'Red beach 2' on Roi Island. (USMC)

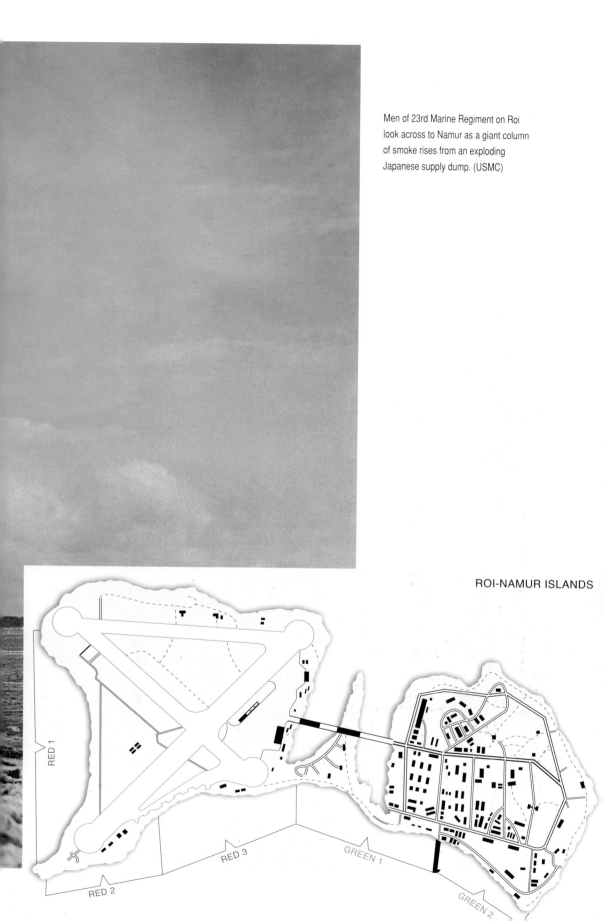

Men of 23rd Marine Regiment on Roi look across to Namur as a giant column of smoke rises from an exploding Japanese supply dump. (USMC)

ROI-NAMUR ISLANDS

RED 1

RED 2

RED 3

GREEN 1

GREEN 2

The two islands were the headquarters of Vice-Adm Yamada's 24th Air Flotilla and were defended by over 2,000 of the enemy – 600 infantry and over 1,400 labourers and administrative staff. Roi was open terrain, the island having been cleared to accommodate the airfield; but Namur, which was attached to Roi by a causeway, was a mass of barracks, administrative buildings and concrete fortifications which the Japanese defenders exploited to the maximum, and their fierce resistance caused the Marines a host of problems (see map on p. 67).

The most spectacular event of D-Day was a massive explosion on Namur. A Marine demolition team had attacked an enemy bunker with high-explosive satchel charges; but, unbeknown to them, the bunker was crammed with torpedo warheads, and the whole complex disappeared in a colossal explosion that was seen and heard for miles around. A column of smoke rose to over 1,000ft and trees were catapulted through the air like matchsticks. Twenty Marines were killed instantly and over a hundred were wounded.

At 7.30 p.m., the order was given to dig in for the night. But the Japanese were not going to allow the Marines any respite and they mounted a series of very determined night attacks which took some time to repulse. On Roi the openness of the airfield allowed the Marines of the 23rd Regiment to deploy their tanks, and the far side of the island was rapidly reached; but there were still many strongholds to be dealt with. Reinforced-concrete blockhouses had to be reduced by 75mm half-track artillery, and many Japanese who had taken refuge in the airfield drainage ditches had to be sorted

Japanese prisoners were a rarity: here, suspicious Marines keep a prisoner well covered on Roi-Namur. (USMC)

out by combat teams using small arms and flame-throwers. However, by 6.00 p.m. most enemy resistance had ceased, allowing the engineers of the 20th Marines and the Naval Construction Battalions (Seabees) to begin preparing the airfield for a Marine aircraft wing. By the afternoon of the following day, all resistance on Namur had been overcome and the twin islands were declared 'secure', despite sporadic rifle fire from fanatical Japanese troops holed up in isolated positions.

Compared with the Tarawa operation, the conquest of Roi-Namur had been a relatively low-key affair. The casualties amounted to 313 Marines killed and 502 wounded; all but a handful of the defenders were killed. All that remained of the northern operation was the occupation of the numerous islets scattered around the atoll, where the Marines were greeted with enthusiasm by the natives, and the mass burial of the dead Japanese defenders, a less happy task.

SOUTHERN ATTACK FORCE – KWAJALEIN ISLAND

The Army's attack on Kwajalein Island was carried out in conjunction with the Marines' assault on Roi-Namur, and both benefited from the massive naval and aerial pounding of the Japanese defences. As in the north, the surrounding islets were rapidly secured, allowing the 17th Infantry Regiment's 145th Field Artillery to blast the target with over 28,000 rounds. Working to well-rehearsed procedures, the 32nd and 184th Infantry Regiments came ashore to find the Japanese well dug in among the demolished buildings, uprooted trees and general debris. Backed up by tanks, the troops slowly advanced along the two and a half miles of the island in column of battalion, as Kwajalein is only 800yd wide. With the backing of artillery and naval gunfire and coordinated air attacks, the Army made slow but steady progress along the island, sealing underground positions with demolition charges and burning out bunkers with flame-throwers. Rear-Adm Akiyama Monzo, the commander of the 4,000-strong garrison, organised a strong resistance, mounting desperate counter-attacks during each night of the battle and making excellent use of the various bunkers that had withstood the pounding by offshore battleships. It took four days to suppress the enemy forces at a cost of 173 US Army killed and 793 wounded; as in the north, the Japanese garrison was virtually annihilated.

A remarkable innovation that was first adopted during the Marshalls campaign was the use of Navajo Indian 'code talkers'. In previous battles the Japanese had been able to intercept and understand messages transmitted by radio or morse. To foil them, groups of Navajo Indians were recruited and trained to use their unique language to send combat messages between various units and from shore to ship; this exotic code would be used for the remainder of the war and was never deciphered by the Japanese. The speed with which the Northern and Southern Attack Forces had completed their assignments encouraged Nimitz to advance by three weeks the next and final phase of 'Operation Flintlock': the occupation of the atoll of Eniwetok in the far north-east of the Marshall Islands.

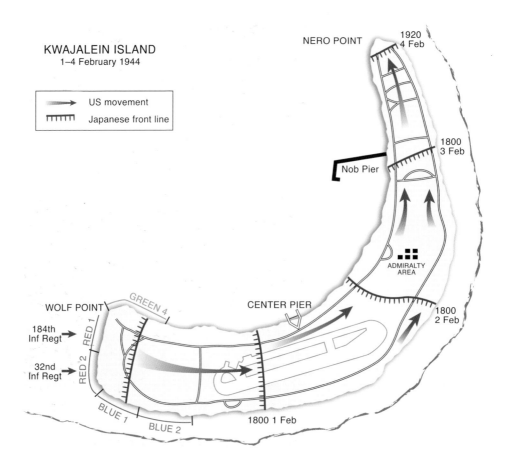

KWAJALEIN ISLAND
1–4 February 1944

US movement	
Japanese front line	

NERO POINT

1920
4 Feb

1800
3 Feb

Nob Pier

ADMIRALTY
AREA

WOLF POINT

GREEN 4

CENTER PIER

1800
2 Feb

184th
Inf Regt

RED 1

32nd
Inf Regt

RED 2

BLUE 1

BLUE 2

1800 1 Feb

A Marine in a shelled storage tank after
the capture of Kwajalein in February 1944.
(National Archives)

Code Talkers. Navajo Indians were recruited to transmit messages in their native tongue, in order to baffle the Japanese. (Charles Waterhouse)

TASK FORCE 58 AT TRUK – 'OPERATION HAILSTORM'

Kwajalein, Roi-Namur and Majuro had all been taken by early February, and Nimitz was determined to maintain the impetus. He flew to the Marshalls from Pearl Harbor to discuss the next move with his commanders, and the atoll of Eniwetok, some 400 miles north-west of Kwajalein, with its excellent lagoon and its proximity to the eastern Caroline Islands, was earmarked as a prime target. However, Eniwetok was dangerously exposed to air and surface attacks from the huge naval base at Truk, the home of Vice-Adm Mineichi Koga's Combined Japanese Fleet, which was only 670 miles to the south-west.

Described as the 'Gibraltar of the Pacific', Truk had a superb natural harbour. The Japanese had made it a formidable bastion with batteries of heavy guns, 4 airfields housing over 400 aircraft, and a garrison which was estimated at over 3,500 troops. On 12 February, Task Force 58, a massive fleet of carriers, battleships, cruisers and destroyers under the command of Vice-Adm Marc Mitscher, left Majuro, arriving off Truk on the 17th. For two days the task force pounded the island: 'Hellcat' fighters strafed rows of parked aircraft; 'Avenger' bombers destroyed hangars and adminis- trative buildings with fragmentation bombs; and 'Dauntless' dive-bombers wreaked havoc among the shipping in the harbour. The Japanese had prior knowledge of the approaching armada and evacuated most of their heavy vessels. However, Mitscher's pilots sank 2 cruisers and 4 destroyers, and over 200,000 tons of merchant shipping;

250 enemy aircraft were also destroyed and heavy damage was inflicted to the airfield and other ground installations.

Nimitz was jubilant and Truk was deleted from his list of possible targets for invasion; the Americans simply bypassed the island, and it was not occupied until after the Japanese surrender in 1945. The loss of Truk obliged the Japanese to move their next line of defence to the Palau Islands hundreds of miles to the west, and, with Truk no longer a threat, Nimitz could now concentrate on the final phase of 'Operation Flintlock' – Eniwetok.

ENIWETOK – 'OPERATION CATCHPOLE'

Eniwetok Atoll is 330 miles north-west of Kwajalein. It has an excellent Lagoon 17 by 21 miles in size and is surrounded by over forty tiny islets; the US Navy saw it as an outstanding natural harbour and a useful stepping-off point for the eastern Carolines. The Atoll's three largest islands, Engebi in the north and Eniwetok and Parry in the south-east, were the obvious targets and accommodated the bulk of the 2,500 troops of the Japanese garrison, the 1st Amphibian Brigade. The commander, Maj-Gen Yoshima Nishida, had deployed his men well, and, despite severe shortages in building materials, the Japanese had constructed an extensive network of tunnels and camouflaged trenches.

Offshore battleships and cruisers soften up Eniwetok Atoll prior to the US invasion. (USMC)

Marines leave their Amtrac under heavy fire on Eniwetok. (USMC)

The Americans had been softening up the defences since the end of January and as D-Day, 17 February, approached, the heavy guns of the old battleships joined in with devastating results. The planners decided to deploy the 22nd Marine Regiment, with 8,000 men, and two battalions of the Army's 106th Infantry Regiment, with 2,000 men, all under Brig-Gen Thomas E. Watson, USMC. Naval support would be supplied by Rear-Adm 'Handsome Harry' Hill. Using Japanese navigation charts captured at Kwajalein, the invasion force entered the lagoon, and the Marine's 2nd Pack Howitzer Battalion and the Army's 104th Field Artillery Battalion set up their guns on the islands adjacent, with the principal objective of providing support for the infantry.

The landings on Engebi on 18 February were spearheaded by the 1st and 2nd Battalions of the 22nd Marines, and the Japanese resistance was fanatical, with extensive use of 'spiderholes' – a series of interconnecting tunnels which enabled the defenders to crawl from one position to another and emerge 50 or 60ft away from the original location. The Japanese pinned down the Marines for much longer than had been anticipated, but with the added firepower of 105mm self-propelled guns the whole island was overrun by the afternoon of D+1; of the garrison of 1,200 Japanese and Koreans, only 19 were taken alive.

After the island had been cleared, documents were found giving the disposition of troops around the atoll. The discovery came as something of a shock; it revealed that Eniwetok and Parry Islands, which the Americans had regarded as being held by a token garrison, were in fact heavily defended, Eniwetok alone housing over 800 defenders. This necessitated a major change of plan, and both islands were soon on the receiving end of an intensified and prolonged naval bombardment.

Instead of attacking both islands simultaneously, as had been originally planned, separate attacks were made, with the Army's 106th Infantry Regiment landing on Eniwetok on 20 February. The advance quickly stalled as the troops encountered heavy mortar fire and dozens of the dreaded spiderholes. Brig-Gen Watson became so frustrated with the lack of progress that he landed the 3rd Battalion of the 22nd Marines in the afternoon and ordered Col Russell G. Ayres, the commander

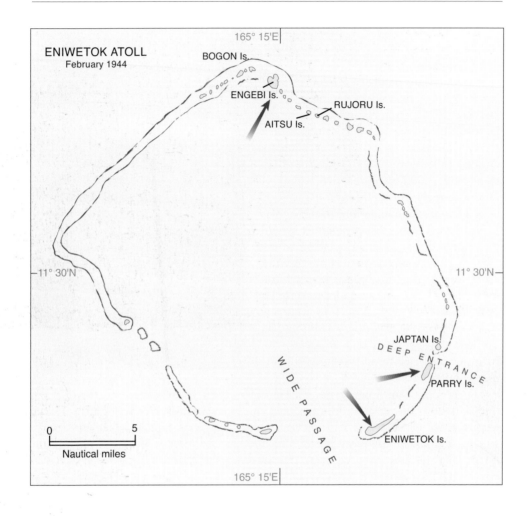

of the 106th, to 'push your attack'. Even with Marine reinforcements, the battle developed into a close-quarter slog between dug-in Japanese defenders and small US assault groups making extensive use of flame-throwers and satchel charges; but by evening the Japanese were reduced to a small area a few hundred yards from the northern end of the island. Throughout the night the enemy harassed the US forces, launching a major attack on the Marine HQ, which was eventually beaten off; and at daybreak the Marines were astonished to discover that the Army units which were supposed to be guarding their right flank had moved back 300yd without notifying them. But the lines were rapidly re-established and the attack resumed with even more ferocity; by mid-afternoon on 21 February the Japanese had finally succumbed.

Parry Island remained defiant and Brig-Gen Watson brought down from Engebi the 1st and 2nd Battalions of the 22nd Marines and also added their 3rd Battalion

Pfc Faris Touhy, 19, front left, and two other Marines recover after the fighting on Eniwetok. (USMC)

A B24 becomes airborne from an island airstrip on Eniwetok, February 1944. (National Archives)

Amid a landscape of shattered palm trees, Marines prepare to storm a blockhouse, having just thrown grenades into it. (USMC)

from Eniwetok. The assault was delayed until the 22nd, by which time the old battleships of Harry Hill's task force had blasted the island with their 14in guns from within a mile of the shore. The 22nd Marines landed behind a dense smokescreen, and the offshore naval bombardment, coupled with artillery fire from the nearby islets, produced a rolling barrage that crept ahead of the tanks and infantrymen as they mounted a relentless assault on Nishida's defences. The last enemy position fell to the Marines in the early hours of the following day. US forces had lost 348 men, with a further 866 wounded; Nishida's garrison of 3,400 was wiped out. Japan's outer defence ring had been breached and thousands of troops in both the Marshalls and the Carolines were virtually excluded from any further participation in the war. Majuro, Kwajalein and Eniwetok became major US naval bases, staging posts for the next phase of the 'island hopping' campaign, against the Marianas. Furthermore, the speed with which the Marshalls had been conquered allowed Nimitz to update his programme by five months.

THE US NAVY IN 'OPERATION FLINTLOCK'

Adm Koga of the Imperial Japanese Navy was reluctant to deploy his depleted carrier force to the Marshall Islands, and his Navy's involvement was minimal. The US Navy, now reinforced and replenished in the two years since Pearl Harbor, fielded a staggering array of vessels. Many of the old battleships from Pearl Harbor had been repaired, and, although most were obsolete, their 14in and 16in guns could provide powerful pre-invasion bombardments. Joining them were the new fleet carriers, battleships and cruisers, all testimony to the amazing achievements of the US shipyards since 1941. The ships involved in the various facets of 'Operation Flintlock' were:

Battleships	*Heavy Cruisers*	*Light Cruisers*	*Aircraft Carriers*
Tennessee (BB13)	*Louisville* (CA28)	*Santa Fe* (CL60)	*Saratoga* (CV3)
Colorado (BB45)	*Indianapolis* (CA35)	*Mobile* (CL63)	*Princeton* (CV23)
Maryland (BB46)	*Portland* (CA33)	*Biloxi* (CL80)	*Langley* (CV28)
Pennsylvania (BB38)	*Minneapolis* (CA36)		*Enterprise* (CV6)
Idaho (BB42)	*San Francisco* (CA38)		*Yorktown* (CV10)
New Mexico (BB40)	*New Orleans* (CA32)		*Belleau Wood* (CVL24)
Mississippi (BB41)			*Intrepid* (CV11)
			Essex (CV9)
			Cabot (CVL27)
			Cowpens (CVL25)
			Monterey (CVL26)
			Bunker Hill (CV17)

Plus six escort carriers, over forty destroyers and hundreds of smaller vessels.

THREE

THE MARIANAS

GATEWAY TO JAPAN

'Bullets we understood, but the hearts and minds of the
Japanese were beyond our understanding.'

(*Charles Carfrae* (Chindit Column, *1985*))

The strategists within Japan's imperial headquarters were shocked at the ease with
which the Marshall Islands had fallen. As they saw MacArthur's troops moving
inexorably westward through the Dutch East Indies towards the Philippines, and
Nimitz sweeping through the Carolines, it seemed obvious that their final defence line
was in danger of being breached. Fresh troops were released from the Japanese mainland and the Kwantung Army was plundered to shore up the garrisons in the Marianas
and Palau Islands. The 4th Fleet and 31st Army, based in Saipan under Adm Nagumo
and Lt-Gen Yoshitsugu Saito, were also reinforced by the 14th Air Fleet. Pivotal to
Nimitz's plans for the Marianas were the three islands of Saipan, Tinian and Guam;
they were needed to provide naval facilities and would be the sites of airfields from
which the US Army Air Force could bomb the Japanese mainland.

Saipan, the most northerly of the three, was 15 miles long and 7 miles wide, with
airfields already in place at the northern and southern extremities; the remainder of
the island was a profusion of mountains, cliff faces, caves and semi-jungle. The highest
peaks were Mt Nafutan and Mt Kagman, both around 400ft, and Mt Tapotchau in
the centre of the island, which rises to 1,554ft. The population, mostly of Japanese
origin, lived in the small towns of Charan Kanoa, Garapan and Tanapag, all on the
west coast.

Only 3½ miles south of Saipan and less than half its size, Tinian is reasonably flat;
there was an excellent site in the north for the expansion of the existing airfield. The
only serious obstacle facing the invaders would be the cliff faces that constitute about
90 per cent of the coastline.

Guam, over 120 miles to the south, is the largest of the Marianas group at 34
miles long and 5–9 miles wide. It had been under US jurisdiction from 1898 until

the Japanese invasion of 10 December 1941. The Americans were aware that the civilian population were still loyal to the USA and they expected a considerable amount of cooperation. An airfield was already in place on the Orote Peninsula on the western coast of the island and despite the generally mountainous terrain, there were numerous other locations for the US Army Air Force to exploit.

Adm King, Chief of Naval Operations and CIC US Fleet, had pressed hard for the inclusion of the Marianas in the strategic planning of the Combined Chiefs of Staff, but it was not until the Quadrant Conference in Quebec in 1943, where he enlisted the support of Gen Henry H. 'Hap' Arnold, Commander of the Army Air Forces, that he was able to get the Marianas on the agenda. As with the Marshalls campaign, the attack on the Marianas, 'Operation Forager', was to be a joint Army and Marine effort under the overall command of Vice-Adm Ray Spruance, who would also command the

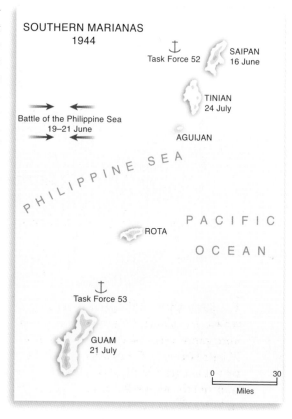

5th Fleet. As at Tarawa, there would be two attack forces – the Northern Attack Force (TF52), under Vice-Adm Kelly Turner, and the Southern Attack Force (TF53) under Rear-Adm Richard Connolly – and tactical control of all troops ashore would be with Lt-Gen Holland Smith. The assault on Saipan would be spearheaded by the 2nd and 4th Divisions of the USMC, with the Army's 27th Infantry Division in reserve, the two Marine Divisions then going on to occupy Tinian; and for the Guam landings the 3rd Division and the 1st Provisional Marine Brigade would lead the attack, with the Army's 77th Infantry Division in reserve. The Americans were guessing at the strength of the Saipan garrison; an early estimation of around 10,000 was later updated to between 15,000 and 17,000, but in fact a figure of over 30,000 would have been more accurate. Although Adm Nagumo was the designated chief of naval forces, his poor performance at Midway had not been forgotten and he was now well down the pecking order; effective control now lay with Saito. It was now becoming customary for the old US battleships to hammer the islands with their heavy guns, but the Marines who stormed ashore on 15 June still came across many strong and undamaged enemy positions.

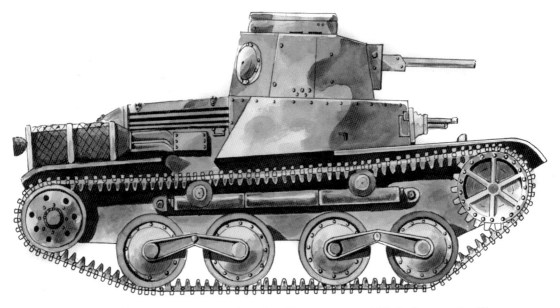

The Japanese Type 95 'Ha-Go', weighing 10 tons and mounting a 37mm gun, was no match for the Sherman and could be easily disabled by bazooka or even machine-gun fire. (Author)

The principal US tank used in the Pacific was the M4 Sherman. Weighing 32 tons, it mounted a 75mm gun. (Author)

SAIPAN – D-DAY

The battle began at 6.00 a.m. with a feint attack off the northern town of Tanapag by elements of the 2nd Marine Division. The Japanese moved one regiment to the area but soon realised that this was a diversion and that the main attack was developing further south. The familiar command, 'Land the landing force', boomed out aboard the troopships of the attack force, and the Amtracs and Armoured Amphibian Tractors (LVT(A)s), with their snub-nose 75mm guns, left the line of departure and headed for the beaches.

The Marines' true destination was two areas of beach between the towns of Garapan in the north and Aginan Point in the south, with the village of Charan Kanoa at the centre (see map on p. 82). The first wave hit the beach at 8.44 a.m., and, with landing craft arriving at around five-minute intervals, over 8,000 troops were ashore within the first twenty minutes.

Things began to go wrong immediately. A strong northerly offshore current pushed many of the 2nd Division craft about 400yd north of their assigned landing areas,

A panoramic view of the Saipan coastline under naval bombardment, 7 July 1944. (USMC)

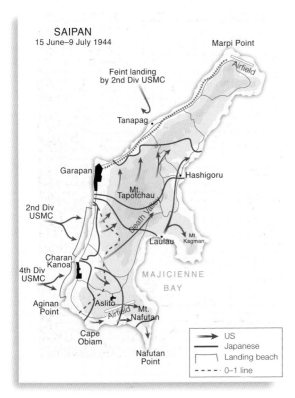

SAIPAN
15 June–9 July 1944

Marpi Point

Feint landing
by 2nd Div USMC

Airfield

Tanapag

Garapan

Hashigoru

Mt.
Tapotchau

Death Valley

2nd Div
USMC

Laulau

Mt.
Kagman

Charan
Kanoa

4th Div
USMC

MAJICIENNE
BAY

Aginan
Point

Aslito

Airfield

Mt.
Nafutan

Cape
Obiam

Nafutan
Point

→ US
   Japanese
   Landing beach
- - - - 0–1 line

and a dangerous gap was created between the two divisions which would require a lot of heavy fighting to close. It had been hoped that the LVT(A)s would carry the first waves of assault troops to the 0–1 line (the first objective), but the fierce enemy resistance prevented all but a few units of the 4th Division from making it that far. Casualties were soon mounting, and evacuating them to the offshore ships was a highly dangerous operation as they ran the gauntlet of heavy Japanese artillery and mortar fire directed by spotters in the hills a few miles inland. As night began to fall the situation was still confused; the gap between the two divisions had not yet been closed and only half of the planned beachhead had been occupied. Over 20,000 troops had come ashore, including Marine artillery, which immediately began

A Marine shot down at the water's edge on the west coast of Saipan. (USMC)

Two Marines fall on the beaches of Saipan as a Japanese sniper finds his target. (USMC)

supporting the infantry. Maj-Gen Harry Schmidt, who had arrived around 7.30 p.m., commented from his command post that it was the hottest spot he had ever been in during the war. Night fighting was not a form of combat that the Marine Corps adopted by choice, but it was undertaken with relish by the Japanese. The night of D-Day saw many attacks across the whole of the US front, the Japanese probing to find weaknesses. At one point they attacked the 4th Division area south of Charan Kanoa, behind a 'human shield' of civilians. But the main attack came from the northern flank, when around 2,000 troops left Garapan, supported by a few tanks, and fell upon the 2nd Division's 6th Marines. After a bitter battle in which over 700 Japanese were killed, the enemy fell back in disarray.

D+1 TO D+2

The following days saw the Marines advancing on a broad front. The 2nd Division finally closed the gap between them and the 4th Division, at the same time pushing north towards Garapan and east to Lake Susupe. On the night of D+1 another major attack developed against the 6th Marines, this time spearheaded by forty-four tanks. The Marines retaliated with rockets, self-propelled 75mm artillery and their

A direct hit on a Japanese fuel dump causes a spectacular blaze as the Marines advance on Garapan. (USMC)

own armour, destroying twenty-four of the Japanese tanks. On the 4th Division front, the 23rd Regiment also reached the swamps around Lake Susupe, where they ground to a temporary halt, while the 24th and 25th Regiments pressed forward to Aslito airfield, the principal objective in the south of the island. To reinforce the 4th Marine Division, Holland Smith sent in the 165th Regiment of the Army's 27th Division under Maj-Gen Ralph Smith, the same commander who had performed so poorly at Makin, thus sowing the seeds for what was to become a major row between the Marine Corps and the Army. US forces were now poised on the northern outskirts of Aslito airfield, the Marines' 25th Regiment in the centre, the 24th on their left and the Army's 165th on their right. A patrol went forward and reported that the airfield had been abandoned, but the 165th, who had been assigned to capture it, decided to wait until the following day.

Meanwhile, a major drama was unfolding elsewhere. Adm Spruance had received news that a Japanese fleet was on the move and apparently heading for the Marianas. A meeting was hastily convened between Spruance, Turner and Holland Smith at which it was decided to disembark the remainder of the 27th Infantry Division, to postpone the landings on Guam, and to move the supply and troopships 200–300 miles to the east. The old battleships and the remainder of the invasion screen would stand by 25 miles west of Saipan.

THE GREAT MARIANAS TURKEY SHOOT – THE BATTLE OF THE PHILIPPINE SEA

Adm Spruance's intelligence from patrolling US Navy submarines informed him that a large Japanese force had left Tawitawi in the Philippines on 13 June and was heading eastward. Under the command of Vice-Adm Ozawa, the 1st Mobile Fleet was an impressive armada of carriers, battleships and cruisers that included the brand new carrier *Taiho*, commissioned in 1944 and displacing 34,600 tons, the veteran carriers *Shokaku* and *Zuikaku*, and the two super-battleships *Yamato* and *Musashi*, at 72,000 tons each the two largest battleships ever built. Ozawa had split his force into two: up front was Force C, centred on the three light carriers *Zuiho*, *Chitose* and *Chiyoda* and commanded by the fiery Vice-Adm Takeo Kurita; Ozawa's main force steamed 100 miles to the rear, prepared for a decisive battle. Impressive as it looked, the 1st Mobile Fleet had a fatal weakness: there were only 450 aircraft available and the crews were almost all poorly trained and lacking any kind of combat experience. Ozawa was also planning on the assistance of land-based planes from the Marianas, but he was to be disappointed: many had been destroyed on Guam by Mitscher's carrier planes and those that remained were to prove ineffectual.

Vice-Adm Mitscher's Task Force 58 could only be described as awesome (it had taken five hours to clear the lagoon at Majuro in the Marshalls): 15 carriers, 7 battle-ships, 10 cruisers and over 60 destroyers were heading westward to square off with Ozawa's fleet. The aircrews of the US Navy were also a formidable bunch; the product of long and intensive training under the supervision of veterans of the Coral Sea and Midway, they outclassed their Japanese counterparts in numbers, skill and experience. The recent introduction of the Grumman F6F–3 'Hellcat' fighter, with a top speed of 375mph and 6 machine-guns, also gave them a huge advantage. On 17 June, Spruance, flying his flag in the cruiser USS *Indianapolis*, issued his battle plan to Mitscher: 'Our aircraft will knock out enemy carriers, then attack battleships and cruisers to slow or disable them. The TF will destroy the enemy fleet either by fleet action if the enemy elects to fight or by sinking slow or crippled ships if [the] enemy retreats. Action against the enemy must be pushed vigorously to ensure complete destruction of the fleet.'

On 18 June, Mitscher's TF58 was some 200 miles west of Saipan when it was located by Japanese reconnaissance planes. Acting on their information Kurita positioned his ships slightly beyond the range of TF58 and prepared for a major attack the following day. Spruance, still unaware of the location of the enemy, launched a pre-emptive strike against the airfields on Guam, where his 'Hellcats' decimated the enemy's fighters and bombers. At 10.00 a.m. on the 19th, the first wave of 64 Japanese planes headed for Mitscher's Task Force 58 and were picked up on radar. More than 200 Hellcats were scrambled from the *Essex*, *Cowpens*, *Bunker Hill* and *Princeton*, and in the ensuing mêlée 41 enemy planes were shot down. None of them reached the US carriers and the only casualty was the battleship *South Dakota*, which was hit by a 551lb bomb that killed 27 of the crew. Ozawa's second wave consisted of 128 planes and again they were picked up on radar, which guided the 'Hellcats' into intercept positions. The inexperienced Japanese flyers were no match for the 'Hellcats', and 97 aircraft were lost. The third wave, only 47 this time, swung round and came in from the north. Seven were shot down and none reached the US carriers. The final attack came at 2.00 p.m., when 82 planes arrived over TF58 and made feeble attacks on the carriers. There were 12 planes shot down in the process, the survivors heading for Guam only to encounter 27 'Hellcats', which shot down another 30.

Ozawa was unaware of the extent of his defeat; he believed that most of the aircraft which had not returned to his carriers had landed in the Marianas and would return later. In all he had launched 373 planes, of which 240 had been shot down, with another 25 being lost to other causes. None of the US carriers had been hit. Lt-Cdr Paul Buie, the leader of fighter group VF-16, coined the phrase 'The Great Marianas Turkey Shoot' for this incredibly one-sided slaughter. Japan's Navy had lost what few experienced pilots it had and the US Navy had displayed its absolute mastery of the skies.

Ozawa's misery was not yet at an end. The US submarine *Albacore* had penetrated his fleet and fired a spread of six torpedoes at the carrier *Taiho*. At least one of them struck home rupturing a large aviation fuel tank. Some hapless seaman activated the ventilation system to clear the fumes and succeeded in distributing the vapours throughout the ship. The inevitable ignition occurred at 3.32 p.m., resulting in a violent explosion that shattered the ship, one witness describing how the flight deck rolled back like a sardine tin. The carrier eventually keeled over and sank, taking 1,650 crewmen with her. A second US submarine, the *Cavalla*, on her maiden patrol, also attacked Ozawa's carriers, slamming three torpedoes into the Pearl Harbor veteran *Shokaku*, which blew up and sank within minutes.

Still unaware of the magnitude of his defeat, Ozawa withdrew to the west of the Marianas to refuel. The extravagant claims of his returning pilots led him to believe that the US fleet had been badly mauled, and he still believed that his missing planes were seeking refuge on Guam and would be back in action on the following day. The loss of two carriers was a serious setback, but no American aircraft had attacked his fleet, a fact that he attributed to the success of his pilots against the enemy carriers. He ordered Vice-Adm Kurita to launch reconnaissance planes to seek out Mitscher's Task Force 58.

In mid-afternoon on the 20th, a scout plane from the *Enterprise* finally located Ozawa's force; it was in three groups heading west and refuelling, Mitscher's Task Force 58 was 280 miles to the east and the sun was getting low in the sky. Mitscher faced a dilemma. If a strike was launched, his planes would reach the Japanese fleet at twilight and would return in total darkness, if indeed they had enough fuel to get back at all; if he didn't attack, the enemy would almost certainly be out of range by the following morning. Mitscher had no doubts and opted to hurl a striking force of 216 'Hellcats', 'Avengers' and 'Helldivers' at Ozawa. With the light failing fast, they finally found the Japanese fleet at around 6.30 p.m. In the gathering dusk Ozawa launched 75 planes, but they were ineffective and the US pilots tore into the enemy ships, hitting the carrier *Hiyo* with two torpedoes, damaging two tankers, which later sank, and crippling the carrier *Chiyoda* and the battleship *Haruna*. The *Hiyo* burned fiercely for some hours and finally sank after dark.

With the sun almost touching the horizon, the Navy pilots turned for home, a 335-mile flight to a blacked-out Task Force 58 over a menacing inky sea. Fuel was running low; few, if any, had been trained for night-time landings; and a radio-silence order was in operation. As engines spluttered to a halt, plane after plane pancaked into the sea. Those that did reach the task force desperately tried to set down on the nearest carrier; one plane even attempted to land on a destroyer. Throwing caution to the wind, Mitscher ordered the fleet to turn on all available lights; one flyer described the sight as being like a seaside resort. Eighty-two planes were lost, either to ditchings or crash landings, and a major air–sea rescue operation the following morning by ships and floatplanes successfully rescued the majority of the crews; only 16 pilots and 33 crewmen were lost.

Spruance had achieved a stunning victory, the Japanese had lost over 480 aircraft, including those destroyed on the ground on Guam, against the Americans' 104. Ozawa retired to Okinawa with only 35 serviceable aircraft. Even so Spruance was criticised by Mitscher for not pursuing the Japanese fleet on the 21st. This was completely unjustified and displayed a lack of understanding of the strategic situation. Spruance's overriding responsibility was to defend the invasion fleet. The fact that he was able to fulfil that obligation and also inflict a massive defeat on the 1st Mobile Fleet is testimony to his outstanding ability.

SAIPAN – THE PUSH NORTH

With Ozawa fleeing for Okinawa the Saipan beachhead was now secure and the troopships and supply vessels returned to their vital work. While the great naval battle was in progress, the Army and Marine forces had captured the airfield at Aslito with the aid of the Army's 105th Regiment, which had moved along the south coast. The bulk of the Japanese troops in south Saipan were now bottled up around Nafutan Point at the south-east end of the island. Further north the 2nd Marine Division, which had landed between Garapan and Charan Kanoa, had swung north and now formed the left flank of a broad front, with the Army's 27th Division in the centre and the 4th Marine Division on the right. The US forces were now approaching some of the most difficult terrain as they headed for the foothills of Mount Tapotchau, the highest point on the island. Lt-Gen Saito's main line of defence ran from west to east across the island in this area, and the Americans had made intensive preparations for the forth-coming attack with a massive increase in

Marines bring in Japanese prisoners, Saipan.
(National Archives)

artillery support and the deployment of rocket-firing P-47 'Thunderbolt' aircraft from the 19th Fighter Squadron US Army Air Force to Aslito airfield.

The offensive to the north began in earnest on the 23rd, and the 27th Division's progress soon stalled; the rugged terrain and a determined rearguard action by the Japanese slowed the Army troops to a crawl. Three principal areas, the so-called 'Hell's Pocket', 'Purple Heart Ridge' and an open area to their front called 'Death Valley', were the main obstacles, and by evening one unit had advanced only 100yd while another dug in for the night only 700yd from their jumping-off point.

By the next day Holland Smith was fuming. While his Marines were grinding forward – the 2nd Division in the tortuous foothills of Mount Tapotchau and the 4th swinging east into the Kagman Peninsula – a gap of over a mile had developed between the Army and Marine lines, and he was faced with the prospect of having to bring his Marines to a halt until the 27th Division caught them up. Recalling Maj-Gen Ralph Smith's poor performance on Makin, Holland Smith took the drastic step of relieving him of command, citing 'lack of aggressiveness', and replaced him with Maj-Gen Sanderford Jarman on 24 June. This was to be the catalyst for one of the most serious incidents in the whole Pacific War. The relief of an Army general by a Marine general caused uproar at the Pentagon, and the 'Smith v. Smith' incident as it became known caused a major rift in interservice relations that was to last for decades.

Holland Smith may have emerged from the furore more damaged than his Army counterpart. His influence was to be diminished to a marked degree: at Iwo Jima his authority was lessened by the appointment of Maj-Gen Harry Schmidt as commander of the Marines on the island – 'they only brought me along in case anything happened to Harry Schmidt', he was to remark during the battle – and at the end of the war, when the surrender was signed aboard the USS *Missouri* in Tokyo Bay, he was conspicuous by his absence, his presence vetoed by Nimitz.

Back at the Nafutan Peninsula, the Army's 105th Infantry were still attempting to clear out the remaining Japanese pockets of resistance; 40mm and 90mm AA guns were using direct-trajectory fire to pin down the enemy while flame-thrower crews dealt with the caves, but the attacks were poorly coordinated. On the night of D+11, over 500 Japanese broke through the 105th's lines ('sneaked through' as the Army report put it) and headed for Aslito airfield, where they destroyed one P-47 'Thunderbolt' and badly damaged two others. Buoyed by their success, they advanced to Hill 500, hoping to break through to their main force south of Mount Tapotchau, but they encountered the 25th Marines, who were resting in reserve, and were annihilated the next day.

The 27th Division's reputation was not enhanced on the following day when their new commander, Maj-Gen Jarman, discovered that elements of the 105th and 106th Infantry were still near the edge of 'Death Valley' and were 'standing when there was no reason why they should not be moving'. More officers were relieved. On the 28th, Maj-Gen George W. Griner took over from Maj-Gen Jarman (Jarman was designated Garrison Force Commander of Saipan; his replacement of Ralph Smith

Ptes V. Harper and L.F. Surfave use a bazooka to blast a Japanese roadblock on the road below them, 9 July 1944. (USMC)

was only temporary) and he soon had a galvanising effect. Over the next few days the 27th Division mounted a series of attacks on the strongholds of 'Hell's Pocket', 'Death Valley' and 'Purple Heart Ridge', and by the 30th they had eradicated the last of the enemy much to the delight of Holland Smith, and the gaps on the flanks of the 2nd and 4th Divisions were finally closed.

The 2nd Division on the left had advanced to the coastal town of Garapan and the US front line now stretched from the centre of the town in the west to Hill 700 at the centre, and from there to just south of Hashigoru on the east coast – a 6-mile advance would complete the battle, but the enemy still had over 3,000 troops and a suicidal determination to resist. The further north US forces advanced, the narrower the island became; Holland Smith withdrew the 2nd Division to become reserve corps, leaving the 27th Infantry Division and the 4th Marine Division to finish the job. The 4th advanced for 3,500yd and on Independence Day (4 July) were north of Tanapag on the west coast. The 27th also made a substantial advance, finding the going much easier now that they had extricated themselves from the 'Death Valley' complex.

Holland Smith was well aware that when Japanese troops were backed into a corner the usual outcome was a wild 'banzai' attack as had happened at Tarawa and on the Marshalls, and he paid Griner a personal visit to warn him of the possibility. True to

A Marine covers a Japanese emerging from a cave. (USMC)

form, Lt-Gen Saito gave the order for a last-ditch 'banzai' attack on 6 July before both
he and Adm Nagumo killed themselves. In the pre-dawn darkness of the 7th, screaming hordes of Japanese launched a frenzied attack against the 105th Infantry Regiment
– two Army battalions were decimated and the attack rolled on to reach the Marine
artillery batteries in the rear. For his counter-attack, Griner sent in the 106th Infantry
with tank support, and in a day of horrendous close-quarter fighting the casualties
mounted spectacularly. The 105th Infantry suffered 918 casualties and the Marine
artillery battalions 127; the Japanese suffered a staggering 4,311 dead.

From 8 July onwards, it was just a case of mopping up. Holland Smith put most
of the 27th Division into reserve and placed the 2nd Marine Division back into the
line alongside the 4th Division. They swept north to the end of the island at Marpi
Point. Although the battle was virtually over in military terms, when the Marines
arrived at Marpi Point on 9 July they were to witness scenes that were as horrific as
anything they had seen on the battlefield. The Japanese civilians on Saipan had been
brainwashed by the military into believing that when the Americans arrived they
would suffer wholesale rape, torture and murder, and the US troops were to witness

the awful sight of women and children jumping off the precipitous cliffs onto the rocks below while others killed themselves by detonating hand grenades left behind by the Japanese troops. The Marines used loudhailers to try to tell the civilians that they had nothing to fear, but the carnage continued unabated and thousands died. In all, an estimated 23,811 Japanese troops were killed; the civilian death count is unknown. US forces suffered 3,225 killed and 13,061 wounded, but Saipan was declared 'secure' on 9 July. All that remained of the campaign in the northern Marianas was the occupation of nearby Tinian.

Realising that the Japanese is holding a hand grenade, the Marine shoots him. (USMC)

TINIAN

Only three and a half miles south of Saipan and less than two-thirds its size, Tinian looked an easy target; the highest point was Mount Lasso, at only 564ft. The Japanese had already built three airfields, one near Gurguan Point in the west and two on the flat northern plain south of Ushi Point (see map on p. 91). The major problem would be the landing itself, as almost 90 per cent of the coastline was sheer cliff. The obvious choice was the area around the capital, Tinian Town, on the south-west coast, where there were areas of beach large enough to take a substantial landing force, and it was here that the Japanese commander, Col Takashi Ogata, concentrated his 8,350-man garrison. Adm Kelly Turner advocated that the landings should take place in this area, but Holland Smith,

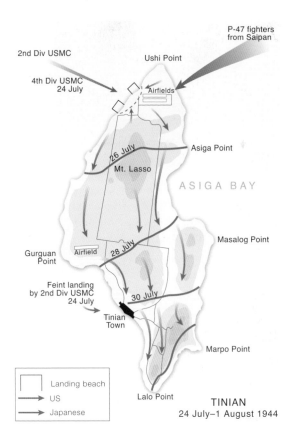

2nd Div USMC
Ushi Point
P-47 fighters from Saipan
4th Div USMC 24 July
Airfields
26 July
Asiga Point
Mt. Lasso
ASIGA BAY
Masalog Point
Gurguan Point
Airfield
28 July
Feint landing by 2nd Div USMC 24 July
30 July
Tinian Town
Marpo Point
Landing beach
US
Japanese
Lalo Point
TINIAN
24 July–1 August 1944

backed by Spruance, had other ideas. Smith argued that a landing around Tinian Town would play into Ogata's hands, and suggested that landing on two narrow beaches in the north-west near the airfields on Ushi Point would achieve the element of surprise, thus reducing the number of casualties. It was a high-risk strategy – the beaches would be congested and the landings would take much longer than usual; if there were a substantial number of Japanese troops in the area, there were all the ingredients for a disaster.

In an effort to distract Ogata, on 24 July a feint attack was made off the coast near Tinian Town by elements of the 2nd Marine Division, and at the same time the 4th Marine Division, followed by the remainder of the 2nd Division, made their landings in the north against minimal opposition. Col Ogata swallowed the bait and imagined that he had frustrated a major American landing. Only at nightfall did he realise that he had been duped, by which time 15,000 Marines were ashore. Ogata rushed troops to the beachheads, and the Marines spent the rest of the night and early morning beating back enemy attacks in which the Japanese lost 1,200 men. The Marines moved rapidly across the open terrain in the north, on the 26th capturing the

Ushi Point airfield on Tinian comes under heavy attack by carrier-based aircraft on 7 July 1944. (USMC)

Marine Corps tankers inspect a dug-in Type 97 'Chi-Ha' tank on Tinian. (George Forty)

airfields at Ushi Point and clearing Mount Lasso. Their advance was only halted on the 29th by appalling weather – the tail end of a typhoon struck the island, destroying two ship-to-shore pontoons and halting the unloading of artillery and supplies. Once the storm had abated, the attack was resumed with increased ferocity as the Marines called in the Army's P-47 'Thunderbolt' fighters from nearby Saipan. They introduced a new weapon to the Pacific War – napalm.

By 31 July, the Japanese were holed up in a tiny pocket in the south only five miles square. A counter-attack that night was a complete failure, and the following morning revealed a scene of utter carnage, with virtually all of the defenders dead or wounded. The battle had lasted for nine days and cost the Marines 328 dead and 1,571 wounded; the majority of the enemy garrison were killed, although a number of defenders hid away in caves and were still being hunted down months later.

Tinian was destined to become one of the US Air Force's prime bases in the assault on the Japanese homeland; and the massively expanded Ushi Point complex, renamed North Field, would be the departure point for a B29 'Superfortress' bomber named *Enola Gay* on 6 August 1945, bound for Hiroshima.

THE RECAPTURE OF GUAM

The largest island in the Marianas group at 34 miles long and between 5 and 9 miles wide, Guam was over 140 miles south of Saipan and Tinian, and the terrain was more tropical than the northern islands, with dense jungle, mountains, cliffs and ravines. The garrison of around 18,500 was only half the size of that on Saipan. They had fewer tanks and less artillery but were still a formidable force, and their commander, Lt-Gen Takeshi Takashina, who had been transferred from Manchuria in early 1944, was an experienced and able leader. The airfield on the Orote Peninsula on the west coast was a prime target for the Americans, and two beachheads, one west of Agana and the other south of Agat, were specifically chosen to allow for a pincer movement to secure the area (see map on p. 94).

For the invasion, delayed until 21 July because of the Philippine Sea battle, Spruance chose the 3rd Marine Division under Maj-Gen Allen Turnage, the 1st Provisional Marine Brigade under Brig-Gen Lemuel C. Shepherd and the Army's 77th Infantry Division under Maj-Gen Andrew Bruce. Once ashore these units would come under the overall command of Maj-Gen Roy S. Geiger, USMC. A massive 'softening up' naval barrage would precede the invasion and for thirteen days the battleships and cruisers of Rear-Adm Richard 'Close in' Connolly's Southern Attack Force (TF53) blasted the island. The Japanese were left in no doubt that the Americans were coming;

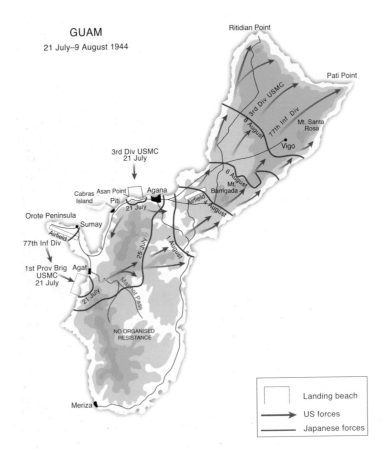

it was just a question of where and when and, as there were only 15 miles of suitable landing beaches on the west coast, they would have an advantage whichever area they chose to defend.

On the morning of 21 July, the Marines came ashore on both sides of the Orote Peninsula: the 3rd Division landed on the northern beach to the west of the town of Agana and the 1st Provisional Brigade on the southern beach to the south of Agat, and both soon ran into stiff opposition. The 3rd landed on the beachhead at Asan-Adelup and found themselves within yards of the command post of the Japanese commander Lt-Gen Takashina, which was carved out of the sandstone cliffs overlooking the beach. Heavy mortar and artillery fire rained down on them from the far left, while snipers and machine-gunners entrenched in the ridges and folds of the Bundschu Ridge covered the remainder of the beachhead with intense fire.

With the arrival of tanks the situation began to improve, and shortly before noon the 12th Regiment's artillery was ashore and was registered and firing by 12.15 p.m.; but the Marines on the far left were still pinned down by intense artillery and mortar fire. On the right of the beachhead, elements of the 9th Regiment overcame the defenders at Asan Point, driving through the initial objectives and gaining partial control of the heights. However, a ferocious 81mm mortar barrage in mid-afternoon failed

A Marine marksman picks off Japanese tank crewmen as they attempt to escape their burning tank. (USMC)

to dislodge the troops of the 320th Independent Infantry Battalion, and by nightfall the beachhead was still dominated by the Japanese. On the next day, 22 July, repeated attacks on the enemy positions gradually wore down the Japanese, and by 7.00 p.m. US forces were on the cliff top. A further advance the following morning confirmed that the enemy had withdrawn.

On the southern beaches near Agat the enemy resistance was even more ferocious than that which the 3rd Division found in the north. A concrete blockhouse at Gaan Point housing two 75mm and one 37mm artillery piece knocked out dozens of Amtracs of the 1st Provisional Brigade's invasion force, and for many hours this stronghold would cause the Marines major problems. The Japanese had made excellent use of the natural features of the Agat beachhead, with blockhouses at Agat Point in the centre, Maanot Ridge on the left and Mt Alifan on the right. In between they had constructed thick-walled concrete bunkers and a series of smaller pillboxes. At the extreme right the tiny island of Yona housed a number of machine-guns which were able to rake the beaches in that area.

As the Marines came ashore they encountered a series of trenches on the beaches from which the defenders poured heavy mortar and machine-gun fire. The Marine Amtracs were expected to drive 1,000yd before disembarking the troops, but the trenches and a heavily mined beach drastically slowed their progress, and it was not until 10.30 a.m. that their target was achieved. Sherman tanks came ashore during the morning and by 1.30 p.m. the Gaan Point blockhouse had been silenced after a surprise attack from the rear, while on the left the 22nd Regiment had advanced as far as the town of Agat. In the centre the Marines had finally moved inland. They were preparing to take the heights of Mt Alifan, but were foiled when the bombs from an aerial assault fell short of their target, halting the attack. On the right the 4th Regiment ran into staunch resistance at Hill 40 near Bangi Point, and it took a fierce infantry attack with tank support to claim the position by nightfall on D-Day. Brig-Gen Shepherd was able to tell Maj-Gen Geiger, 'think we can handle it – will continue as planned tomorrow'.

From his command post on Mt Alifan, the commander of the 38th Regiment, Col Tsunetaro Suenaga, witnessed the American landings and urged Lt-Gen Takashina to mount a counter-attack. The General was initially unwilling but finally relented, and Suenaga directed his forces against Hill 40 at the southern end of the beachhead. The brunt of the attack fell on the 3rd Battalion of the 4th Regiment, who just managed to hold on during a frenzied night-time assault in which 750 Japanese were killed. Suenaga pushed his men forward time and time again only to see them mown down. Four Japanese 'Ha-Go' tanks – small, poorly armed and armoured, and totally inferior to the Marines' Shermans – supported the attacks, but were destroyed by bazooka fire or by the 75mm guns of the Shermans. A day and a night of ferocious fighting saw the 38th Regiment decimated; amid the dead was Col Suenaga, cut down by machine-gun fire. Lt-Gen Takashina ordered the remnants of the regiment to join the reserves.

Back on the northern beaches at Asan Point the 3rd Division were consolidating their gains. They had suffered 615 men dead, wounded or missing, and they were still only a

War is Hell. War artist and correspondent Kerr Eby made a series of moving charcoal drawings in the Solomons and later at Tarawa. (US Navy Art Collection)

Jungle Rot. Amid the horrors of battle, Eby was able to depict a more humorous incident as a Marine receives embarrassing medical treatment (US Navy Art Collection)

few hundreds yards inland. Cabas Island to the west of Piti was occupied after a heavy naval and aerial bombardment; the only serious obstacle that the Marines encountered was a dense minefield. The 3rd Amphibian Corps Commander Maj-Gen Roy Geiger was well aware that the bulk of the Japanese troops had not yet been put into the field and stressed the need for close contact between his units, who were spread thinly over a wide front holding individual strong points covered by interlocking fire.

Since the Marine landings on 21 July, Takashina had been bringing up troops from all over Guam in preparation for an all-out counter-attack. By 25 July, he had amassed over 5,000 men, principally from the 48th Independent Mixed Brigade and the

A Marine falling after being hit by shrapnel from an exploding Japanese mortar shell. (USMC)

10th Independent Mixed Regiment. A major battle for control of Fonte Ridge south-east of the village of Asan took place on the 25th. Fighting at very close quarters and with many hand-to-hand encounters, the Marines stormed the entrenched Japanese with the aid of tanks and offshore naval gunfire. Battling through the night, they reached the crest in the early hours of the 26th, leaving over 600 of the enemy dead in front of the 2nd Battalion, 9th Regiment positions.

The battle was not yet over. The reverse slopes of the ridge were yet to be secured, entailing more hand-to-hand fighting and many more Japanese counter-attacks; but by 28 July Fonte Ridge had been taken for the loss of 62 Marines killed and 179 wounded. A determined counter-attack hit the whole of the 3rd-Division front on the night of 25/26 July as dozens of Japanese troops infiltrated US lines. In the early hours of the morning more troops flooded down the hill in a wild 'banzai' charge; the Marines held the line but a few of the intruders penetrated as far as the divisional hospital, where they were disposed of by cooks, stretcher-bearers and the walking wounded. The 'banzai' charge marked the end of any serious Japanese opposition on the northern beachhead, leaving the way open for the 3rd Division's advance to the north of the island.

THE OROTE PENINSULA

As the Marines of the 1st Provisional Brigade moved north through the town of Agat, the Army's 77th Division took over the southern beachhead and moved in their artillery. Further north, on Cabas Island, the 14th Defense Battalion also brought forward their artillery; the Orote Peninsula was now covered by flanking fire from both directions. There were an estimated 5,000 enemy troops on the peninsula, and they had no intention of allowing the Americans an easy occupation of this strategically important area. On the morning of 26 July, Lt-Gen Takashina mounted a large-scale counter-attack. The Japanese troops, many half-drunk on sake, stormed out of the mangrove swamps at the eastern end of the peninsula and charged the Marine front line. Brig-Gen Shepherd called in artillery fire from the 77th Division and from Cabas Island, and more than 26,000 rounds landed among the enemy over a three-hour period.

The attacks continued unabated throughout the night: at 12.30 a.m., 1.30 a.m. and 3.00 a.m., hordes of screaming troops sacrificed themselves against a steadfast line of 4th and 22nd Regiment Marines, and the body count soon exceeded 400. Shepherd ordered an intense artillery barrage in the morning and the 105mm and 155mm guns of the 77th Infantry blasted the enemy positions prior to the Marine advance, which was scheduled for 7.30 a.m. When it came, the Marines found themselves up against a blistering wall of artillery, machine-gun and small-arms fire, and the attack ground to a halt until 8.15 a.m. to allow tanks to be brought forward. The mangrove swamp was still manned by large numbers of the enemy and the demolition teams and flame-throwers were heavily engaged before the bottleneck was cleared in late evening.

Another heavy artillery barrage preceded the renewal of the advance on the following day, but a well-defended ridge close to the old US Marine barracks at the end of the airfield runway slowed down the Americans, and it took heavy tank support to clear the area (see map on p. 99).

By the 28th, the Japanese resistance was beginning to wane. The horrendous artillery barrages were decimating the defenders as they steadily retreated to Orote airfield. Brig-Gen Shepherd called in yet another barrage together with a 45-minute air strike and a 30-minute naval bombardment as a prelude to the attack on the airfield, but the stubbornness of the defenders amazed even the most battle-hardened Marines as the machine-gun and small-arms fire continued to frustrate the advance. The now-familiar

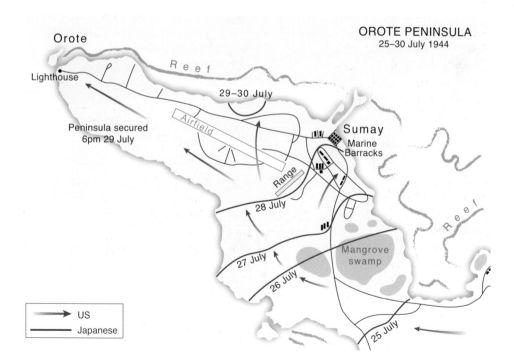

barrage ushered in the dawn on the 29th as massed tanks of the Marines and the Army spearheaded the assault on the airfield. Resistance was now reduced to a few fanatical defenders (many were committing suicide by jumping off cliffs or exploding grenades), and by early afternoon both the airfield and the old Marine barracks were again in US hands. The capture of the peninsula had cost the Marines 115 dead and 721 wounded; the Japanese toll was 1,633 killed, with many so badly mutilated by the artillery barrages that they could not be accounted for.

With the Orote Peninsula secure, the Americans could now consolidate. Pushing inland they reached the area of Mt Chachao in the east, where they met strong resistance in the foothills; 135 Japanese were killed in a close-quarter mêlée with grenades and bayonets, while further west the 305th Infantry secured Mt Tenjo. Gen Takashina was killed by machine-gun fire from a Sherman tank while supervising the withdrawal of his men in the Fonte area. He was succeeded by Lt-Gen Hideyoshi Obata, who had now only a few staff officers to rally the increasingly disheartened troops.

THE BITTER END

The Japanese were aided in their withdrawal when Maj-Gen Geiger decided to rest his battle-weary Marines before launching the final drive to the north of Guam. Meanwhile, intensive aerial reconnaissance and foot patrols in the south of the island revealed that there were only around 6,000 Japanese troops in the area. Geiger would

Shermans of C Company, 3rd Marine Tank Battalion, pass through Agana on Guam, July 1944. (Sgt Robert Riebe)

Shermans of C Company, 3rd Marine Tank Battalion, involved in fighting around Agana. (Sgt Robert Riebe)

now be able to concentrate his main thrust to the north. Lt-Gen Obata conducted a skilful rearguard withdrawal to Mt Barrigada midway across the island, where he constructed defences on the south-west slopes as his main force moved to their final defensive positions near Mt Santa Rosa in the north-west corner of the island.

Geiger's final assault started on 31 July, with the 3rd Marine Division on the left and the 77th Infantry Division on the right, while the 1st Marine Brigade secured the Agat areas and continued to mop up in the south. Against ever-weakening opposition the Marines and Army moved north, the Marines liberating Agana and the Army rescuing 2,000 Guamanians from a hellish detention camp at Asinan. Maj-Gen Geiger employed the 77th to free Yigo and Santa Rosa, and the Marines entered Finegayan and the remainder of north-west Guam. Obata was now reduced to a few isolated pockets near Mt Santa Rosa.

The American attack began at noon on 7 August as bulldozers carved trails through the rocky terrain and tanks and infantry overran the outlying Japanese positions. Soon the northern half of Mt Santa Rosa was in US hands, and by 2.40 p.m., the Army had captured the other half of the mountain. Only 600 bodies were accounted for, leaving Geiger to suspect that there were still significant numbers of the enemy elsewhere. Ritidian Point, the extreme north-west tip of Guam, was reached on 8 August by the 22nd Marine Regiment, and patrols of the 9th Regiment advanced to Pati Point, the north-east extremity. Intelligence reports came through that there were up to 2,000 Japanese troops holed up at Savana Grand, a wild area near the coast; artillery

A Marine rests under a tree during a lull in the fighting on Guam, July 1944. (National Archives)

was directed to the area and a total of 2,280 rounds rained down on the unfortunate men, killing most of them.

On 10 August at 11.31 a.m., Maj-Gen Geiger declared Guam 'secure'; but the mayhem was not yet over. On the morning of the 11th, Lt-Gen Obata was in his HQ at Mt Mataguac when elements of the 306th, supported by tanks, made their attack. The Japanese resisted fanatically, killing 7 Americans and wounding another 17 before they were annihilated. Lt-Gen Obata was either killed or took his own life in these last hours. Small units of Japanese troops continued to fight all over the island, but illness and starvation forced many into the ultimate degradation – surrender. The battle had lasted for 21 days and the Marines reported 1,190 men killed in action and 5,308 wounded, the 77th Division had 177 men killed and 662 wounded. The few remaining Japanese were hunted down by US patrols that were killing or capturing up to 80 a day. Amazingly, the last soldier to surrender did so in 1972 after living in a cave for 28 years. He returned to Japan as a national hero.

Four

PELELIU

THE FORGOTTEN BATTLE

'Some people wonder all their lives if they've made a difference – the Marines don't have that problem.'
(President Ronald Reagan)

As Adm Nimitz drove through the central Pacific, leading his five Marine divisions and the largest navy the world had ever seen on the 'island hopping' campaign that would eventually bring them to the very doorstep of the Japanese mainland, Gen MacArthur, Supreme Commander South-West Pacific, was making a series of brilliantly executed leaps through the Solomons and the Dutch East Indies. He had taken Manus, Los Negros and Biak and had isolated the important Japanese stronghold of Rabaul. He was now poised to invade the island of Morotai in the Molucca Sea, from where he intended to mount the invasion of Mindanao, the largest of the southern Philippine Islands. He had an irresistible passion to fulfil his pledge of 'I shall return', made when he had been ignominiously evacuated from Corregidor in 1942. MacArthur was adamant that his eastern and western flanks should be secure before embarking on the invasion of the Philippines in mid-November 1944. To the west lay Borneo, and he was confident that he could handle the small enemy garrison there; to the east were the Palau Islands, home to a substantial Japanese force and the site of at least two airfields and an excellent harbour. In a directive issued in March 1944, Nimitz had been instructed to occupy the Marianas–Palau line, so the responsibility for securing MacArthur's right flank lay with him. A chain of command was established under the code-name 'Stalemate', with a proposed invasion set for September.

'Stalemate' was a very ambitious operation, which envisaged the occupation of the whole of the Palau Islands. The 1st Division USMC and the 81st Division of the US Army were to occupy the islands of Peleliu and Angaur at the southern end of the chain, while the Army's 7th and 77th Divisions were assigned the larger island of Babelthuap in the north; in reserve would be the Army's 27th Division. However, the campaigns in the Marianas caused Nimitz to make a radical alteration to the plan. The 77th Division had been diverted to Guam, and the reserve went to Saipan. At the same time, intensive aerial surveys of the Palaus raised grave doubts about the northern phase of the operation on Babelthuap, which was revealed as a mass of dense jungle in which the Army troops could be bogged down for months. Consequently, the operation was drastically modified and a second order was issued, code-named 'Stalemate 2'. This order omitted Babelthuap altogether, and the atolls of Yap and Ulithi in the Carolines were substituted. The operation would now be divided into two phases: the Eastern Attack Force, comprising the Army's 7th and 96th Divisions, would occupy Yap and Ulithi; and the Western Attack Force, which would remain the 1st Division USMC and the Army's 81st Division, would take Peleliu and Angaur.

In September 1944, Adm 'Bull' Halsey, Commander of the 3rd Fleet, arrived in the Philippine Sea to oversee both operations. Adm Mitscher informed him that he had encountered little opposition to a series of carrier-based air attacks and reconnaissance fights that he had ordered throughout the island of Mindanao. Halsey ordered more flights on 12–13 September involving over 2,400 sorties, but the Japanese response was virtually nil. Further evidence of the lack of an enemy presence came from a Navy pilot who had been forced to land on the island due to mechanical problems. He was informed by the locals that there were very few Japanese on Mindanao. Halsey contacted Nimitz, MacArthur and King (Chief of Naval Operations), expressing his belief that Mindanao was virtually unoccupied and that MacArthur should move his scheduled invasion further north. There followed a series of messages between the various commands and the Joint Chiefs of Staff in Washington, and the final outcome was a confirmation that MacArthur would abandon his invasion of Mindanao and go directly to Leyte further north. The final decision about the Peleliu invasion remained with Nimitz.

COMMAND STRUCTURES

For the proposed invasion, Maj-Gen Julian Smith, USMC, was designated Commander, Expeditionary Troops, 3rd Fleet. Smith was of course the Commander of the 2nd Division during the invasion of Tarawa and was therefore experienced in amphibious operations. The Western Attack Force that would assault Peleliu and Angaur was the responsibility of III Amphibian Corps under Maj-Gen Roy S. Geiger, USMC, whose major components were the 1st Division USMC under Maj-Gen William H. Rupertus and the 81st Division US Army under Maj-Gen Paul J. Mueller, an experienced First World War veteran. The 1st Marine Division known as 'The Old Breed', was composed of three regiments, each comprising three battalions. The 1st Regiment's commander was Col Lewis B. 'Chesty' Puller, already an admired figure; he would later retire as the most decorated marine in the history of the corps. The 5th Regiment was under the command of Col Harold D. Harris; something of an intellectual, he had attended the École Supérieure de Guerre in Paris shortly before the war. And the 7th Regiment's commander was Col Herman H. Hanneken MOH, nicknamed 'hard head' by his men because of his German ancestry. As with all

Marine divisions, the infantry regiments were accompanied by a plethora of support and service units: tanks, transport, medical, supply – the list was long and included everything from musicians to war dogs. The Army's 81st Division, known as 'The Wildcats', had been re-formed in 1942 at Camp Rucker in Alabama, and trained in Arizona and California before being shipped out to Oahu in Hawaii.

The Marine numbers looked impressive – 26,417 all ranks but these numbers were deceptive, as only around 10,000 of them were infantrymen, giving a realistic ratio of assault troops to defenders of little better than 1–1, very low given the experience of previous landings. The capture of Angaur would occupy two Regimental Combat Teams (RCTs) from the 81st Division. Another RCT had been earmarked for the occupation of Ulithi, which meant that there would be virtually no reserves during the first phase of the operation. The Navy had no such problems. Vice-Adm Theodore S. Wilkinson's Task Force 31 was responsible for getting the troops ashore; and Task Force 34, with its Fire Support Group, under Rear-Adm Jesse B. Oldendorf, was to soften up the two islands. All opposition to the landings was expected to be suppressed by fire from the battleships *Maryland*, *Idaho*, *Mississippi* and *Pennsylvania*, supported by the cruisers *Louisville*, *Portland* and *Indianapolis*. Air cover would be provided by hundreds of planes from eight aircraft carriers; Japanese air cover would be non-existent as the devastating raids on the Palaus in late March 1944 ('Operation Desecrate') had virtually wiped out all of the enemy opposition from the airfields on Peleliu and Babelthuap Island.

As the islands and atolls of the outer perimeter of the Japanese defences began to crumble, those that were nearer to the homeland began to take on an added significance as part of the new 'Absolute National Defence Zone'. The 14th (Utsunomiya) Division, stationed in Manchuria, was transferred to the Palaus. Its commander, Lt-Gen Sadae Inoue, had been summoned to Tokyo by Prime Minister Gen Tojo, who left him in no doubt about his mission: hold the island for as long as possible and kill as many Americans as possible; he and his garrison were not expected to return.

For the defence of Peleliu Gen Inoue deployed the 3,280-strong 2nd Infantry Regiment under Col Kunio Nakagawa, a tough and experienced veteran of the China wars. Additional units were added from the 15th Infantry Regiment and the 53rd Independent Infantry Brigade and for the defence of Angaur he sent two battalions of the 59th Infantry Regiment under Maj Ushio Goto. Nakagawa soon realised that almost everything was against him. The Americans would have total control of the air and the sea; he was not certain where the enemy would land but anticipated, correctly, that the long straight stretch of beach to the west of the airfield would be the most suitable site. The Japanese commander did enjoy one advantage. North and north-west of the airfield was an area known as the Umurbrogol Mountains. Although the maximum height in this range was only 550ft above sea level, it was a defender's dream: a mass of ravines, ridges, cliffs, valleys and caves, all hidden under an umbrella of dense foliage. To this labyrinth the Japanese were to add even more caves and obstacles to deter the invaders.

DESECRATE 1 – TASK FORCE 58

Five months before the Marines and Army invaded Peleliu and Angaur, Task Force 58, a huge armada of carriers, battleships, cruisers and destroyers under the overall command of Adm Spruance, attacked the Palau Islands. Split into three task groups (58–1, –2, and –3), the task force arrived off the islands on 29 March and immediately set about attacking the airfields on Peleliu and Ngesebus and the seaplane base at Arakabesan, together with the anchorages at Urukthapel, Komebail, Malakal and Rock Island. In a series of brilliantly coordinated air attacks, the 'Hellcats', 'Dauntless' and 'Avengers' wreaked havoc throughout the islands as they had earlier done at Truk. Barracks and airfield installations were destroyed, harbours mined, and all shipping, apart from two hospital ships, was either sunk or left burning. By the 30th, 'Hellcat' pilots were reporting a shortage of targets.

The two-day foray was an overwhelming success and eliminated virtually all Japanese naval and airborne presence throughout the islands. Over 110 enemy aircraft were destroyed along with most shipping. The Imperial Navy abandoned all hope of making the Palaus their next line of defence after the loss of Truk and moved their HQ to Tawitawi. The US Navy had proved that they could neutralise the Japanese presence in the islands in a mere two-day operation. MacArthur's eastern flank had been secured long before the first marine ever hit the beach on Peleliu.

'OPERATION DESECRATE' 1 – 29–30 MARCH 1944

Overall Commander – Adm Raymond Spruance

Task Force 58
Task Force Commander – Vice-Adm Marc Mitscher

Task Group 58–1
Rear-Adm J.W. Reeves, Jr

Carriers: *Enterprise, Belleau Wood, Cowpens.*
Cruisers: *Santa Fe, Mobile, Biloxi, Oakland,* plus 25 destroyers.

Task Group 58–2
Rear-Adm A.E. Montgomery

Carriers: *Bunker Hill, Monterey, Hornet, Cabot.*
Battleships: *Iowa, New Jersey.*
Cruisers: *Witchita, San Francisco, Minneapolis, New Orleans, Boston, Baltimore.*

Task Group 58–3
Rear-Adm S.P. Ginder

Carriers: *Yorktown, Lexington, Princeton, Langley.*
Battleships: *Massachusetts, North Carolina, South Dakota, Alabama.*
Cruisers: *Louisville, Portland, Indianapolis, San Juan,* HMAS *Canberra,* plus 16 destroyers.

Submarines deployed for 'lifeguard' duties.

THE 1ST DIVISION USMC – 'THE OLD BREED'

In 1941, the 1st Marine Division numbered only 7,389 officers and enlisted men, but patriotic fever and a massive recruiting campaign boosted the numbers to around 19,000 by May 1942. As with other divisions of the USMC, the 1st was built around three infantry regiments, the 1st, 5th and 7th, each with three battalions. Each marine belonged to a rifle squad consisting, at full strength, of a sergeant and 12 men divided into 'fire teams', one man carrying a Browning automatic rifle (BAR) and the others semi-automatic rifles, carbines and grenades. Three squads plus an HQ element made up a rifle platoon of 45 men led by a 2nd lieutenant. Three rifle platoons plus a machine-gun platoon made up a company of around 230 men led by a captain, and the company HQ element included a 60mm-mortar platoon. Three rifle companies and an HQ made up a battalion of just over 1,000 men commanded by a lieutenant-colonel and supported by 3 majors, with further support that could be attached as required: 81mm mortars, bazookas, flame-throwers and demolition teams. Three battalions made up a regiment of over 3,000 men led by a colonel, and supporting the three regiments were a multitude of components that allowed them to fight as a self-sufficient unit. The 11th Marine Artillery Regiment had four battalions, two each of 75mm pack howitzers and 105mm howitzers. The 1st Marine Tank Battalion had four companies each of fifteen M4 Sherman tanks. In addition were the non-combatant groups: corpsmen (US Navy medics), engineers, drivers, ordnance, communications, clerks, MPs, cooks and war-dog handlers. The sum total was a complex and carefully balanced miniature army of almost 20,000 highly trained and motivated specialists.

1st Marine Division badge.

PAVUVU

In 1942, the commander of the 1st Division was Maj-Gen Alexander A. Vandegrift. A highly regarded First World War veteran, he led the division through the vicious battles for Guadalcanal and Cape Gloucester before being awarded the Medal of Honor and promoted to Commandant of the Marine Corps. After receiving his new appointment in Washington, 'Archie' Vandegrift flew to Melbourne in Australia, where the 1st were resting and regrouping after their gruelling campaigns, and handed over his division to his second in command, Maj-Gen William H. Rupertus. A less appropriate choice would have been difficult to make. Rupertus was heartily disliked by both officers and men, who dubbed him 'Rupe the stupe'. His leadership inspired little confidence. One battalion commander commented on his performance during the battle for Tulagi: 'he sat on his ass while the others did the work'.

The 1st Division had originally been allocated a training area on Guadalcanal to prepare for 'Operation Stalemate 2', but the 3rd Division beat them to it. Instead they went to Pavuvu, one of the British-administered Russell Islands some 60 miles west of Guadalcanal. The island, which had been used for the production of copra, had been hastily evacuated by the Unilever Company. It was 10 miles long and 6 miles wide and when approached by the troopships had a pleasant appearance, but the Marines were soon to find that the area allocated to them was little more than a thinly crusted swamp.

There were no roads, just muddy tracks, and there was no accommodation – the fifty Seabees sent to set up camp had not received any materials. Rats wandered about in their thousands, and cattle abandoned during the Unilever evacuation now roamed wild and had adopted serious attitude problems. Lt Bruce Watkins recalled, 'When the rains let up, the rats came by the thousands, ran over tents, gear, and us. Many were hit by throwing knives or decapitated with machetes.' Another problem was the land crabs who arrived by night, filling boots and covering blankets. The Marines soon gave up killing them as the stench was overpowering. Eventually they just let them crawl around until they finally disappeared. Adding to the stink were the millions of rotting coconuts, the remains of the copra trade. For a long time the only food consisted of C-Rations, dehydrated potatoes, powdered egg and the inevitable Spam. Bathing facilities were non-existent; the trick was to wait for one of the frequent tropical downpours and hope that it lasted long enough to have a shower. More serious was the lack of space. Tons of coral were dug up and tracks laid, but there was a chronic shortage of room for tank movements, parking for amphibious tractors and DUKWs, rifle practice and flame-throwing.

Morale was very low during the Pavuvu period and many went 'Asiatic', a marine term for extreme boredom, depression and loneliness. There were a few humorous moments, however. Ollie Sweetland of the 3rd Amphibian Tractor Battalion recalled an encounter with one of the wild beasts: 'These moo-cows were not just the normal farm critters by any means. They had huge sets of sweeping horns similar to the famed Texas longhorns and had a mean temperament to match. They had been wild for about two years and some of the bulls would not back down even for a tank.'

One of the few highlights of the time on Pavuvu was a show given by Bob Hope and members of his troupe. Hope had been performing at the Navy's 4th Base Depot on the island of Banika when he heard that the Marines were on the God-forsaken hole of Pavuvu. He insisted that he and a few of his company be flown there to entertain the troops. They landed in Stinson Sentinel aircraft, which made precarious landings on the rough roads that had been carved out by bulldozers. Hope's company gave a show that still remains in the memory of many veterans.

Gradually, the camp took shape, and tented accommodation, decking and even a makeshift movie screen appeared. Many of the 1st Division Marines had been in the Pacific since 1942 and were overdue for replacement. Some 4,860 officers and men were rotated back to the States, to be replaced by over 5,000 young Marines straight out of boot camp. Most had only been in the corps for a few months and the average age was 18–19. Enthusiastic and patriotic as they were, they were no match for the toughened and experienced men who were leaving.

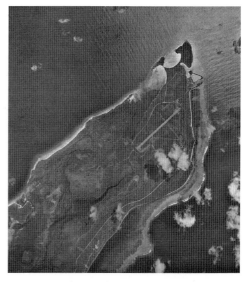

An aerial view of Peleliu, taken some years after the battle. A dock has been constructed near the unnamed island. The east and west roads and remains of the airfield can be clearly seen. (USAF)

At the same time as the division were training on Pavuvu, the Army's 81st Division were assembling on Tulagi south of Guadalcanal for the forthcoming invasion of Angaur. It was during this time that Maj-Gen Rupertus suddenly disappeared from the scene – for six weeks he was in Washington with his wife, and the training, planning and organisation were left in the hands of his second in command, Brig-Gen Oliver Smith. This absence, only weeks before a major amphibious operation has never been satisfactorily explained and was unprecedented during the whole of the Pacific War. When he finally returned, most of the detailed plans had been formulated by the very capable Smith, and it was becoming increasingly evident that he would be shouldering a significant part of the responsibility for the operation. In all earlier operations the planning had been in the hands of Nimitz's 'big three' – Spruance, Turner and Holland Smith – but they were now preoccupied with the Marianas campaign and from there would go directly to the Iwo Jima operation; their expertise would be sorely missed at Peleliu.

During training exercises a few weeks before the division embarked, Rupertus fell and broke his ankle while climbing into an Amtrac. Normally this would have been just an inconvenience, but on the eve of a major operation it posed a serious problem. He did not report the injury, which would become a serious restriction to his mobility during the battle. Other accidents dogged the preparations leaving many 'Leathernecks' to believe that 'Stalemate 2' was jinxed from the start: the battleships *California* and *Tennessee* collided off Guadalcanal and the former had to be withdrawn; two oil tankers also collided and were sent for repair; days before embarkation a destroyer and a troopship collided, and the empty troopship sank; seven transports capable of holding 6,000 troops failed to arrive and only two tank landing ships (LSTs) turned up, which meant that only 30 of the 46 available Shermans were loaded. Days before the division sailed for Peleliu, Rupertus called a meeting of his officers. 'We're going to have some casualties, but let me assure you this is going to be a fast one, rough but fast. We'll be through in three days – it may only take two.'

PELELIU

Six miles long and two miles wide at its extremities, the island of Peleliu is a very irregular shape and could be roughly compared to a three-pronged fork pointing to the north-east (see map on p. 111). Most of the important features were at the western side of the island; the airfield was at the base, with its sizeable HQ and barracks area attached. Just north of the airfield was the Umurbrogol, as previously described, a mass of cliffs, ravines and caves encircled by the East and West Roads. To the north lay another group of hills, which included Hill Row and Radar Hill, with the now-defunct phosphate refinery at their side. And beyond that was a causeway leading to Ngesebus Island, with its unfinished fighter airstrip. The remainder of the island was a mass of jungle, coral and mangrove swamp.

The airfield was the obvious first objective. Built in the 1930s, it had two main runways of around 1,000yd and adjacent hangars and servicing facilities, and it was on the beaches to the west of the airfield that the Marines intended to make their landings. Five beaches of approximately 500yd were chosen. Here the offshore reef was 700–800yd from the shoreline, leaving nearly half a mile of shallow water to negotiate. From north to south the beaches were code-named 'White 1', 'White 2', 'Orange 1', 'Orange 2' and 'Orange 3', and the plan was to drive straight across the island to seize the airfield and split the defenders. 'Chesty' Puller's 1st Regiment

A view of the airfield today, looking north to the ridges. (Eric Mailander)

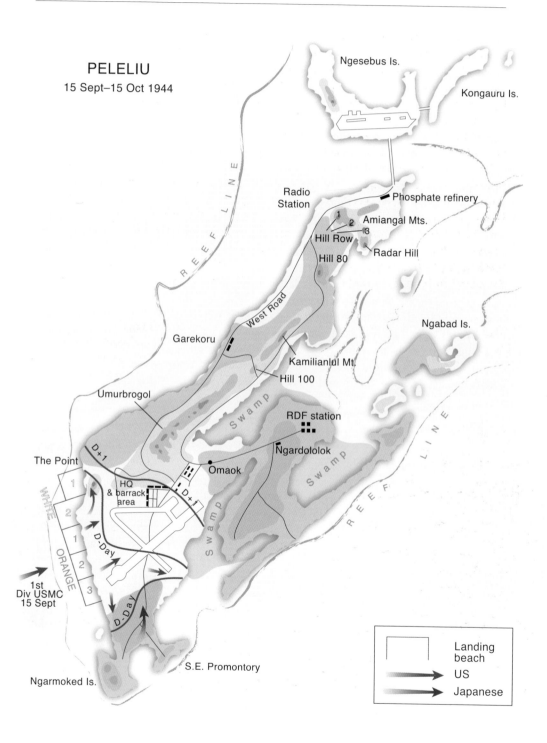

PELELIU
15 Sept–15 Oct 1944

Ngesebus Is.

Kongauru Is.

Radio
Station

Phosphate refinery

1
2
3

Amiangal Mts.

Hill Row

Radar Hill

Hill 80

West Road

Garekoru

Ngabad Is.

Kamilianlul Mt.

Hill 100

Umurbrogol

Swamp

RDF station

Ngardololok

D+1

Omaok

Swamp

The Point

Ngardololok

WHITE

1

HQ
& barrack
area

D+1

2

ORANGE

1

D-Day

2

3

D-Day

1st
Div USMC
15 Sept

REEF LINE

REEF LINE

S.E. Promontory

Ngarmoked Is.

Landing
beach

US

Japanese

would land on both 'White beaches', drive inland to the barracks area and swing north to the edge of the Umurbrogol; Harris's 5th Regiment in the centre would tie up with Puller on its left and the remainder would drive straight ahead across the airfield to the mangrove swamp beyond; the 7th Regiment under Hanneken would press straight ahead to the swamp and swing south to mop up the enemy forces in the south of the island.

The Japanese were aware that these eastern beaches were the most likely sites for the US landings and had planned accordingly. Artillery was sited in the Umurbrogol foothills, from which the whole invasion zone could be swept, and the labyrinth of cliffs and caves in the Umurbrogol had been well prepared and supplied as the ultimate stronghold for the inevitable final stand.

As the eve of the operation approached there were many doubts: 'Adm 'Bull' Halsey did not believe that the invasion was necessary; the assault force was inadequately rested and trained and had a disproportionate number of untested 'rookies' in its ranks; and there were grave doubts in the minds of many of the officers about their division's commander. Shortly before leaving, Rupertus called another meeting of his staff. He told them, 'You have your orders. I will not be ashore on D-Day and may not be there on D+1. It depends on the course of the action. But I want you to understand now that there will be no change in orders regardless. Even if General Smith attempts to change my plans or orders, you regimental commanders will refuse to obey.' This astonishing undermining by Rupertus of his second in command must have been deeply embarrassing for Smith and very worrying for his senior officers.

D-DAY

On 12 September, the Fire Support Group under Rear-Adm Jesse Oldendorf began their bombardment of Peleliu. Lying 7,500yd offshore and spread over 12 miles of sea the huge flotilla was an awesome sight. The battleships *Tennessee*, *Idaho*, *Maryland* and *Pennsylvania* blasted the island's beaches with their 16in and 14in guns, and then moved their fire inland to the airfield and foothills beyond. From 15 miles offshore, 400 aircraft from 3 fleet and 5 escort carriers ravaged the island, dropping 500lb bombs and napalm canisters until their ammunition was exhausted. As the planes returned to their carriers the battleships resumed their pounding, and so it continued until the evening, when a reconnaissance plane photographed the whole of the southern end of the island. The results showed massive destruction to the airfield installations and runways, and all fortifications at ground level appeared to have been destroyed. A third day of intensive bombardment led Oldendorf to conclude that he had 'run out of targets'. Holland Smith was scathing in his criticism of this and other pre-invasion bombardments carried out by the Navy. In his postwar memoirs he described the Peleliu and Iwo Jima contributions as inadequate and ineffectual.

D-Day dawned slightly overcast but dry, and Oldendorf's battlewagons again pounded the shoreline, leaving it under a huge pall of smoke and dust. On the

LCI(G) rocket-firing gunboats pound the invasion beaches on D-Day. (USMC)

The US bombardment from air and sea was awesome, yet when the smoke had cleared it was obvious that dozens of US landing craft and DUKWs had been destroyed by Japanese artillery and mortar fire. (US Navy)

command ship *Mount McKinley*, Maj-Gen Julian Smith and Roy Geiger anxiously scanned the island through their binoculars, while Rupertus, ensconced on a deck-chair on the troop transport *DuPage*, was as optimistic as ever. The goal was to get 4,500 men ashore in 19 minutes – a formidable task, but one that Kelly Turner had already perfected. Up front were the Landing Vehicles Tracked Armoured (LVT(A)s) of the 3rd Armoured Amphibian Tractor Battalion. They were developments of the original Amtracs used at Tarawa and had armoured superstructures and a turret with either a 37mm or snub-nosed 75mm gun. Their task was to drive straight across the reef for some 700–800yd and clear the beaches for the first wave of Marines in their LVTs.

The presence of the offshore reef forced the planners to adopt an unusual system for getting the Marines ashore: the first waves of Amtracs would depart the Landing Ships, Tank (LSTs) and drive straight onto the beaches; the remainder of the Marines would have to embark first into Landing Craft Vehicle/Personnel (LCVPs), which would take them to the 'transfer line' at the edge of the reef, where they would then

Amtracs and landing craft head through the smoke of the naval bombardment towards the beach on D-Day.
(US Navy)

Marine Amtanks of 3rd Armored Amphibian Tractor Battalion lead the assault towards the bank of smoke and dust concealing the beaches. The closest vehicle, an LVTA-1, mounts a 37mm gun, while the others carry short 75mm guns, making them LVTA-4s. (US Navy)

clamber from their LCVPs into Amtracs running a shuttle service between reef and beach. The Sherman tanks of the 1st Tank Battalion, all waterproofed, would leave their LCTs and cross the half-mile of shallow water and provide close gunfire support. What actually happened was not exactly what the planners had envisaged; the 'Old Breed's' previous 'landing luck' ran out on the beaches of Peleliu.

THE BEACHHEADS

As the Navy barrage moved from the shoreline to targets further inland, the Japanese emerged from their well-prepared bunkers and manned their guns. With ranges worked out to the nearest yard the Japanese artillery and mortars laid a barrage all along the 'White' and 'Orange beaches', and within minutes twenty-six Amtracs were reduced to blazing wrecks. The smoke and dust finally cleared enough for the onlookers on the offshore ships to get a clear view of the island; what they saw

Smoke rises from disabled US amphibious craft, seen from above 'White' and 'Orange' beaches. The reef edge where soldiers waited to board Amtracs and head towards the beach, is marked by the line of white water. (US Navy)

came as a sharp shock. Gone was the bush foliage that had covered the Umurbrogol Mountains; in its place was a mass of unsuspected ravines and cliffs, while on the beaches clouds of oily smoke rose from battered Amtracs and DUKWs.

At the reef the situation was becoming chaotic. Rows of Marines who had arrived in their Higgins Boats were waiting for Amtracs to shuttle them to the beaches, but these were becoming fewer and fewer and, despite the build-up, the troopships continued to embark more troops for the beaches. 'Chesty' Puller's 1st Regiment arrived on 'White beaches 1 and 2' only two minutes behind schedule, but, as the Japanese artillery and mortar fire intensified, the first casualties were the Amtracs carrying the radio equipment. Its loss was to be a severe blow that resulted in a serious breakdown in communications early in the battle. Eighteen Shermans of the 1st Tank Battalion ground across the reef to support Puller's men, but such was the intensity of the enemy fire that only one arrived undamaged. At the southern end of the beachhead Col Hanneken's 7th Regiment were also having a rough time. Tom Lea, an artist and correspondent for *Time/Life* magazine recalled:

I fell flat on my face just as I heard the 'whishh' of a mortar that I knew was too close. A red flash stabbed at my eyeballs as it smashed down among four men from our boat. One figure seemed to fly to pieces. With terrible clarity I saw the head and one leg sail in the air. Moments later I saw another man stagger in the direction of the LVTs. His face was half bloody pulp and the mangled shreds of what was left of an arm hung down like a stick. The half of his face that was still human had the most terrible look of abject patience I have ever seen. He fell in a red puddle on the white sand.

'Orange beach 3' was the narrowest of the five beaches and the 7th Regiment had to land in column of battalion (one behind the other). They were soon engaged by heavy machine-gun fire from a small unnamed island on their right, causing many coxswains to veer to the left and deposit their passengers onto 'Orange beach 2'. The Japanese had inadvertently aided the Marines by digging a tank trap that ran

On D-Day, Marines take cover around LVTA-4 number B-6, near 'White beach 2'. (USMC)

Left: Artist Tom Lea landed with the Marines on Peleliu. He later produced a series of paintings illustrating the events. (Tom Lea/US Army Center for Military History)

Below: Lea made a rough drawing of the scene that he vividly describes on p. 117. (Tom Lea/US Army Center for Military History)

Left: Going in – *First Wave*, another of Tom Lea's graphic pictures of the Peleliu landings. (Tom Lea/ US Army Center for Military History)

parallel to 'Orange 3', it provided excellent cover in which the Marines could rest and reorganise before pushing forward to their objectives, and it also became an artery for moving troops into proper positions for deployment. In the centre of the beachhead, on 'Orange 1' and 'Orange 2', the 5th Regiment encountered slightly less resistance and the terrain was more favourable for manoeuvre. The 5th pushed forward to the airfield but were forced to halt, partly because the 1st Regiment from 'White 2' were unable to link up with them and partly because of the artillery and mortar fire raining down on them from the foothills of the Umurbrogol. 'When we reached the shore I saw one hell of a sight. The sands were littered with the dead and mutilated bodies of Marines and all the armoured amphibs I could see were knocked out and burning', recalled Jim Johnston, a machine-gunner with the 5th. Brig-Gen Oliver Smith came ashore about an hour and a half after the first wave and set up his HQ in an anti-tank ditch. He was soon in contact with the 5th and 7th Regiments and with Rupertus aboard the *DuPage*, but all attempts to contact Puller failed. According to plans, Rupertus should have come ashore about four hours after Smith, by which time his over optimistic predictions should have had the whole of the southern end of Peleliu under American control. But the reality of the situation ensured that he stayed at sea. However, he insisted on committing the 5th Regiment reserve, much to Smith's puzzlement and Col Harris's annoyance.

HELL ON WHITE BEACH

The 1st Regiment's radio equipment was largely destroyed when the five Amtracs carrying the command group were shot up crossing the reef. On 'White 2' the resistance was heavy, but within an hour the Marines had advanced some 350yd. Lt Bruce Watkins remembered the sprint to the shoreline:

> there I found Sgt Stasiak on his back, holding his stomach, with blood all over himself. He asked me to check and see how it was. A bullet had torn through flesh and muscle clean across at hip height and it looked real bad. I told him it looked worse than it was and counted on his toughness to keep him going. We joined up with the 3rd Platoon, who had just lost their lieutenant, 'GoGo' Meyer. Typically out in front of his men, he refused help when hit, knowing he was dying and not wanting to risk his men in a futile rescue attempt.

The stiffest resistance of the day was encountered on 'White 1'. Directly to their front the Marines faced a coral ridge about 30ft high. It was dotted with gun emplacements from which a steady withering stream of machine-gun and small-arms fire was directed at them as they left the shore. At the extreme left of the beach, rising to a height of 30ft and protruding into the sea was a rock and coral promontory identified on the maps as the Point. It housed a 47mm artillery piece and a number of machine-guns, and had been developed into a strongpoint from which the Japanese were able to sweep the whole of 'White 1' and about half of 'White 2'. Puller and his men were in serious trouble: Lt-Col Sabol's 3rd Battalion were pinned down in front of the coral ridge; and Capt George Hunt's K Company was cut to pieces attempting to storm the Point. In the bloody mêlée, Hunt's men battled their way with hand grenades and small arms to the edge of the Point and lobbed smoke grenades through the firing apertures of the 47mm gun. A lucky rifle grenade landed among the ammunition, and three screaming Japanese soldiers ran out of the rear exit to be shot down by waiting Marines who eventually fought their way to the top of the Point and established a defensive perimeter. Hunt made a rough estimate that K Company had lost almost two-thirds of its strength – they had been on Peleliu for less than two hours.

'ORANGE 3'

The 0–1 line, the boundary that the 7th Regiment was expected to reach at the end of day one, stretched to the eastern coast and included the promontory called Ngarmoked Island and the small unnamed island to the south of 'Orange 3'. However, in the face of unexpectedly heavy opposition there had to be some modifications made. Within an hour, two companies of the 3rd Battalion came upon a large concrete blockhouse and the advance ground to a halt. Tanks had already landed and were called in to reduce this obstacle, but for some unknown reason the Shermans had been attached to the 5th Regiment and it was some time before they returned to the 7th. As the day wore on the 0–1 line looked to be an impossible target; the blockhouse was still intact and the Japanese were directing heavy artillery and mortar fire into the Marines' right flank.

General Rupertus, still offshore in the *DuPage*, was seeing his 'three-day quickie' beginning to deteriorate. It was obvious that the 7th Regiment were not going to reach the 0–1 line on day one, while on the left the 1st Regiment were bogged down around the Point. In another of his dubious decisions he committed the Divisional Reconnaissance Company and the sole reserve of the 7th Regiment, the 2nd Battalion, to the battle. Both Oliver Smith and Col Hanneken were scathing in their condemnation of these deployments: Smith considered it an improper use of the Reconnaissance Company and Hanneken wondered why the 2nd Battalion had been sent when he had not requested it. 'I've shot my bolt when they go in,' Rupertus told his Chief of Staff, Col John Selden.

The Marines were now facing another enemy – the weather. When the sun was at its zenith the temperature was reaching 105°Fahrenheit in the shade, and the demand for water was intense. The Marines each carried two canteens, but these were rapidly used up, and it was discovered that the water arriving from the transports in 55-gallon drums was tainted with diesel fuel. The contamination was caused by inadequate steam-cleaning of the drums, and there were dozens of cases of stomach cramps and violent sickness, while the numbers suffering from heat exhaustion outnumbered the dead and wounded.

A view along 'Orange beach' today. (Tom Climie)

THE BATTLE FOR THE AIRFIELD

As the afternoon wore on, a spotter plane reported Japanese tanks grouping in the foothills of the Umurbrogol beyond the barracks area. It was known that the Japanese had a tank company on the island as a standard component of an infantry division, and the Marines had taken appropriate measures. The principal tank in the Pacific was the Type 95 'Ha-Go', which weighed under 10 tons and mounted one 37mm gun and two 7.7mm machine-guns. It was powered by a Mitsubishi 110hp diesel engine and was thinly armoured – 14mm maximum. The 'Ha-Go' was totally inferior to the Sherman, which weighed 35 tons and mounted a 75mm gun and had 76mm armour. At 4.50 p.m., the 'Ha-Gos' began their attack. Between 13 and 19 tanks accompanied by 400–500 infantry moved across the airfield towards the beachheads, but they had left it too late and the Marines were prepared.

The initial advance was well coordinated, but as they reached about halfway across the airfield the tanks surged forward, leaving the accompanying infantrymen in a cloud of dust. As they came within range, the Marines opened up with 37mm anti-tank guns, bazookas, mortars, rifle grenades and machine-guns; a Navy dive-bomber added a 500lb bomb for good measure. Within minutes tanks began to explode and burn all over the airfield and the Japanese infantry fell under a hail of American gunfire.

The ruins of the airfield administration buildings are gradually being taken over by the jungle. (Tom Climie)

From the south of the airfield a platoon of Shermans burst out into the open and joined the mêlée. Corpsman Jack McCombs watched as a bazooka knocked out one 'Ha-Go': 'a Jap was cut in half by machine-gun fire as he tried to get out of his tank. As a joke the guys carried his pants with the parts of his legs in them and threw them to one another. I know it sounds gruesome but it helped break the tension.'

The few survivors kept on coming, and they overran a Marine sector before being wiped out; what little was left of the infantry retired across the airfield back to the barracks area. The attack had been a total disaster for the Japanese, who lost 450 men and virtually all of their tanks. The Marines suffered 59 dead and wounded. The 5th Regiment, taking advantage of the enemy's disorganisation, advanced across the airfield in the late afternoon and arrived at the eastern swamp. Elsewhere they reached the southern runways, but encountered stiff opposition and decided to dig in for the night.

THE POINT

'Chesty' Puller and his men were still catching hell on 'White beach 1' and 'White beach 2'. His lack of communications equipment meant that he could not call for reinforcements, and his need for them was certainly more urgent than Hanneken's. Little headway had been made against the ridge directly in front of the 3rd Battalion, and Capt Hunt and the remains of his company were isolated near the Point, hanging on like grim death under a barrage of mortar fire. Hunt was down to about thirty-four able men and he was getting desperately short of ammunition and water. Puller sent his liaison officer to make contact with Oliver Smith, to inform him of the situation. Puller estimated that he had lost around 40 men, a massive underestimation – the true figure was nearer 500. Smith also had another visitor that afternoon. Maj-Gen Roy Geiger slid into the tank trap where Smith had made his HQ, and an astonished Smith said, 'Look, General, according to the book you are not supposed to be here.' 'Where's Rupertus?' asked Geiger. 'He's out on the *DuPage* with a broken ankle,' replied Smith. 'If I'd known that I'd have relieved him,' said Geiger.

As evening fell the Americans had secured a beachhead some 3,000yd long and averaging 500yd in depth. In the centre, Hanneken's men had reached the mangrove swamp at the far side of the island, virtually cutting off the south-east promontory and Ngarmoked Island. The 11th Artillery had one and a half battalions of 75mm pack howitzers and one battalion of 105mm howitzers in position. Estimated casualties were 210 men killed and 90 wounded, with a large number of men suffering heat prostration and fatigue. At the Point, an Amtrac had managed to deliver ammunition, food and water, and evacuate the wounded, but Hunt still had to fight a running battle throughout the night against Japanese infiltrators.

D+1

Rupertus and his staff came ashore around 9.50 a.m. on the second day of the battle and set up his HQ in the tank trap with Oliver Smith. He was briefed on the current situation and soon became irritated when he heard that Puller had not yet secured the areas assigned to him for D-Day. 'Goddamnit, Lewie, you've got to kick asses to get results,' he told Puller on the field telephone. Clearly, he had little grasp of the true situation on the 'White beaches'.

The objectives for D+1 were unambiguous: Puller was expected to take the ridge to his front and link up with the isolated Capt Hunt and his men at the Point; he was also expected to seize the northern sector of the airfield, link up with the 5th Regiment and swing northward to the foothills of the Umurbrogol; the 5th, in the centre, were to occupy the remainder of the airfield and barracks area; while in the south Hanneken's 7th were to clear the southern peninsula.

The temperatures which had been such a problem on D-Day rose even higher on D+1. In mid-afternoon it peaked at 115°Fahrenheit, and cases of heat exhaustion, sunstroke and stomach problems from drinking contaminated water reached near-epidemic proportions. With the heat came the smells. Dozens of bodies lay where they had fallen and soon became stinking, swollen fly-blown horrors. Marines were quickly removed to the beaches, where they were identified and tagged, but the Japanese were left where they lay and were avoided like the plague by one and all until they could be finally disposed of.

At the Point, Capt Hunt had repulsed a series of attacks by the Japanese which had continued throughout the night. Dawn saw some relief as Amtracs delivered more ammunition and some reinforcements and evacuated the freshly wounded. Bloody fighting continued as Maj Raymond Davis with the regimental reserve tried to close the gap between Hunt and the 1st. It would not be until the morning of D+2 that Hunt and his gallant men would finally be relieved. The Japanese were forced back inch by inch until the arrival of two Sherman tanks finally tipped the balance and the last 500yd was secured. Hunt's men had been isolated for over thirty hours and were reduced at one point to only eighteen men. Of the 235 men in the company, only 78 of the original combatants remained when they were relieved. Hunt was awarded the Navy Cross, much to the disgust of his men, who thought of him as a certain candidate for the Medal of Honor.

The 2nd Battalion of the 1st Regiment jumped off at 8.30 a.m. and fought their way across the northern half of the airfield to join up with the 5th Regiment before noon, and the combined force were soon engaged in a fierce battle for control of the barracks and airfield hangars. The attack across the southern half bore all the hallmarks of the Battle of the Somme in the First World War – rows of infantry walking across open ground in the face of entrenched elevated enemy positions. Jim Jordan called it the

Marines H.T. Backous (left) and C.E. Schneider stand in front of Maj Parker's knocked-out command tank. Backous drove the tank while Schneider was in the turret with Parker. (USMC)

worst experience of his life: 'shimmering heat, deafening noise, shells whistling and exploding all round us, tracer bullets flashing past waist height, steel splinters falling like rain, men stumbling and falling'. As corpsman Brooking Gex recalled, 'the Japs began picking off stretcher-bearers. They were easy targets. Four men were gunned down trying to reach a Marine who looked like he would not make it. Finally I ran to the wounded man myself. He had a hole in his abdomen the size of my two fists side by side, and his stomach was leaking from this hole. "God help me", I gasped, "I don't think I can do anything for these men."'

In the south the 7th Regiment, with tank support, began the task of clearing the bottom half of the island. The first major obstacle was a large blockhouse supported by three dual-purpose guns. The guns were soon disposed of, but the blockhouse proved to be a major problem, and it took a demolition team, working under cover

'Looking up at the head of the trail I could see the big blockhouse that commanded the height.' (Tom Lea/US Army Center for Military History)

of smoke, to blast the position into silence. On the southern shores the Japanese had constructed a series of pillboxes and trenches in the belief that the Americans would mount a seaborne invasion on this part of the island. With all guns facing seaward the complex was soon overwhelmed, and the way lay open to the south-east promontory. A patrol also went out at low tide to the unnamed island to the south of 'Orange 3', but it soon discovered that shelling from Sherman tanks had done a good job and not a single Japanese was found alive.

The searing heat had taken its toll. Dehydrated and exhausted, the troops called it a day, and as darkness fell tanks arrived in preparation for the next day's advance. By nightfall Rupertus was a little happier: the first day's targets had almost been achieved, albeit a day late. He believed that a rapid advance up the East and West Roads would isolate the Umurbrogol, leaving only Ngesebus to the north to complete the operation. His 'three-day quickie' might only have to be extended by a few days. Little did he know that the battle had barely started.

WITH THE ARMY ON ANGAUR

Two reasons were given for the occupation of the island of Angaur, six miles to the south of Peleliu: the first was to prevent the Japanese from using the island to reinforce

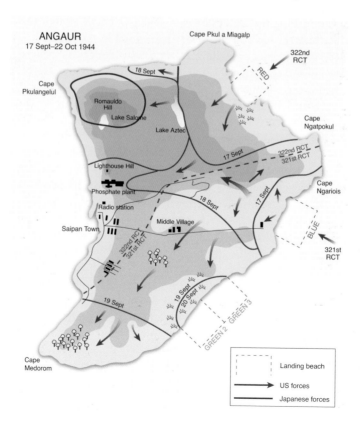

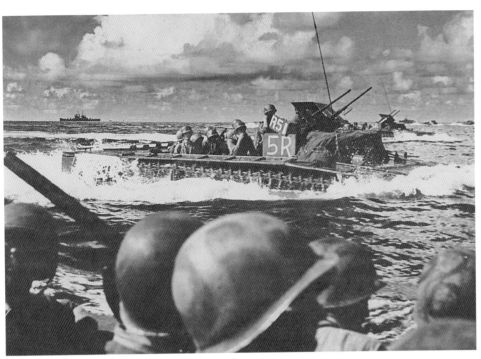

Assault infantry, probably Army GIs, head towards the shore in LVT-2 Amtracs. (US Navy)

the Peleliu garrison during the US landings; and the second was that the US Air Force wanted to build a bomber base on the low-lying ground in the south. It turned out that neither reason proved to be compelling. Contrary to American beliefs, the garrison on Angaur only numbered around 1,400 men, mainly from the 1st Battalion of the 59th Infantry Regiment commanded by Maj Ushio Goto. The Major had a problem deciding how to defend the many possible landing sites with his small garrison and, deciding to concentrate on an area to the south-east (which the Americans had designated as 'Green 2' and 'Green 3' on their maps), he built a series of bunkers, pillboxes and machine-gun emplacements. These were soon spotted by US aerial reconnaissances and the invasion beaches were selected elsewhere (see map on p. 127).

The invasion of Angaur was to be an all-Army operation by the 81st Division (the 'Wildcats') under Maj-Gen Paul Mueller, with two regimental combat teams (RCTs) – the 321st and the 322nd – with additional artillery, engineers and armour. Maj-Gen Geiger considered the situation on Peleliu to be sufficiently stable by D+1 to issue the order for the invasion and, on the morning of 17 September, the battleship *Tennessee*, together with the cruisers *Denver*, *Cleveland* and *Columbus*, began bombarding the selected invasion beaches at 8.00 a.m. 'Dauntless' bombers from the carrier *Wasp* blasted the woodland areas behind them as the Army's 726th Amphibian Tractor Battalion and the 776th Amphibian Tank Battalion spearheaded the troop-carrying Amtracs.

The Army had selected two beaches: 'Red' in the north-east would be attacked by the 322nd RCT, and 2,000yd further south the 321st RCT would land on 'Blue'. The plan was for the 322nd under Col Benjamin W. Venable to push towards the main built-up areas of Saipan Town, while the 321st under Col Robert F. Dark pushed west. The two RCTs were to join up somewhere in the centre of the island and swing south for the final drive.

The landings went well: on 'Red' beach the Army came ashore against only a few mortar rounds and were soon established; on 'Blue beach' the resistance was a little stiffer and by evening the troops had a foothold over 1,500yd long and 500yd into the undergrowth. The 322nd moved rapidly inland and by evening were almost halfway across the island, but on 'Blue beach' a determined Japanese counter-attack during the night held the 321st within their beachhead, leaving a 700yd gap between them and the 322nd. A strafing run by carrier planes the next morning directly to the enemy's front, coupled with the arrival of Sherman tanks, soon had both RCTs moving again, and by 2.00 p.m. the 322nd had reached the phosphate plant a few hundred yards north of Saipan Town. But they were delayed when a 'friendly fire' incident occurred in which carrier planes bombed the advancing troops, killing seven men and wounding a further forty-six. The 321st RCT finally made contact with the 322nd, closing the gap between them, and their 1st Battalion soon came upon the fortifications that Maj Goto had built around 'Green beach 2' and 'Green beach 3'. Most of these strongpoints faced the sea, giving Col Dark's men the advantage, and with the support of tanks US forces overran them early the next day.

By D+2 the Japanese were retreating on a broad front and Maj Goto was rallying the remains of his command for a final stand around Romuldo Hill in the north-west

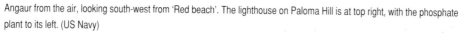

Angaur from the air, looking south-west from 'Red beach'. The lighthouse on Paloma Hill is at top right, with the phosphate plant to its left. (US Navy)

corner of the island. The Romuldo Hill area was a natural defensive stronghold, and the Major made full use of it. By occupying a maze of caves, he and his men kept RCT 322 occupied for another month. Goto was killed on 19 October and resistance finally ceased three days later. The operation had cost the 81st Division 260 men killed and 1,354 wounded; the Japanese casualties were estimated at 1,338 killed, with only 59 taken prisoner. The Seabees and the 81st Division engineers built the airfield in the south of the island, which became operational on 15 October, housing B-24 'Liberator' bombers of the 494th Bomb Group, though these were never used for their intended purpose of supporting MacArthur's advance through the Philippines.

BLOODY NOSE RIDGE

Back on Peleliu the Marines now had a firm line across the island just north of the airfield, while in the south Ngarmoked Island and some of the south-east promontory were still held by the Japanese. The 1st Regiment had suffered heavy casualties – over 1,000 dead and wounded in just two days – and the heat and lack of clean drinking water was having a serious impact on the fighting efficiency of everyone.

The 7th Regiment moved out on the morning of the 17th and headed for Ngarmoked Island. A large blockhouse at the end of a causeway slowed down their progress and caused many casualties. 'The whole causeway was littered with wounded and dead Marines,' recalled Sgt Jim Moll. 'I ran at full speed and halfway across I recognised a young Marine who was no more than 16. His leg was shot off above the knee and still attached to his body by a piece of thigh, and blood was pouring out. I took his belt off and used it as a tourniquet and yelled for a Corpsman and wished him good luck – I shall never forget that kid if I live to be a hundred.' The island finally succumbed and the Marines transferred their attention to the nearby promontory.

The attack had to be delayed for two hours while the 1st Engineers cleared a minefield. Once this was done the Marines, accompanied by tanks, swarmed across the sand spit, and by 1.30 p.m. the remaining Japanese had taken to the water's edge, where they were shot down one by one.

Rupertus now concentrated on driving north into the Umurbrogol and east to the village of Ngardololok, where the Japanese had a radio direction finder (RDF on the map on p. 111). The 2nd Battalion of the 5th Regiment swung to the east towards the village of Omaok and encountered little resistance, but the heat slowed progress to such an extent that they postponed their advance until the following day. Moving out early in the morning they soon reached the road connecting Omaok to Ngardololok. At a point about halfway between the two villages the road narrowed to a 200ft-wide neck, and fearing the prospect of strong resistance they called in an air strike to 'soften up' the area. It was here that another 'friendly fire' catastrophe occurred.

The attacking carrier planes dropped their bombs way off target, so an artillery barrage was substituted. Assuming that it was over, the 2nd Battalion started to cross the neck only to be bombed by a second, an uncalled-for, air strike. To add to the chaos, the battalion's command group was blasted by misdirected Marine artillery and mortar fire. These incidents were responsible for the deaths of eighteen men. The attack on the RDF installation on 19 September proved to be an anticlimax, as the Japanese had abandoned the area and only scattered resistance was encountered. Mopping up continued until the 20th, as the Marines occupied the whole of the eastern area, including the island of Ngabad. The Marines could now devote their attention to the main objective – the Umurbrogol.

'Chesty' Puller had already taken a mauling on the 'White beaches' and at the Point, so the divisional reserve that Rupertus had landed earlier, the 2nd Battalion of the 7th Regiment, was assigned to him. The first Marines to face the Umurbrogol were the 2nd Battalion of the 1st Regiment (2–1). They overran the point where the East and West Roads met, and advanced for 150yd to the base of Hill 200, where they ground to a halt in the face of withering enemy fire. Artillery and naval gunfire was directed at the hill, reducing the enemy resistance slightly, and by nightfall 2–1 had slogged their way to the summit, only to be pinned down by heavy fire on their left flank from another hill 10ft higher – Hill 210. To the west the 3rd Battalion of the 1st Regiment (3–1) had advanced 700yd along the flat coastal strip to the west of the Umurbrogol, where they halted, fearing that they would overextend the front line. Only four days into the battle, the Marines had suffered 1,236 casualties and were calling on engineers, dog handlers and clerks as front-line replacements.

The complex of hills, cliffs and rocks that was the southern end of the Umurbrogol was renamed 'Bloody Nose Ridge' by the Marines, and with good reason. The fourth day of battle began with a massive bombardment by artillery, naval guns and carrier planes, as 3–1 advanced further up the west coast. But it was in the centre, on Bloody Nose Ridge, that the hardest fighting would take place. Capturing Hill 210 and infiltrating beyond Hill 200 was the main objective, but the battle see-sawed as the Americans drove the Japanese off Hill 210 only for the enemy to recapture Hill 200; 3–1 also captured another Hill – 205 – which was to the side of Hill 210 and was useful only as an observation point. But as they moved forward the battalion came across another row of hills, soon to be named 'Five Sisters'.

Casualties throughout the day had been appalling as the troops crawled and slithered across diamond-sharp coral under constant mortar, artillery and small-arms fire from the hills above. 'The men surged forward, slugging their way upwards over razor-sharp crests, shinning coral pinnacles and plunging down into sheer-sided gullies and ravines and dodging behind boulders,' said Maj Ray Davis. Out of touch with the plight of his men, Rupertus issued the order 'All units will resume the attack with maximum effort in all sectors on September 19th'. Now reduced to using cooks, military police, laundry workers and non-combatant troops as front-line infantry, Puller desperately tried to implement the General's orders.

Overleaf: The dead were brought to the rear, where the grisly task of identification and recording got under way. (USMC University Archives)

After the usual naval and artillery barrage the Marines moved forward across the entire front; 3–1 advanced another 40yd up the west coast, but in the centre the true nature of the 'Five Sisters' was becoming apparent. It was not, as indicated on their maps, a series of interlocking hillocks but a sheer wall that barred any progress forward. Far from being connected, the 'Sisters' were separated by precipitous ravines, and even if one 'Sister' was captured there was no way they could move directly to the next.

Lt-Col Russ Honsowetz, the 2nd Battalion Commander, attempted to break the deadlock by a manoeuvre to outflank the 'Five Sisters'. To the left of the East Road and to the rear of the 'Sisters' lay Hill 100; if this could be taken it might provide a route to the rear of the enemy. A ninety-man company under Capt Everett P. Pope advanced through a mangrove swamp, but were pinned down by machine-gun fire for two hours. Tanks were called in, but the first one bogged down on a causeway; a second tank attempted to move it and also became stuck. Utterly frustrated, Pope and his men stormed across the causeway and surprisingly suffered no casualties. After regrouping, they charged the slopes of Hill 100 and reached the summit, only to realise that they too had become the victims of the map-makers. Hill 100 was not an isolated summit as indicated, merely the southern slope of a long ridge (later named 'Walt Ridge' after Lt-Col Lewis W. Walt) which was dominated by a higher position 500yd to their front.

This is Sad Sack Charlie. (Tom Lea/US Marine Corps Art Collection)

Tom Lea's famous image was originally captioned, *Down from Bloody Nose Ridge too late, he's finished, washed-up, gone*. It has since become famous as *The Two-Thousand-Yard Stare*. (Tom Lea/US Army Center for Military History)

Marooned for the night the Marines fought a prolonged battle against Japanese infiltrators until their ammunition ran out, whereupon they were reduced to fighting for their lives with knives, stones and bare fists. As dawn broke, the order to evacuate was finally given and the survivors scrambled down under a smokescreen. Only nine men, including Capt Pope, returned to the foot of the hill. Pope was later awarded the Medal of Honor and four of his men the Navy Cross, the Marine Corps' second-highest decoration.

Meanwhile, the shattered 1st Regiment was badly in need of reinforcements. Puller's men were being systematically slaughtered on 'Bloody Nose Ridge' and were constantly being harried by Rupertus to make the magical breakthrough that he so desperately needed. Reinforcements were readily available from the Army's 81st Division, but Rupertus was bitterly opposed to their use, a reluctance that probably had its origins

US MARINE CORPS COMMAND AND STAFF – PELELIU

Expeditionary Troops
Commanding General – Maj-Gen Julian C. Smith
Chief of Staff – Col Dudley S. Brown

III Amphibian Corps
Commanding General – Maj-Gen Roy S. Geiger
Chief of Staff – Col Merwith H. Silverthorn

Corps Troops
1st Amphibian Tractor Battalion:
Commanding Officer – Maj Albert F. Reutlinger

6th Amphibian Tractor Battalion:
Commanding Officer – Capt John I. Fitzgerald Jr

3rd Armoured Amphibian Tractor Battalion:
Commanding Officer – Lt-Col Kimber H. Boyer

1st Marine Division
Commanding General – William H. Rupertus
Ass. Divisional Commander – Brig-Gen Oliver P. Smith
Chief of Staff – Col John T. Selden

Regiments

1st Regiment	*5th Regiment*	*7th Regiment*
CO – Col Lewis B. Puller	CO – Col Harold D. Harris	CO – Col Herman H. Hanneken
1st Btn – Maj Raymond Davis	1st Btn – Lt-Col Robert Boyd	1st Btn – Lt-Col John J. Gormley
2nd Btn – Lt-Col Russell E. Honsowetz	2nd Btn – Maj Gordon Gayle	2nd Btn – Lt-Col Spencer Berger
3rd Btn – Lt-Col Stephen V. Sabol	3rd Btn – Lt-Col Austin C. Shofner	3rd Btn – Maj E. Hunter Hurst

11th Regiment
CO – Col William H. Harrison
1st Btn – Lt-Col Richard W. Wallace
2nd Btn – Lt-Col Noah P. Wood Jr
3rd Btn – Lt-Col Charles M. Nees
4th Btn – Lt-Col Louis C. Reinberg

81ST INFANTRY DIVISION – COMMAND STAFF AND ATTACHMENTS, PELELIU AND ANGAUR

Commanding Officer – Maj-Gen Paul J. Mueller

321st Regimental Combat Team
Commanding Officer – Col F. Robert Dark

Attachments: 316th Field Artillery Battalion
154th Engineer Combat Battalion
481st Amphibian Truck Company (DUKW)
Coy A, 726th Amphibian Tractor Battalion
Coy D, 776th Amphibian Tank Battalion
Coy A, 710th Tank Battalion

322nd Regimental Combat Team
Commanding Officer – Col Benjamin W. Venable

Attachments: 317th Field Artillery Battalion
Coy B, 306th Engineer Battalion
52nd Engineer Combat Battalion
Coy B, 710th Tank Battalion
726th Amphibian Tractor Battalion
Coy D, 776th Amphibian Tank Battalion

323rd Regimental Combat Team
Commanding Officer – Col Arthur P. Watson

Attachments: 906th Field Artillery Battalion
Coy C, 306th Engineer Battalion
155th Engineer Combat Battalion

81st Infantry Division Artillery (3 × 105mm Battalions)
HQ and HQ Battery: 318th Field Artillery Battalion

Attachments: 710th Tank Battalion (Coys A and B)

ESTIMATED JAPANESE STRENGTH – PELELIU AND ANGAUR

Imperial Army

14th Division: 2nd Infantry Regiment (incl. 1 Artillery Battalion)	3,283
3rd Battalion. 15th Infantry Regiment (incl. Artillery Coy)	1,030
Divisional Tank Company (Type 95 'Ha-Go')	100
Misc. Units (signals, field hospital, etc.)	300
53rd Independent Mixed Brigade (HQ, Infantry Battalions, Artillery and Engineer)	3,815
346th Independent Infantry Battalion	685

Imperial Navy (Combatant)

45th Naval Guard Force (part of)	200–400
114th and 126th Anti-Aircraft Units	600

Imperial Navy (Labour)

204th and 214th Naval Construction Battalions, 43rd and 235th Naval Construction Battalions (parts of)	2,000–2,200

Imperial Navy (Airfield Personnel)

Peleliu	1,270
Angaur	950
Estimated Maximum Strength	10,418–10,818

in the 'Smith v. Smith' feud that reached its climax on Saipan and soured Army–Marine Corps relations for the remainder of the war and beyond. Puller made one more effort to break the deadlock by attacking 'Walt Ridge', where Pope and his men had fought so valiantly the previous day, but the attack floundered as the exhausted men struggled against impossible odds. The 1st Regiment was a spent force; the men had given more than any reasonable commander could expect and were replaced in the line by elements of the 7th Regiment.

This changeover was due to the intervention of Maj-Gen Geiger. He had visited Puller's command post (CP) and found the Colonel limping around on a swollen leg; a fragment of shrapnel that he had picked up on Guadalcanal had turned septic and would later require an emergency operation. A heated conversation took place and Geiger then went to Rupertus's HQ and asked for the latest casualty figures. His worst fears were confirmed: the 1st Regiment had suffered the heaviest losses by any regiment in Marine Corps history. Geiger told Rupertus that he was bringing in the Army, whereupon Rupertus became agitated and insisted that he could secure Peleliu in another day or two. But Geiger was adamant and instructed that the remnants of the 1st should withdraw and await evacuation to Pavuvu.

At 6.25 a.m. the following day, an urgent message was sent to Maj-Gen Mueller's divisional HQ to supply a regimental combat team. Within hours Col Dark's 321st were making ready. The 1st Regiment and 'Chesty' Puller left Peleliu on 2 October in two hospital ships, and during the voyage he underwent an operation for the removal of the shrapnel in his leg. He did not know it but his war was over: after recuperation and long-overdue leave in the USA he was due to return to the Pacific, but before that could happen the atomic bomb on Hiroshima ended the war. He would eventually return to his beloved 1st Regiment during the Korean conflict, this time under Oliver Smith, and he retired as the most decorated marine in the history of the corps, with an unprecedented five Navy Crosses.

ENTER THE WILDCATS

The relief of the 1st and the arrival of the Army's 321st RCT signalled a new phase in the battle. Few people had placed much faith in Rupertus's 'quickie' scenario, but now it was becoming evident to everyone that the Japanese holed up in the Umurbrogol were only going to be prised out by the use of point-blank artillery fire, flame-throwers, bazookas and demolition charges. In the past the Japanese had relied on halting the invader at the water's edge. When this failed, as it usually did, they resorted to a wild, suicidal 'banzai' charge that inevitably ended in wholesale slaughter. Peleliu heralded a new and more sinister defence technique: a garrison determined to die where they stood while taking with them as many Americans as possible – these techniques were later perfected at Iwo Jima and Okinawa, which would no doubt have been the cause of millions of casualties had the Americans and their Allies ever been forced to invade the Japanese homeland.

Lt-Gen Sadae Inoue, on Babelthuap in the north, was still holding on to a large number of troops in the belief that US forces were contemplating an attack. However, on the night of 22 September, during a heavy rainstorm, he ferried the 2nd Battalion of the 15th Infantry Regiment to northern Peleliu by barge. US Intelligence sources confirmed that 300–600 men succeeded in reaching the island, a serious blow to the Americans. They rapidly sealed off this route with amphibious patrols and air-search missions.

Brig-Gen Oliver Smith was to observe:

There were two Pelelius after the first two weeks of the battle. The flat ground we had captured in the southern third where we brought in our men and supplies, and the other third that began at 'Bloody Nose Ridge' and extended northward into the Umurbrogol and on to Ngesebus Island. This was a brutally different ball game, where the score was kept by the number of ridges taken and how many Marines were killed in a seemingly endless process.

D+8, 23 September, saw the start of the encirclement of the Umurbrogol. RCT 321 advanced up the West Road towards the village of Garekoru and almost reached it by evening, but had to halt for the day when they came under heavy fire from the ridges to their right. Next morning the advance continued and Dark's GIs discovered a trail that led up into the hills. Leaving E Company to investigate, he pressed forward and secured Garekoru around 4.00 p.m., then dug in for the night. Meanwhile, E Company continued up the trail, ending up in a sharp firefight which lasted through the night. Next morning they stormed down the eastern slopes of the Umurbrogol and reached the East Road. This ranked as a major breakthrough. The trail, later named the 'Wildcat Trail', was narrow but could be improved. Its capture meant that the bulk of Col Kunio Nakagawa's garrison were isolated and contained in an area that soon became known as 'The Pocket'.

Rupertus now turned his attention to the East Road and an area beyond the Umurbrogol called Kamilianlul Mountain (see map on p. 111). He transferred the 5th Marine Regiment from the east of the island to undertake the task, and Lt-Col Lewis Walt (deputising for Col Harold D. 'Bucky' Harris, who was indisposed by injuries sustained on D-Day) took command. Simultaneously, the 1st and 3rd Battalions of the 7th Regiment were assigned to support RCT 321 in their advance up the West Road. This operation went well and with the support of Shermans and LVT-4 flame-thrower tanks in the vanguard they reached the radio station 600yd north of Garekoru by dusk. As night fell the Japanese mounted a fierce counter-attack with infantry supported by two 70mm artillery pieces and artillery and mortar fire from Ngesebus to the north.

Next morning 3–5 stormed a coral ridge called Hill 80 and pushed on to the east coast, while 1–5 advanced to the phosphate refinery at the end of the island, where the opposition was strong. To the right of the West Road lay a group of hills collectively known as the Hill Row – Hills 1, 2 and 3, and Radar Hill – which were to prove hard work for the Marines.

CORSAIRS AND HELLCATS

Since the occupation of the airfield the Seabees and Marine Engineers had been busy clearing the wreckage and levelling the runways in preparation for the arrival of the Marines' own pilots. On 26 September the base was declared 'operational', and a squadron of twenty-four F4U 'Corsair' fighter-bombers under the command of Maj Robert F. 'Cowboy' Stout was landed from the aircraft carrier *Lexington* fifty miles offshore. Two days later, twenty-four F6F Hellcat fighters arrived from the *Wasp*, and the combined force, 2nd Marine Air Wing, became operational immediately. For the remainder of the battle the wing flew close-support sorties against enemy positions throughout the island. They must have been some of the shortest operational flights ever recorded. The planes would take off and drop a bomb or napalm canister within half a minute, do a tight turn and return to the runway – most pilots didn't even bother to retract their undercarriages. Spotter planes were also stationed at the airfield and provided invaluable information for the Marines and Army artillery. Smaller aircraft were used to spray DDT over the battlefield to kill off the millions of mosquitoes and flies that plagued the combatants – even the Japanese let these low-flying and fragile planes pass by unmolested.

MOPPING UP IN THE NORTH AND ON NGESEBUS ISLAND

The 5th Marine Regiment continued their operations along Hill Row on 27 September. The phosphate plant was proving to be a hard nut to crack, and Maj Gordon D. Gayle's 2–5 had to call on Shermans and LVT flame-throwers to reduce the garrison; they killed more than sixty enemy troops in the process. The Marines battled on until noon, when the attack ground to a halt before a mass of bunkers, caves and pillboxes to their front. They had come across one of the most elaborate cave systems on the island, which had at one time housed over 1,000 Japanese troops. Col 'Bucky' Harris devised an ingenious plan to resolve the problem. While the 11th Marine Artillery laid down a barrage on Ngesebus Island to suppress the enemy fire, nine Shermans moved along the shore under a heavy smokescreen and blanketed the beaches of Ngesebus with smoke shells. With the offshore island effectively blinded, five LVTA-4s mounting 75mm howitzers churned out to the reef and blasted the enemy positions at short range. This enabled tanks and LVT flame-throwers to hose down the whole complex, and by nightfall the Marines had consolidated the area.

The capture of Ngesebus Island was one of the highlights of the whole battle. Lying some 330yd off the northern coast, it was the site of a short fighter airstrip and an important gun position from which the enemy could bombard Hill Row. Again it was Col Harris who would plan and implement the attack. At 9.00 a.m., the battleship *Mississippi* and the cruisers *Denver* and *Colorado* plastered the island for 40 minutes with their heavy guns, and when the barrage lifted Maj Stout's 'Corsairs' roared in at treetop height, terrifying the 550-strong garrison. The 3rd Armoured

Amphibian Tractor Battalion provided 35 Amtracs for the assault, which was spearheaded by 13 waterproofed Shermans that crossed the channel between Peleliu and Ngesebus at positions previously marked out by the Underwater Demolition Team. Three tanks were swamped out, but the remainder hauled themselves onto Ngesebus beach 6 minutes later. Companies I, K and L of 3–5 under Maj John H. Gustafson led the attack and by mid-afternoon on the following day the island was in US hands.

The Ngesebus operation was a textbook example of good planning and execution, with a small battalion of Marines defeating an enemy force of around 500 (most of them elite troops from the Kwantung Army) killing 440 and capturing 23. Rupertus, true to form, had invited a party of 'brass', including Rear-Adm Jesse Oldendorf, to witness the 'show' from a vantage point that provided safety and comfort. Had they known, one can readily imagine the reaction of the Marines who provided this entertainment.

THE UMURBROGOL POCKET

With operations in the north virtually at an end – only a few pockets of resistance remained around Radar Hill in Hill Row – the Umurbrogol 'Pocket' became the focus of the US attack. Holed up in an area only 1,000yd long and 500yd wide, Col Nakagawa and the remains of his 14th Division occupied a defensive fighter's dream: a labyrinth of hills, caves, valleys and ravines; the Japanese troops' only concern was how many Americans could they take with them when they died.

Col Hanneken's 7th Regiment were ordered to start the final push and an area known as the 'Horseshoe' was chosen as the jumping-off point (see map on p. 142). At its northern end was the 'Freshwater Pond', on the right was 'Walt Ridge' and on the left a line of hills called the 'Five Brothers'. D+15, 30 September, saw Hanneken's 1–7 moving along the East Road to attack the adjacent ridges while part of 3–7 assisted on their right, but little ground was given up by the fanatical defenders. Rupertus now ordered the 7th to seize 'Walt Ridge' and also 'Boyd Ridge', which was at the northern end of the 'Horseshoe'. On 2 October, 2–7 followed the same route that had been taken earlier by Capt Pope – up the East Road and across the causeway – and achieved a complete surprise, reaching the summit of Hill 100 without suffering any casualties. Meanwhile, 3–7 advanced against 'Boyd Ridge' but were soon bogged down under heavy fire. Moving through the swamps alongside the East Road they made a flanking attack, and by evening most of 'Boyd Ridge' had been cleared and a link-up with 2–7 was achieved. Next it was the turn of 'Wildcat Bowl' on the far side of the 'Five'. With tanks in support, 3–5, now rested and reinforced, attacked the 'Five Sisters' and succeeded in taking most of the area.

A bizarre incident at the time was the death of Col Joseph F. Hankins, CO of the 1st Division's HQ Battalion and the highest-ranking casualty of the battle. Sgt Tom Climie of the Army's 321st witnessed the incident:

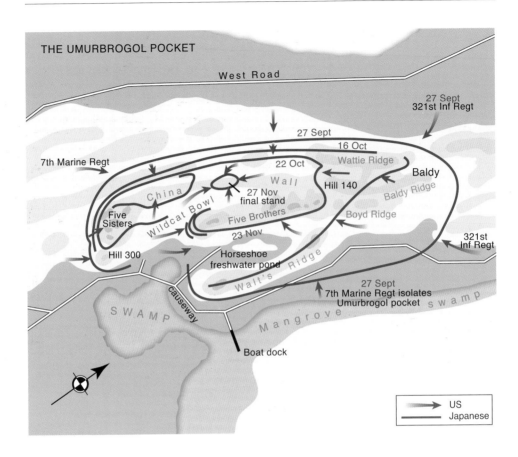

THE UMURBROGOL POCKET

West Road

27 Sept
321st Inf Regt

27 Sept

16 Oct

22 Oct

Wattie Ridge

Baldy

7th Marine Regt

W a l l

Hill 140

Baldy Ridge

China

27 Nov
final stand

Wildcat Bowl

Five Brothers

Boyd Ridge

Five
Sisters

23 Nov

321st
Inf Regt

Hill 300

Horseshoe
freshwater pond

Walt's Ridge

27 Sept
7th Marine Regt isolates
Umurbrogol pocket

S W A M P

causeway

M a n g r o v e   s w a m p

Boat dock

US
Japanese

Rusting amphibious tractors. (David M. Green)

Rusting Amtracs continue to litter the battlefield today. (David M. Green)

We were with a convoy of trucks pinned down by enemy fire on the West Road. Bullets were flying everywhere from a Japanese machine-gun position and eventually we found cover behind some big rocks. I looked down the road: Jeeps, three-quarter-ton trucks – nothing was moving. Then to my amazement, down the centre of the road came this man cursing and swearing and telling everyone to get out and get the convoy moving. I yelled for him to get down – too late. He went down in a hail of bullets. I learned later that he was a marine colonel.

On 5 October, 3–7 commenced the assault on 'Baldy Ridge', a 200ft-high barrier in the northern sector of the 'Pocket'. The approach was guarded by three dome-like hills called the 'Knobs'; it looked a daunting task, but surprisingly the 'Knobs' were taken without much difficulty and 3–7 pressed on to 'Baldy Ridge', but were repulsed with heavy casualties. This was the final action for the 7th Regiment. Brig-Gen Oliver Smith said, 'purely and simply there were not enough men left to continue the fight'. Of the 3,217 men who had landed on D-Day, 1,486 were dead or wounded, amounting to losses of over 46 per cent. The 7th were moved to Ngarmoked Island and were soon on their way back to Pavuvu.

A Company, 1/7th Marines, before leaving Peleliu. Of the 235 men that landed on D-Day, 94 survived. (USMC)

The only Marine regiment now operational on Peleliu was 'Bucky' Harris's 5th, and on 7 October the Colonel launched a two-pronged attack: 2–5 were ordered to continue the assault on 'Baldy' while 3–5 were to probe the 'Horseshoe', 'Walt Ridge' and the 'Five Brothers'. On 9 October a patrol from 2–5 reached the summit of a ridge to the west of 'Baldy' which provided direct access to 'Baldy' itself. The ridge was promptly named 'Wattie Ridge' after Lt Wattie, the platoon leader, and the following morning a direct attack on 'Baldy' was mounted with the support of Army howitzers. The enemy resisted strongly, but by noon 'Baldy' was in US hands. Pressing home their advantage, 2–5 secured Hill 140 and, despite a vicious night-time Japanese counter-attack, held it with few casualties. This achievement was to mark the end for 2–5, who were relieved the next day by 3–5. On 12 October, twenty-eight days into the battle, Adm George E. Fort declared the assault phase of 'Operation Stalemate' to be over and ordered the replacement of the USMC 1st Division by the Army's 81st Division; within two days Col Dark's 321st RCT began taking over from the Marines around 'Baldy' and Hill 140, and Col Venable's 322nd RCT was ordered over from Angaur to garrison southern Peleliu. On the 30th, Maj-Gen Geiger officially handed over to Maj-Gen Mueller; Geiger and Rupertus flew to Guadalcanal and Oliver Smith stayed behind to liaise with Mueller during the transition.

SIEGE WARFARE

With the full weight of defeating the Japanese in the Umurbrogol falling on his shoulders Maj-Gen Mueller made his deployments around the 'Pocket'. The 3rd Battalion of the 321st RCT, 3–321, were to cover 'Walt Ridge', 'Boyd Ridge' and the entrance to the 'Horseshoe', 2–321 held the top of Hill 140 and the surrounding area, and 1–321 faced the 'Five Sisters' and 'Death Valley'.

The initial attacks were countered by murderous Japanese troops deeply entrenched in almost invulnerable positions. The 2–321 moved against the first of the 'Five Brothers' but were forced to retire under shredding machine-gun fire; 1–321 could only advance for 100yd before they were beaten back from the 'Five Sisters'. And a further attempt by 2–321 to secure the 'Five Brothers' on 19 October was partially successful when they took 'brothers' one and two; but by the end of the day they were forced back to their original positions.

Seeing the futility of these frontal assaults, Mueller opted for a policy of siege warfare. Nakagawa's men were now contained in an area little more than 800yd by 400yd, ammunition and food were rapidly diminishing, and his men in the 'Horseshoe' were being picked off as they attempted to get water from the Freshwater Pond. The intermittent heavy rain and shrouding fog that had characterised the weather since the beginning of October continued to slow down operations, and it was well into November before there was any improvement. But the attacks on the 'Horseshoe' continued and Mueller's force was bolstered by the arrival of RCT 323, who had been involved in the occupation of the atoll of Ulithi a few weeks earlier.

As the weather improved renewed assaults were mounted in the southern sector; 2–323 gained control of Hill 300 and the 'Five Sisters' as 3–323 advanced along the top of the 'China Wall'. Unbeknown to the troops, they were within yards of Col Nakagawa's and Maj-Gen Kenijiro Murai's HQ. By now, tanks and LVT flame-throwers were roving at will in the 'Horseshoe' and 'Death Valley', and Army engineers constructed a ramp from the bottom of 'Wildcat Bowl' to the crest of the 'China Wall', enabling tanks and flame-throwers to bring the last enemy strongholds under direct fire.

The remnants of the Japanese garrison were now confined to an area about 150yd long. Nakagawa sent a final message to Lt-Gen Inoue on Koror, saying that he could only last for one more day and that he was reduced to fifty able-bodied men with seventy wounded. On that day, the seventy-first of the battle, Col Nakagawa and Maj-Gen Murai committed suicide, and the battle was over. Odd pockets of resistance were being mopped up for months; and the last survivor came down from the hills to surrender in 1954, returning to Japan as a national hero.

A QUESTIONABLE BATTLE

Peleliu was one of the major battles of the Pacific War. Most veterans equate it with Tarawa, Iwo Jima and Okinawa; many think it was worse. But questions still hang

High in the almost
inpenetrable
Umurbrogol Mountains,
the Japanese defenders
still maintain their grim
vigil. (Eric Mailander)

A Japanese gun that
covered all of 'Orange
beach' in 1944 still
protrudes from the
mouth of a cave. (Eric
Mailander)

over the planning and execution of the operation. 'Operation Stalemate' was planned
to neutralise the Japanese presence in the Palau Islands and to secure MacArthur's
flank prior to his invasion of Mindanao in the southern Philippines, but 'Operation
Desecrate 1' in late March had already destroyed all Japanese shipping and most of the
aircraft on the islands. The Japanese had no means of transporting their troops from
the Palaus to the Philippines, and, even if they had had, the overwhelming superiority
of the US Navy task forces would have devastated them. The acceptance of 'Bull'
Halsey's recommendation to move the invasion north was the final confirmation that
the Palau garrison posed no threat to MacArthur.

Shortcomings in the planning and direction of the battle are easier to pinpoint. The planning skills of the 'big three' – Turner, Spruance and Holland Smith – were sadly missed. An aide to Oliver Smith described communications between Pearl Harbor and Pavuvu as being 'like jungle drums'. Aerial photos and invasion maps of Peleliu were woefully inadequate in showing the true nature of the Umurbrogol area; ships failed to arrive on time, resulting in a third of the available Sherman tanks being left behind; a large proportion of the Marines were young inexperienced recruits fresh from boot camp; and the choice of Pavuvu as a training area was appalling.

Perhaps the biggest question mark hung over the choice of Maj-Gen Rupertus to command the operation. His presence cast a dark shadow over the whole battle; moody, unimaginative, and uncommunicative he was disliked by both his officers and his men. At one point during the battle, Col 'Bucky' Harris called at Divisional HQ and found Rupertus in tears: 'I'm at the end of my rope,' he said. 'Two of my fine regiments are in ruins. You usually seem to know what to do and get it done – I'm going to turn over to you everything we have left. This is strictly between us.' This outburst clearly shows that the battle had become too much for him to handle. Shortly after the battle was over, he was flown to Washington, where he had a meeting with Maj-Gen Vandegrift, the Marine Corps Commandant. Nothing is known of what was said, but shortly afterwards Rupertus was appointed to command the Marine Corps Training Schools, a move generally regarded as a demotion. In March 1945, after attending a dinner party at Washington Navy Yard, he collapsed and died of a massive heart attack. He was fifty-five years old.

THE BATTLE OF LEYTE GULF

Peleliu had been officially declared 'secure' by 12 October, and the next objective in the 'island hopping' campaign was the island of Iwo Jima; but sandwiched between the two was the largest naval encounter in history, a mighty battle that lasted for three days from 23–5 October. Leyte Gulf was the Imperial Navy's last chance to force a decisive engagement with the US Navy, and it followed the usual complicated plan. 'Operation SHO-1' called for Japanese naval forces in northern Borneo to divide into three groups: from Borneo, Force A, part of the First Strike Force under Vice-Adm Takeo Kurita, would pass through the San Bernardino Strait to attack US

landing forces off the island of Samur; from the north, the Second Strike Force under Vice-Adm Kiyohide Shima would head south to join up with Force C, also from Borneo, and, under Vice-Adm Shoji Nishimura, pass through the Surigao Strait to attack the landing force from the south; and finally, the main carrier force from Japan under Vice-Adm Ozawa hoped to lure Halsey's Task Force 38 away to the north, thus enabling the First and Second Strike Forces to destroy the US invasion fleet.

Halsey did not know that the Japanese were at sea until 23 October. On that day US submarines sank two of the heavy cruisers of Kurita's A Force; as they passed through the Sibuyan Sea, the Japanese fleet came under heavy air attack, and the huge 73,000-ton battleship *Musashi* succumbed after nineteen torpedo hits. Around noon on 24 October US reconnaissance planes spotted the combined Second Strike Force and Force C and assumed that they were heading for Surigao Strait. Rear-Adm Jesse Oldendorf deployed his old battleships with cruisers, destroyers and motor torpedo boats to ambush the enemy at the northern end of the Strait. A fierce battle began in the early hours of the morning during which the battleship *Fuso* was torpedoed and blew up and the battleship *Yamashiro* took two torpedo hits. By 4.00 a.m., Nishimura had had enough and both Force C and Shima's Second Strike Force retired.

At 3.00 p.m., reconnaissance planes from TF38 located Ozawa's decoy force and Halsey immediately gave chase. By doing so he played into the enemy's hands, as Ozawa's carriers were almost devoid of aircraft and pilots. During that night Kurita's A Force passed through the San Bernardino Strait and by morning were heading towards the US landing areas. A Force consisted of four battleships, six heavy cruisers and dozens of destroyers and posed a very serious threat to the US forces. Luckily for them Kurita blundered into Taffy 3, a group of six escort carriers with a six-destroyer escort. A frantic battle ensued as Kurita strove to overwhelm the carriers but the Navy pilots excelled themselves by mounting non-stop attacks in which they sustained heavy losses. Although he had sunk two carriers and four destroyers, Kurita lost his nerve when he heard that the Second Strike Force and Force C had been routed in the Surigao Strait, and at 12.36 p.m. he turned tail.

Halsey was still steaming northward in pursuit of Ozawa's carriers and came within striking distance at 8.00 a.m. – throughout the day Task Force 38 launched strike after strike and by early evening Ozawa had lost four carriers, the *Chitose*, *Chiyoda*, *Zuikaku* and the *Zuiho*. Halsey by now had been notified of the situation to the south and his error of leaving the San Bernardino Strait unguarded. He sent his fast battleships to the scene, but by this time Kurita had fled. Nimitz was furious and his message to Halsey, 'Where is, repeat, where is Task Force 34, the world wonders', was regarded by him as a huge insult that he never forgave. The Battle of Leyte Gulf signalled the end of the Imperial Navy. With little fuel available for further operations and no aircrew to man the carrier planes, it would now only offer token attacks, such as the suicidal one-way sortie by the super-battleship *Yamato* off Okinawa.

FIVE

IWO JIMA

'DO NOT PLAN FOR MY RETURN'

Long before the last Japanese soldier had been prised out of his dugout in the Marianas, the Seabees and the Army and Air Force Engineers were busy building airfields on Guam, Saipan and Tinian to house the B29 'Superfortress' bombers of the 20th Air Force. Before the Marines and the US Army secured the Marianas, the US Army Air Force had been limited to carrying out raids on the southern islands of Japan from bases in eastern China. These missions involved the transportation of all of their high-octane aviation fuel over thousands of miles of inhospitable country using specially adapted tanker aircraft, small bomb loads, and poor navigation by inexperienced aircrews. The offensive proved to be ineffective and was abandoned by the Air Force chiefs, who turned their attention to the islands of the Central Pacific. The Marianas, particularly the islands of Saipan, Guam and Tinian, would put their B29 'Superfortress' bombers within range of the whole of the Japanese mainland and, long before the Japanese had been defeated, Navy Seabees were busy carving out great swathes of the jungle and scrubland to provide five huge airfields.

Each airfield was to become a small town. Apart from the standard workshops and administration facilities, shops, banks, post offices and cinemas sprang up to service the large numbers of air and ground staff. On Guam alone, at the height of operations in 1945 there were over 65,000 Air Force personnel. Five bombardment wings were housed on the islands: the 314th and 315th on Guam, the 58th and 313th on Tinian, and the 73rd on Saipan. Together they formed the 21st Bomber Command of the 20th Air Force under the overall command of General of the Air Force Henry 'Hap' Arnold, who was based in Washington. The first local commander was Brig-Gen Haywood S. Hansell Jr – 'Possum' to his friends – who took over on 12 October 1944 and wasted little time in initiating an intensive training programme. Starting with a raid on the island of Truk, the results were not encouraging, with only fourteen of the eighteen planes managing to bomb the target and three failing to locate the island. After further training, Hansell mounted his first raid on the Japanese mainland, bombing Tokyo on 24 November with a force of 111 B29s. It was the first raid on the capital since the Doolittle attack of April 1942, but the results were poor, with only eighty-eight of the planes dropping their bombs on account of bad weather.

Brand-new B29 'Superfortress' bombers stand outside the specially built factory at Wichita, Kansas. (Boeing Company Archives)

Hansell had adopted the strategy that had proved so successful for the 8th Air Force in its campaign against Germany – high-altitude, daylight precision bombing against industrial targets – but the slow build-up of the bomber force, combined with lack of fighter escort, indifferent weather and a high number of engine troubles due to an inherent overheating problem, played havoc with his strategy and he became disillusioned: 'In my opinion you people haven't earned your pay over here. Unless you do better, this operation is doomed to failure,' he said in a bitter attack on his aircrews.

Pressure was also mounting in Washington for better results, and by mid-January 1945 it was decided that Hansell must go. His replacement was Maj-Gen Curtis E. LeMay, former commander of the 3rd Division of the 8th Air Force in England. LeMay was a volatile but innovative tactician. His nickname of 'Iron Arse' was not inappropriate. The cigar-chewing General surveyed the problem and came up with a completely new and radical solution. Instead of the high-altitude bombing favoured by Hansell, LeMay would mount low-level attacks at night with an all-incendiary bomb load. There was talk among the crews of a 'suicide mission' and LeMay was very much aware that his reputation, and possibly his job, was on the line. But the first raid, on 9 March vindicated his new policy. A 3-mile by 5-mile area of Tokyo was saturated

A flight of B29 bombers return to North Field on Guam after a fire-raising attack on the Japanese mainland. (National Archives)

by 334 'Superfortresses', and a firestorm soon developed. At its centre, temperatures reached a staggering 1,800°Fahrenheit. Only fourteen aircraft were lost, and reconnaissance pictures the next day indicated that sixteen square miles of the city had been destroyed. The official death count was later recorded as 83,793 killed and 40,918 injured – and thousands made homeless.

Mounting an attack on the Japanese homeland was a daunting task. Tokyo was some 1,500 miles from the Marianas and involved a very long and tiring flight. Aircraft that sustained damage over the target had a precarious return trip, with the possibility of having to ditch in the vast expanses of the North Pacific; to bail out over Japan meant at best imprisonment under inhuman conditions or at worst death. Ships patrolled the seas from the Marianas to north of Iwo Jima, and from there to the Japanese coast the rescue operations were taken over by submarine; but the survival rate among downed aircrews was depressingly low, and so the occupation of Iwo Jima became an overriding priority. From Iwo Jima the Navy could dispatch 'Catalina' and 'Coronado' PBY flying boats to pick up ditched crews, and P51 'Mustang' fighters based on the island could offer a much-needed fighter escort for the second leg of the long trip. But the main advantages of Iwo Jima was an emergency base for damaged B29s – during the whole of the 20th Air Force bombing campaign against the Japanese mainland an estimated 24,761 lives were saved because of its availability.

In addition to the 20th Air Force campaign, hundreds of carrier-based planes from the Fast Carrier Task Forces joined in the assault on Japan. The first strike was by Marc Mitscher's TF58 which attacked aircraft-engine factories in the Tokyo suburbs on 16 February and returned the following day to complete the job. In two days the Navy pilots downed 341 enemy aircraft for the loss of 88 Navy planes in combat or in landing accidents. Adm Nimitz also requested the 20th Air Force to carry out an extensive mining operation on most of the routes used by Japanese merchant shipping. Commencing on the night of 27 March, the 313th Wing, operating from Tinian, began the systematic mining of the harbours of Tokyo, Kure, Hiroshima, Sasebo, Tokuyama and Nagoya in 'Operation Starvation'. The results were dramatic: 18 ships sunk in April, 83 in May and 85 in June. The 313th Wing dropped a total of 12,053 mines, making it the largest operation of its kind ever undertaken: 'You were eventually starving the country', said the commander of the minesweeping force after the war.

20TH AIR FORCE COMMAND STRUCTURE
APRIL 1944–JULY 1945

Joint Chiefs of Staff

HQ US Army Air Force
Gen Henry 'Hap' Arnold

HQ 20th Air Force – Gen Henry 'Hap' Arnold
Chief of Staff: Brig-Gen Haywood S. Hansell, Jr (April–August 1944)
Brig-Gen Lauris Norstad (August 1944–July 1945)

HQ 21st Bomber Command
Commanding Generals: Brig-Gen Haywood S. Hansell (August 1944–January 1945)
Maj-Gen Curtis E. LeMay (January 1945–July 1945)

58 Bomb Wing	313 Bomb Wing	314 Bomb Wing	315 Bomb Wing	73 Bomb Wing
West Field	North Field	North Field	North-west Field	Isley Field
Tinian	Tinian	Guam	Guam	Saipan
40 Bomb Group	6 Bomb Group	19 Bomb Group	16 Bomb Group	497 Bomb Group
444 Bomb Group	9 Bomb Group	29 Bomb Group	33 Bomb Group	498 Bomb Group
462 Bomb Group	504 Bomb Group	39 Bomb Group	501 Bomb Group	499 Bomb Group
468 Bomb Group	505 Bomb Group	330 Bomb Group	502 Bomb Group	500 Bomb Group
	509 Composite Group (Nuclear)			

A 7th Air Force reconnaissance picture of the south of Iwo Jima. The landing beaches can be seen on the right.
(US Navy)

On 3 October 1944, the Joint Chiefs of Staff issued Adm Nimitz a directive to seize the island of Iwo Jima – 'Operation Detachment' would be masterminded by the 'big three' – Spruance, Turner and Holland Smith – and would be an all-Marine-Corps operation, utilising the 3rd, 4th and 5th Divisions in what would be the supreme test of the amphibious techniques that had been developed over the previous three years.

Iwo Jima – Japanese for 'Sulphur Island' – lies at the end of the Nanpo Shoto, a 750-mile-long chain of bleak islands reaching into the Pacific from Tokyo Bay. It is 660 nautical miles south of Tokyo and 625 miles north of the Marianas, a location that gave the island immense strategic importance at this stage of the war. Four and a half miles long, with its axis running south-west to north-east, it tapers from two and a half miles wide in the north to a mere half-mile in the south, giving a total area of seven and a half square miles. At the base of the island is Mt Suribachi, a 550ft-high dormant volcano with commanding views all over the island. The beaches that stretch north from the volcano are terraced at various heights and widths by storms and constant wave action. There is no harbour or anchorage, and the surf conditions are not conducive to amphibious operations. On a plateau on the south of Iwo Jima lay Airfield No. 1, and a little further north at the wider section was Airfield No. 2, with an unfinished third airfield beyond. The ground that slopes away to the north is a mass

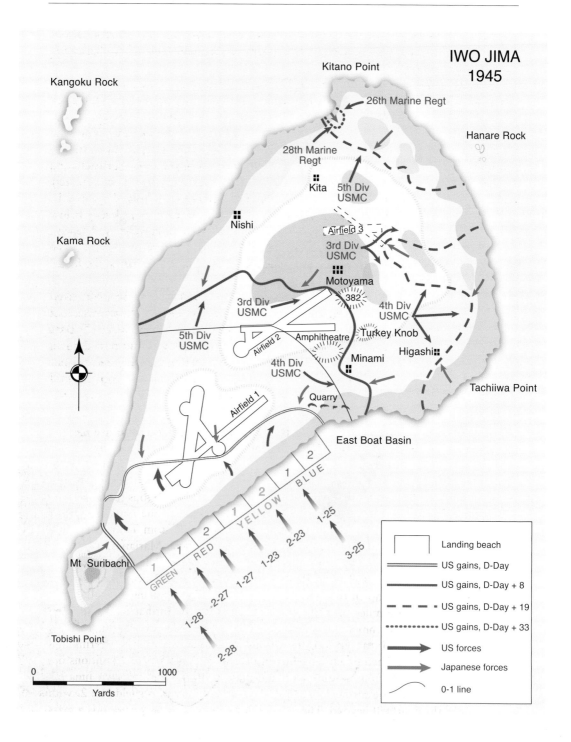

IWO JIMA
1945

Kitano Point

Kangoku Rock

26th Marine Regt

Hanare Rock

28th Marine
Regt

Kita   5th Div
        USMC

Nishi

Airfield 3

Kama Rock

3rd Div
USMC

Motoyama

382   4th Div
        USMC

3rd Div
USMC

Turkey Knob

5th Div
USMC   Airfield 2   Amphitheatre

Higashi

Minami

4th Div
USMC

Tachiiwa Point

Quarry

Airfield 1

East Boat Basin

2

1

BLUE

1-25

2

YELLOW

1

1-23   2-23   3-25

2

RED

1-27   2-27

Mt Suribachi

1

GREEN

1-28

2-28

Tobishi Point

0   1000

Yards

	Landing beach
	US gains, D-Day
	US gains, D-Day + 8
	US gains, D-Day + 19
	US gains, D-Day + 33
	US forces
	Japanese forces
	0-1 line

of gorges, valleys, ridges and hills – ideal ground for defensive fighting – and at various points throughout the island clouds of sulphurous vapours are vented from fissures in the earth (see map on p. 154).

The combined three divisions of the USMC totalled over 70,000 men, most of whom were seasoned veterans of earlier campaigns, and they were to be supported by the Navy who were scheduled to provide a massive 'softening up' bombardment from the old battleships *Arkansas*, *Texas*, *Nevada*, *Idaho* and *Tennessee*. The plan of attack devised for Maj-Gen Harry Schmidt's 5th Amphibian Corps looked simple. The Marines would land on the two-mile stretch of beach between Mt Suribachi and the East Boat Basin. The area would be divided into seven sections of approximately 550yd each. Under the shadow of Mt Suribachi lay 'Green beach', flanked by 'Red 1', 'Red 2', 'Yellow 1', 'Yellow 2', 'Blue 1' and 'Blue 2'. 'Blue beach 2' lay directly below the quarry overlooking the East Boat Basin, a known hot spot for enemy defences; it was decided that the troops in this area would all come ashore on 'Blue 1'. The isolation of Mt Suribachi was the primary objective. Once this was achieved the forces would swing north on a broad front.

The length of the pre-invasion bombardment became controversial, Schmidt asked for ten days of continuous shelling, but Adm Hill rejected the idea on the grounds that there would be insufficient time to rearm his battleships and cruisers before D-Day. Schmidt persisted and modified his request to nine days but this was also turned down – the Navy thought that three days would be sufficient. Schmidt again protested but again failed to convince the Navy. 'I know your people will get away with it,' said Spruance, small comfort for the Marines destined to land on D-Day.

Mount Suribachi under bombardment on D-Day, 19 February 1945. Several small vessels can be seen operating inshore. (National Archives)

The first day of softening up was a disappointment; bad visibility hampered the gunners and the results were poor. The second day was disastrous: the cruiser *Pensacola* was hit 6 times by Japanese guns, with the loss of 17 of her crew and a further 120 wounded. The third and final day again brought rain squalls and poor visibility with inconclusive results. Rear-Adm William H.P. Blandy informed Turner, 'I believe the landings can be accomplished tomorrow.' 'We got about 13 hours of fire support during the 34 hours of available daylight,' complained Gen Schmidt's Chief of Staff.

'OPERATION DETACHMENT'

In overall command of 'Operation Detachment' was Adm Raymond Spruance; the Joint Expeditionary Force Commander was Adm Richmond Kelly Turner; commanding the 5th Amphibian Corps (VAC), composed of the 3rd, 4th and 5th Divisions of the USMC, was Lt-Gen Holland Smith. Smith was out of favour by this stage of the war, largely because of the 'Smith v. Smith' affair, and he was content to take a low-key approach in favour of Maj-Gen Harry Schmidt. 'I think they asked me along in case anything happened to Harry Schmidt', he was to say later.

The operation benefited from having three outstanding divisional commanders: the 3rd was under Maj-Gen Graves B. Erskine, a tough veteran of the First World War; commanding the 4th was another First World War campaigner, Maj-Gen Clifton

B. Cates, who in 1948 rose to become Commandant of the Marine Corps; while the 5th would be under Maj-Gen Keller E. Rockey, who had distinguished himself at the famous Battle of Chateau Thierry in 1918. In late December, the 4th and 5th Divisions were ordered to leave their camps in the Hawaiian Islands and join up with the 3rd, who were stationed on Guam.

A REDOUBTABLE ADVERSARY

The choice of Lt-Gen Tadamichi Kuribayashi as the Commander in Chief of the Iwo Jima garrison was a stroke of genius. A samurai with thirty years' experience, he had been an attaché in Washington between 1928 and 1930 and later served in China and Hong Kong. In 1943, he was appointed to command

Lt-Gen Kuribayachi, organising the defences of Iwo Jima with his staff before the battle. (Taro Kuribayachi)

the Tokyo Guard, a responsibility that included the protection of the Imperial Palace and the Emperor. In May 1944, he was summoned to the office of the Prime Minister, Gen Hideki Tojo, and told of his appointment. His feelings would not be difficult to imagine; he knew that Iwo Jima would certainly fall to the Americans and that there would be few survivors from the Japanese garrison. 'Do not plan for my return', he wrote to his wife as he left Japan in June 1944.

Kuribayashi had been given a free hand to organise the Iwo Jima defences as he saw fit. His first decision was to evacuate the entire civilian population; they could serve no useful purpose and would be a drain on the food and water supplies. With them went a number of officers who he considered to be disruptive; the General was a stern disciplinarian and would not tolerate anyone who questioned his judgement. The defences of the island were a shambles. Dissent between the Army and Navy units had resulted in little being done to prepare for the invasion and he set about reshaping the whole island. He soon realised that the two beaches stretching away from Mt Suribachi were the prime sites for the Marine landings. He measured distances and flung himself on the ground, using his cane as if it were a rifle. 'The enemy must come here, there is no alternative,' he said to Maj Yoshitaka Hori, a member of his staff. Work progressed at a furious pace. Dozens of surface blockhouses and bunkers were constructed, and a total of 15,000 men worked around the clock, digging an amazing labyrinth of underground chambers and passages that could hold scores of men, tons of ammunition, food and water and even a hospital.

Lt-Gen Kuribayashi had followed the progress of the war with growing dismay. He realised that the traditional tactic of attempting to halt the invader at the water's edge was a failure and that the 'banzai' charge was stupid and wasteful. Lt-Gen Inoue had rejected these tactics at Peleliu and opted for a battle of attrition, fighting a rearguard action to previously prepared positions in the hope that the enemy would sicken of the slaughter and sue for peace. The General approved of the new strategy and intended to make Iwo Jima an almost impregnable fortress from which he would bleed the enemy white.

STORMING THE BLACK BEACHES

"'How do you remember that far back?" people ask me.
"That is not the problem", I tell them. "The problem is how do I forget?"'

(Lt John Keith Wells, Iwo Jima veteran)

After the poor weather that had hampered the pre-invasion bombardment, D-Day dawned bright and sunny, with only a brisk wind and fairly calm sea. During the night Vice-Adm Spruance with Mitscher's Task Force 58 arrived fresh from their successful attacks on the Japanese mainland. The order 'Land the landing force' was given at 6.30 a.m., and the mammoth task of ferrying thousands of troops to the island got

Lt-Gen Tadamichi Kuribayachi, Commander of the Iwo Jima garrison. Holland Smith described him as, 'Our most redoubtable enemy'. (Taro Kuribayachi)

Spaced at five-minute intervals, rows of landing craft head for the beaches. Two destroyer escorts can be seen in the foreground. (US Navy)

under way. The Navy added their final salvos; from 250yd offshore rocket-firing gunboats blasted the invasion beaches from the East Boat Basin to Mt Suribachi; and a massive air strike by planes from TF58 hammered the whole of the southern end of the island. To spearhead the landing, 68 LVT(A)s were to penetrate some 50yd into the beachhead to cover the first waves of Marines, but, as at Peleliu, the troops fell foul of the planners.

The invasion beaches were described as being ideal for landings: 'troops should have no difficulty in getting off the beach'; 'sand and silt have been deposited and form an easy approach inland'; 'there should be little difficulty in pushing well up onto the beach'; so ran the various reports. What the first wave of Marines actually found were steep terraces of black volcanic ash, some of them 15ft high. 'All I could see were mountains of black sand – did intelligence know about them?' said Chuck Tatum, an 18-year-old from one of the first landing craft. As the troop-carrying LVTs arrived and the ramps were lowered, the Marines hit the beaches at a fast run that soon turned into a trudge as they sank ankle-deep into the soft ash. As they struggled to move forward, successive waves of Marines arrived at five-minute intervals and the situation rapidly deteriorated. Within minutes over 6,000 men were crammed onto the

4th Division Marines at Iwo Jima, a painting by Col D.J. Neary. (USMC Art Collection)

Instead of the easy exit that the planners had indicated, the Marines were confronted by walls of black volcanic ash up to 15ft high. (National Archives)

beachhead, and LVTs, jeeps, and tanks got bogged down and added to the chaos. The men tried to dig in, but the soft sand just piled back into the holes as fast as it was dug out – 'like trying to dig a hole in a mound of corn', as one Marine described it.

For Lt-Gen Kuribayashi the logjam on the beach was an added bonus; he had expected the Americans to move inland more rapidly towards Airfield No. 1, but seeing the clutter at the water's edge he decided to implement the first phase of his defence strategy. At 10.00 a.m., the full fury of the Japanese artillery was unleashed. Firing from well-concealed positions and with distances worked out to the nearest yard, the Japanese guns raked landing areas from Mt Suribachi to the Quarry from end to end and then back again; 'catching all hell from the Quarry', 'mortars killing us', 'machine-gun and artillery fire heaviest ever seen' ran the frantic messages flashed to the control ship *Eldorado* from the regimental commanders. By 10.40 a.m., Harry Hill had a few bulldozers ashore and they were hacking at the terraces in an attempt to clear a lane for tanks and transport; and US artillery was gradually getting into a position where it could return the enemy fire.

The first breakthrough came under the shadow of Mt Suribachi. Here the mountains of ash petered out and gave way to a mass of rocks and boulders. Ignoring the volcano to their left, the 1st Battalion of Col Harry Liversedge's 28th Regiment pressed on

A Japanese position at the base of Mt Suribachi is eliminated by a high-explosive charge, set off by men of 5th Marine Division. (USMC)

across the half-mile isthmus towards the far shore. Fierce battles erupted halfway across when 1–28 came upon Capt Osada's 312th Independent Infantry Battalion entrenched in a series of bunkers and pillboxes. Some of these positions were destroyed and others bypassed in the relentless push across the island. At 10.35 a.m., the first Marines, six men from B Company, hit the west coast, and Mt Suribachi was isolated after only ninety minutes of savage and bloody fighting. Meanwhile, 2–28 had landed in support and were catching hell from elevated strongpoints to their left in the foothills of the volcano; but the bulldozers on the beach had finally cleared enough ash to allow Shermans to penetrate inland and add their support. Kuribayashi had inflicted grievous losses on the invaders, but, as the morning wore on, more and more Marines were advancing towards their objectives; despite minefields and heavy machine-gun fire, the southern end of Airfield No. 1 was reached by 11.30 a.m.

The battle had now developed into two phases: the Marines in the southern sector had isolated Mt Suribachi and some were approaching the airfield; while further north on 'Yellow' and 'Blue' beaches the Marines were still bogged down and attempting to survive Kuribayashi's furious bombardment. Surviving on 'Yellow beach' was an horrendous ordeal for 2Lt Benjamin Roselle, a member of a naval liaison team. A mortar shell exploded among the group and Roselle and two others went down.

While some Marines wait on the rim of the sand wall, others attempt to dig in below. (National Archives)

A dramatic shot, taken from inside one of the landing craft, of Marines storming out on to the invasion beaches. (National Archives)

Wrecked landing craft and a bogged-down jeep litter the congested beaches. In the foreground the body of a dead Marine awaits collection. (Marine Corps University Archives)

The Lieutenant's left foot and ankle hung from his leg, held only by a ribbon of flesh. Pinned down with no hope of advancing, they dug in and sweated out the barrage. Within minutes another mortar shell exploded among them and fragments tore into his other leg. For nearly an hour they lay, trying to anticipate where the next shell would land. They were soon to find out as an artillery round burst almost on top of them, tearing off one man's leg and wounding Roselle for the third time, in the right shoulder. A fourth hit bounced him several feet in the air and hot steel ripped into both thighs. He lifted his arm to look at his watch as a mortar round exploded only feet away, blasting the watch from his wrist and tearing a jagged hole in his forearm. 'I was beginning to know what it must be like to be crucified,' he said later.

Amid the chaos on the beaches the Seabees and Naval Construction Battalions were working miracles. The bulldozers attacked the terraces, carving passages through the walls of ash as cranes unloaded vital supplies, ammunition, water, food and fuel, all under constant artillery and mortar fire, and, as news of the congestion reached the *Eldorado*, Adm Turner decided that it was unwise to land any more troops and closed the beaches for two hours.

On the 'Blue' beaches, Col John R. Lannigan landed with the 1st and 3rd Battalions of the 25th Regiment on 'Blue 1'; 'Blue 2' was overlooked by the cliffs of the Quarry and in the opinion of Gen Clifton B. Cates was unsuitable: 'If I knew the name of the man on the extreme right of the right-hand squad of the right-hand company, I'd recommend him for a medal right now,' he said. Lannigan's men made a two-pronged attack, the 1st Battalion moving straight ahead as the 3rd swung to the right to clear

Once ashore the troops were confronted with Japanese machine-guns and minefields. Here a group awaits a lull in the fighting to move forward. (US Navy)

'Blue beach 2' and assault the cliffs of the Quarry. Although the Japanese gunners had the range down to the last foot, little fire was encountered by the first group of Marines and by 11.30 a.m. the 1st Battalion had advanced to within 600yd of the north end of the main runway of Airfield No. 1. A few tanks of the 4th Tank Battalion had succeeded in coming ashore on 'Blue 1', and at 2.00 p.m. the 3rd Battalion under Col 'Jumpin' Joe' Chambers began scaling the cliffs of the Quarry. Resistance was fanatical and the Marines were soon down to 150 men from the original 900 who had landed five hours earlier. In the centre, the 25th and 27th Regiments were gradually moving off the beaches and heading for Airfield No. 1, and by 11.30 a.m. they had reached the southern end. Hundreds of Japanese were killed as they charged down the main runway, while the remnants took refuge in the pipes of the drainage system.

By evening the Marines were prepared to consolidate their tenuous hold on the island. Night fighting was not favoured by the Marines, but the Japanese were very adept at making night-time attacks and infiltrations, and the Marines always kept a good watch on their nocturnal activities; it would be the height of folly not to. The temperature dropped dramatically and the Japanese maintained a constant artillery and mortar barrage throughout the night. A shuttle service began between the offshore transports and the beachhead, bringing in supplies and evacuating the wounded. On the slopes of Mt Suribachi, Maj Subashi Yonomata had had a grandstand view of the day's activities: 'It is getting dark now and the flashes of our shells make an eerie spectacle. The Marines of the Yankees are in the midst of a flaming hell.' Aboard the *Eldorado* Holland Smith studied the day's reports: 'I don't know who he is,' he mused, 'but the general running this show is one smart bastard.'

ROUND TWO D+1

The weather deteriorated dramatically on the second day of the battle; gone were the blue skies as dawn broke with chill winds and rain. The 28th Regiment, having isolated Mt Suribachi, were now faced with the unenviable task of capturing it. At 8.30 a.m., the troops began a simultaneous attack, the 28th against Mt Suribachi and the remainder to the north against Airfield No. 1 and towards Airfield No. 2, with the right flank hinged on the East Boat Basin.

Under Col Kanehiko Atsuchi, 2,000 troops defended the volcano, and he had orders to hold it as long as possible. Although naval gunfire had silenced some of his guns, his defences were still formidable: seventy concrete blockhouses and fifty other reinforced positions faced the Marines on the lower slopes alone. The 28th Regiment attacked on a broad front with artillery support but had gained only 75yd by noon, suffering heavy casualties all along the line. Tanks joined the battle around 11.00 a.m. and provided valuable support, but by late afternoon the Marines had dug in for the day and awaited reinforcements and additional tanks for an all-out assault the following day.

Col Atsuchi was wavering. He radioed Lt-Gen Kuribayashi that the US bombardment was very heavy and suggested that his men attempt a 'banzai' charge; the General didn't even bother to reply.

To the north the other regiments began their offensive around 8.30 a.m., with the right flank holding the Quarry and the left moving north to straighten the line; by noon the whole of Airfield No. 1 had been taken. This was a blow to Lt-Gen Kuribayashi, who had not expected the Americans to advance so rapidly. Maj-Gen Harry Schmidt decided to commit the 21st Regiment of the 3rd Division, an indication that the top brass did not think the advance had been fast enough; and although the front line now ran straight across the island to the north of Airfield No. 1, the D-Day objective, the 0–1 line, still eluded them. The second day was coming to an end; although the Marines had control of almost a quarter of the island it had cost them nearly a thousand dead and wounded.

A Curtiss SC-1 seaplane taxis alongside the USS *Alaska* (CB-1), to be picked up by the ship's crane during 'Operation Detachment'. (National Archives)

D+2

'You knew that other guys were going to be killed – not you, other guys.'

(Unknown Marine)

The plan for Wednesday was straightforward, or so it seemed. The 28th at the base of Mt Suribachi would attack again, while the remainder would move north on a broad front – the 26th and 27th Regiments in the west, the 23rd in the centre, and the 24th in the east. The bad weather of the previous day had deteriorated even further.

US Navy TBF 'Avengers' blast enemy installations north of Airfield No. 1. The cliffs of the Quarry can be seen in the foreground. (National Archives)

Sherman tank 'Cairo' sheds a track. The wooden boards were fitted to prevent the Japanese from attaching magnetic mines.
(National Archives)

A gale-force wind howled down the island from the north-east, rain clouds gathered and 6ft-high waves closed the beaches.

At 7.40 a.m., a massive artillery barrage rained down on the Japanese lines immediately to the front of the Marines, and sixty-eight carrier planes added rockets and bombs. As the gunfire lifted, the 4th and 5th Division Marines moved out and casualties soon mounted. In the west the 26th and 27th, supported by Sherman tanks, advanced for 1,000yd, good going by Iwo Jima standards, and finally reached the D-Day objective, the 0–1 line. In the east the 24th made little impression on the enemy; the rugged terrain and a large minefield limited the advance to only 300yd. In the centre the 23rd were having difficulties in keeping contact with the 26th and 27th on their left, and a reserve company had to be brought forward to fill the gap. Forty carrier planes loaded with bombs, rockets and napalm canisters opened the attack on Mt Suribachi, and supported by fire from offshore cruisers and destroyers the Marines began their attack at 8.25 a.m.

A patrol worked its way around the volcano from the east coast and by afternoon had reached Tobiishi Point, the southernmost point of Iwo Jima. On the land side the Marines were only 200yd from the main Japanese defence line, and they moved forward under cover of a continuous artillery barrage. The Sherman tanks that were supposed to be supporting the attack were late; problems with refuelling delayed their arrival until midday and little was achieved until mid-afternoon. By nightfall the 28th Regiment had formed a semicircle around the north side of Mt Suribachi, and the lines had advanced by 650yd on the left, 500yd in the centre and 1,000yd on the right.

The ships of the offshore task force were to become targets for one of the early kamikaze attacks of the war. In the fading light fifty Japanese aircraft arrived from the north-west. They were from the 2nd Milate Special Attack Unit based at Katori Airfield and had refuelled at Hachijo Jima, some 125 miles south of Tokyo. They were located by the radar of the carrier *Saratoga*, and six fighters were sent to intercept them. Two Mitsubishis were shot down, but others ploughed on to slam into the side of the carrier, turning the hangars into an inferno, while another plane hit the flight deck, leaving a gaping hole. Damage-control crews worked wonders and within an hour the fires were under control and the *Saratoga* was able to recover a few of her planes. The remainder were taken aboard the escort carriers *Wake Island* and *Natoma Bay*. But the kamikazes were not yet finished. A 'Betty' (Mitsubishi G4M) twin-engined bomber tore into the escort carrier *Bismarck Sea*, whose deck was full of aircraft, starting uncontrollable fires. Within minutes a massive explosion ripped off the entire stern of the carrier and she rolled over and sank. The attack had been a success for the Japanese: the *Saratoga* returned to Pearl Harbor and was out of action for the rest of the war; 358 men had been killed and another escort carrier, the *Lunga Point*, had been severely damaged. It was a grim preview of what was to happen at Okinawa later in the war.

A Marine flame-thrower operator, with an escort of riflemen, burns out a Japanese foxhole. (US Navy)

D+3

There was no let up in the weather on Wednesday. The Marines were soaked to the skin and bent by the wind as the assault on Mt Suribachi was renewed. Ammunition and supplies had been brought up during the night, but by morning the Sherman tanks were bogged down in the mud and the Navy decided that the weather was unsuitable for air support. Col Atsuchi still had 800–900 men on the volcano and no intention of allowing the Americans an easy ride. With little room for manoeuvre and reduced artillery support because of the close proximity of the lines, it was left to the Marines to employ the familiar weapons of rifle, grenade and flame-thrower. The difficulty in fighting an almost invisible enemy in such conditions soon became apparent: each pillbox saw a life-and-death struggle; mortar fire rained down from the heights above; guns clogged in the mud; and one Marine fought a battle with a sabre-wielding officer, while another threw a grenade at a Japanese soldier standing in the mouth of a cave, but forgot to pull the pin – the grinning enemy threw it back again with the pin still in place.

By afternoon the struggle for the northern slopes was being won. The enemy were down to a few hundred men and Col Atsuchi was weakening. Further north, Maj-Gen Schmidt concentrated on the centre line between the 4th and 5th Divisions. Here, around Airfield No. 2, Col Masuo Ikeda and his 145th Regiment held the strongest point in the Japanese defence line, where hundreds of well-sited bunkers and artillery positions barred the US advance. After four days of ferocious fighting the Marines were suffering – lack of sleep, heavy casualties, no hot food and appalling weather were taking their toll. Maj-Gen Cates and Maj-Gen Keller E. Rockey decided that it was a good time to relieve some of the more hard-pressed units, but the changeover did not go smoothly, as the unremitting Japanese artillery and mortar fire continued.

A war dog-handler catches a few minutes of sleep while his Dobermann stands guard. (National Archives)

The most famous photograph of the Second World War, Joe Rosenthal's magnificent shot of Marines raising the flag on Mt Suribachi on 23 February 1945. (US Navy)

For the troops who had been 'relieved' to the rear, the enemy shells fell almost as thickly as they had at the front – a hot coffee and a doughnut and perhaps a couple of hours of shallow sleep was the best they could hope for.

In the east, 'Jumpin' Joe' Chambers's 3rd Battalion continued to blast the area around the Quarry. He requested that rocket-firing trucks be brought forward to blast the hills to his front. It was a sound idea, for the ensuing fusillade caused the enemy to flee their hideouts in droves. This was what the Marines had been waiting for. The machine-gunners caught the enemy in the open and cut them to ribbons. Unfortunately 'Jumpin' Joe' was caught by a burst of machine-gun fire which punctured his lung, and he was carried to the beach for evacuation to a hospital ship.

During the night Task Force 58 left Iwo Jima for a second strike against the Japanese mainland, significantly reducing the number of aircraft available to support the land forces. Adm Spruance accompanied them in his flagship, the *Indianapolis*. It is difficult to understand why yet another attack on Japan was considered more important than supporting three Marine divisions in a battle that was only a few days old and whose outcome was still far from certain.

FLYING THE FLAG

The date of 23 February, D+4, was the day on which Mt Suribachi was finally conquered. When Lt-Gen Kuribayashi heard the news he was furious; he had not expected so important a feature to fall so early in the battle. The survivors, who had threaded their way through the US lines along the maze of underground tunnels, arrived at his HQ to be severely reprimanded.

The weather had improved significantly, and Lt-Col Chandler W. Johnson gave orders to occupy the volcano's summit. Marines from the 3rd Platoon, a forty-man patrol led by Lt Hal Schrier, started off at 8.00 a.m. Labouring up the northern slopes, they found the opposition to be surprisingly light and by 10.00 a.m. had reached the rim of the crater, where they engaged a few enemy troops who attacked them with hand grenades. At 10.20 a.m., the Stars and Stripes was raised and the scene was recorded by Marine photographer Lou Lowery; at around 12.00 noon a larger flag was raised by six men, five Marines and a corpsman, and this event was photographed by Associated Press cameraman Joe Rosenthal, the image becoming the most famous photograph of the Second World War (see p. 196). On a landing craft halfway between the *Eldorado* and the beach, Holland Smith and James Forrestal, Secretary of the Navy, saw the flag fluttering on the summit of Mt Suribachi: 'Holland, the raising of that flag means a Marine Corps for the next five hundred years', said Forrestal.

Contrary to popular mythology, the raising of the flag was not the end of the battle; the capture of Mt Suribachi was an important achievement, but the worst was yet to come. D+4 was largely a day of consolidation elsewhere in the island. The generals were leaving their ships and coming ashore, and Schmidt was planning a major offensive for the following day.

BREAKING THE DEADLOCK – D+5

Maj-Gen Harry Schmidt's objective for 24 February was to break the stalemate on the northern front, so Airfield No. 2 became the target for the US thrust. From the west coast the battleship *Idaho* plastered the area just north of the airfield with her 14in guns, while from the east the cruiser *Pensacola*, now repaired after her D-Day mauling, added her support. Marine howitzers joined in, as did the planes from the escort carriers left behind by Task Force 58.

The spearhead was the 21st Regiment, who advanced to the area between Airfields 1 and 2. Tanks were expected to support the advance, but Col Ikeda had anticipated such a move and both taxiways were heavily mined and covered by anti-tank guns; the first two tanks were blown up by mines and the tank commander called a temporary halt to the operation. Deprived of their armour the Marines were reduced to the now-familiar grenade and flame-thrower attacks and advanced only 400yd. As the numbers of pillboxes and bunkers increased the advance slackened, but, unwilling to give up their gains, the Marines became embroiled in hand-to-hand battles with the enemy; in

A Marine howitzer in action. The artillery provided vital support for the Marines, with heavy bombardments before each advance. (National Archives)

A 155mm howitzer of 3rd Marine Division goes into action. (USMC)

a frenzied mêlée of stabbing, clubbing, punching and kicking, legs were broken, skulls smashed and bodies slashed until over fifty of the enemy lay dead before them.

A badly needed breakthrough had been achieved at the intersection of the runways of Airfield No. 2, and the Marines were ordered to 'hold at all costs'. With only four hours of daylight remaining, the Marines, exhausted and short of ammunition, were determined to hold their ground. On the right flank the 24th Regiment of the 4th Division were battling for 'Charlie Dog Ridge', an escarpment south of the main runway on Airfield No. 2, and with support from howitzers and mortars they blasted their way to the top, despite suffering heavy casualties. Col Walter I. Jordan ordered the men to dig in for the night at 5.00 p.m.

By Iwo Jima standards the day's gains had been impressive, but so too had been the casualties. Since D-Day, 773 men had died, 261 had died of wounds, 3,741 were wounded, 5 were missing and 558 had suffered combat fatigue. Dale Worley, a tank man who kept an unofficial diary throughout the battle, remarked of this day: 'Had to go through the 5th Division cemetery. Plenty of dead lying about – they sure smell awful.'

THE MEATGRINDER

By Sunday 25 February, the Marines held a line across the island that approximated to the 0–1 line, the first day's objective. To the south of the line the Seabees and Marine Engineers were working non-stop at repairing and extending Airfield No. 1, and a small town of Nissen huts and tents had sprung up around the perimeter, housing field hospitals, ammunition dumps, cookhouses and even a bakery, while to the west of the airfield the divisional cemeteries were being established.

North of the line the situation was totally different. The central plateau that housed Airfield No. 2 and the unfinished Airfield No. 3 gave way on all sides to a mass of valleys, canyons, hills and cave-ridden ridges – perfect defensive terrain to which Kuribayashi had added a maze of fortified positions. Having secured a foothold on Airfield No. 2, Harry Schmidt sought to press his advantage by pushing northward across the relatively flat central plateau to the northern coast, thus splitting the enemy in two. At 9.30 a.m., the 3rd Division began its drive through the centre of the line. The aim was to clear the remainder of Airfield No. 2, advance to the village of Motoyama, and then to the unfinished Airfield No. 3. On the left the 5th Division consolidated their position – they were already 400yd ahead of the 3rd and could afford to wait – while on the right the 4th Division faced a complex of four formidable defence positions. At 150yd east of the end of the east–west runway of Airfield No. 2 stood Hill 382 (named after its elevation above sea level), which was a mass of caves and pillboxes; 400yd to its south lay a shallow rocky depression called the 'Amphitheater'; and immediately to the east was 'Turkey Knob', a hill surmounted by a massive blockhouse; the fourth obstacle was the ruins of the village of Minami. All four were within 600yd of each other. Collectively, they became known as the

'Meatgrinder' and were destined to become one of the last positions on the island to fall to the Marines.

The 'Meatgrinder' was defended by Maj-Gen Sadasue Senda's 2nd Mixed Brigade and included the remains of Lt-Col (Baron) Takeichi Nishi's 26th Tank Regiment. The flamboyant baron, a former Olympic gold-medal horseman, had lost most of his tanks to a US submarine attack before the battle, and the remainder had soon succumbed to the superior Shermans. His men were now reduced to fighting as infantry under Maj-Gen Senda.

At 8.00 a.m., the now-customary naval barrage heralded the assault on the 'Meatgrinder'. Men of the 23rd and 24th Regiments of the 4th Division tackled Hill 382, the major strongpoint, with one platoon battling their way to the summit, only to find themselves surrounded when the enemy mounted a massive counter-attack.

4th Marine Division badge.

All day long the Marines fought vicious battles with the enemy before they had to withdraw to the base of the hill under cover of smoke. Ten of the wounded had to be left behind to be rescued under cover of darkness by gallant volunteers. Sherman tanks had been used in the attack, but the increasingly difficult terrain proved to be so rough that they had to be diverted through the 3rd Division lines, a sign of things to come.

The assault on the 'Meatgrinder' had ended in stalemate; about 100yd had been gained at a cost of nearly 500 casualties. In the centre, the 3rd Division moved against high ground at the end of Airfield No. 2. The strongest point was 'Hill Peter', a 360ft-high prominence just off the runway. Marines stormed the hill repeatedly, but by 2.30 p.m. they had only gained 200yd; 9 Shermans had been knocked out and 400 men were either killed or wounded. 'Hill Peter' remained in Japanese hands.

WEEK TWO – D+7

Most Marines couldn't believe that they had been on Iwo Jima for only a week; it seemed more like a month. The second attack on Hill 382 began with the replacement of the 24th Regiment by the 25th, causing the jump-off to be delayed by half an hour. The initial attack looked promising – the 1st and 3rd Battalions gained over 100yd, a substantial advance in this area – but the attack ground to a halt as shredding machine-gun fire from the emplacements around the 'Amphitheater' and 'Turkey Knob' brought the advance to a grinding halt. The 23rd Regiment on the left flank worked its way through a minefield and turned towards the ruined radio station below Hill 382. The enemy immediately laid down a mortar barrage from the hill, killing seventeen men and wounding a further twenty-six, but the remnants pressed forward to the base of the hill. Much of the credit for the advance went to 19-year-old Pfc Douglas Jacobson,

3rd Marine Division badge.

who destroyed sixteen strongpoints with a bazooka, killing seventy-five of the enemy and earning himself the Medal of Honor. In the west the 5th Division attacked Hill 362A, 600yd south of the village of Nishi; tanks from the 5th Tank Battalion ground through the rocks and boulders of the increasingly hostile terrain, but the complex proved to be impregnable. The weather had deteriorated during the day, with heavy rain in the afternoon. Maj-Gen Cates called it a day, the lines were consolidated and much needed ammunition was replenished. 'Our casualties are frightful. If it doesn't end soon the 5th Division will be past history', wrote Dale Worley in his diary.

BOGGED DOWN – D+8

'You got so blasé that you could sit next to a dead, mutilated Jap and eat your dinner – if you had any dinner to eat.'

(4th Division Marine)

'Hill Peter' still barred the way of the 3rd Division. Supported by artillery and flame-thrower 'Zippo' tanks, the Marines inched forward against a murderous hail of machine-gun and mortar fire; the leading elements of the 9th Regiment reached the top, but were pinned down by fire from the reverse slopes and from bypassed positions to their rear. The breakthrough came around 1.00 p.m. A coordinated attack by the 1st and 2nd Battalions of the 9th relieved the beleaguered troops on the summit, and they stormed on to take Oboe Hill to their front. The 3rd Division were now in possession of Airfield No. 2 and in a good position to continue their northward thrust towards Motoyama village, the unfinished Airfield No. 3 and, eventually, the north coast.

In the east the 4th Division were still bogged down in the 'Meatgrinder'. Maj-Gen Cates committed five battalions to the attack: two against Hill 382 and three against 'Turkey Knob'. A convoy of rocket-firing trucks was brought as far forward as the terrain would allow, and they blasted over 500 rockets into Hill 382 before being forced to race away under a torrent of enemy mortar fire. Throughout the day the battle see-sawed up and down the slopes of the hill. One intrepid group actually reached the top but had to fall back when they ran out of ammunition. At the foot of the hill other Marines fought a series of close-quarter battles against dug-in Japanese troops and by mid-afternoon had succeeded in surrounding the hill. They spent the rest of the day desperately trying to hold on to their precarious gains.

All day long the Marine Engineers had been trying to clear a way through the mass of rocks and boulders to allow Sherman tanks to operate within range of Hill 382 and 'Turkey Knob'. Bulldozers hacked their way through by afternoon and Shermans of B Company began shelling 'Turkey Knob' from close range, allowing the infantry to advance 100yd. But the enemy were not prepared to give up any more ground and by late afternoon the Marines were back to their original positions. Yet another day

One of the rocket-launcher crew makes an undignified exit as Japanese mortars home in on the trucks. (National Archives)

in the 'Meatgrinder' had resulted in insignificant gains and heavy casualties. The only grim consolation for the Americans was that their casualties could be replaced; for the Japanese the losses were irreplaceable.

During the night the enemy attempted to drop supplies to their beleaguered troops; three of the Japanese aircraft were shot down by night-fighters of the US Navy escort carriers, but a few got through to drop medical supplies and ammunition. 'I pay many respects to these brave aviators. It is difficult to express how the fighting youth of Iwo Jima who stood before their death felt when they saw these brave flyers', commented Lt-Gen Kuribayashi.

BREAKTHROUGH IN THE CENTRE – D+9

The last day of February – the day given by Maj-Gen Schmidt for the end of the battle – saw the Marines in control of almost half of the island. In the centre it was to be a good day for the 3rd Division. The 21st Regiment relieved the battered 9th and

moved out behind a massive naval and artillery barrage that appeared to have stunned the Japanese. Good progress was made as the troops swept aside the few remaining 'Ha-Go' tanks of Baron Nishi's 26th Regiment; the flimsy 'tankettes', as the Americans called them, were easily destroyed by bazookas and marauding fighters, and the Baron now had only three serviceable tanks left. By midday the Japanese had recovered sufficiently to stiffen their resistance, and the advance slowed to a crawl; but, working on the principle that what had worked once could work again, another huge barrage was laid on and by 1.00 p.m. the Marines were on the move once more. Storming through clusters of bunkers and pillboxes, the Marines reached the ruins of Motoyama, the largest village on Iwo Jima, and soon overwhelmed the snipers and machine-gunners who had set up defences among the rubble. Maintaining their momentum, they pushed on and by the end of the day had established themselves on high ground overlooking Airfield No. 3. By Iwo Jima standards this had been an outstanding day; an advance of over 600yd was a great achievement, and the Marines felt that they were in an excellent position to press on to the north coast.

Things did not go so well elsewhere. On the 5th Division front the troops were still stalled in front of Hill 362A. The base was lined with defensive positions, the slopes bristled with machine-guns and the top was dotted with anti-tank guns and mortars. US attacks were mounted all day, with tanks in support, but little progress was made and the impasse continued. Meanwhile, at the 'Meatgrinder', operations closed down at 4.45 p.m. after a frustrating day in which the 4th Division failed to gain any ground.

The most spectacular event of the day was to occur in the south of the island. Japanese artillerymen were still lobbing the occasional shell over towards Airfield No. 1 and on this day they struck lucky. Shortly after 2.00 p.m., a shell found a large ammunition dump and the whole of the southern end of Iwo Jima erupted in a giant pyrotechnic display. Shells shot hundreds of feet in the air, mortar and artillery rounds exploded with ear-shattering violence, bullets popped and crackled, and a huge cloud of smoke covered everything from Mt Suribachi to the approaches of Airfield No. 2. To add to the chaos the gas and air-raid warnings sounded. The Seabees manned their bulldozers and risked life and limb to pile mounds of earth onto the exploding ammunition, but the flames raged until dawn. There were no casualties, but the 5th Division lost almost a quarter of its ammunition stocks.

Opposite, top: A row of rocket-launchers blast away with their 4.5in missiles. The trucks were a prime target for Japanese mortars and had to make a rapid exit once they had fired off their rockets. (National Archives)

Opposite, bottom: Sunset off Iwo Jima, D+8, 27 February 1945, photographed from USS *Wisconsin* (BB-64). (National Archives)

5th Marine Division badge.

D+10 – STALEMATE

By 1 March the divisional commanders were becoming worried about the combat efficiency of their divisions. It was not uncommon in some units for command to have passed from captain to lieutenant and down to sergeant, or even in some cases to private. Gen Graves B. Erskine of the 3rd Division was scathing of the quality of the replacements: 'They get killed the day they go into battle,' he said. His concerns were justified in one case. A replacement was sent to a machine-gun unit and when asked if he had any questions replied, 'Yes, how do you fire this thing?'

After spending the night overlooking Airfield No. 3, the 21st Regiment of the 3rd Division moved out against surprisingly light opposition and by noon were across the main runway. Tanks moved forward in support, and all went well until they reached Hills 362B and 362C and the advance ran out of steam. On the west coast the 5th Division was bolstered by the arrival of the 28th Regiment, the conquerors of Mt Suribachi, and the attacks on Hill 362A began with a 45-minute bombardment from the battleship *Nevada* and the cruisers *Pensacola* and *Indianapolis*, Adm Spruance's flagship. The Marines stormed the slopes and by noon were on the summit, only to find that the Japanese had abandoned the position and had moved through a labyrinth of tunnels to establish themselves on Nishi Ridge some 200yd to the front.

Amid a pile of spent ammunition, a machine-gun crew blasts Japanese positions just north of Mt Suribachi. (National Archives)

The capture of Hill 362A was a significant achievement and helped to break the deadlock on the west coast, but the cost had been appalling. In the 'Meatgrinder', Hill 382 was the key. Until it was taken there could be no further progress in the area. In the pre-dawn darkness the 24th Regiment replaced the 23rd and in a day of unremitting savagery the battle flowed back and forth. The Japanese took to their caves under a furious attack by naval guns, artillery and carrier aircraft; but as US forces resumed their attacks the Japanese emerged and renewed their machine-gun and mortar fire from the high ground. By afternoon the generals had to concede another stalemate.

NOT ANOTHER RIDGE – D+11

The pressure continued on Hill 382 and 'Turkey Knob'. Sherman tanks and 'Zippo' flame-thrower tanks expended over 1,000 gallons of fuel on the caves, but the enemy simply retired to the depths of their tunnels and sat out the inferno. In the centre the hopes for a dash to the north coast were flagging; the sea was only 1,500yd to the north, but the 3rd Division had yet to deal with Hills 362B and C. Four thousand Marines were deployed in a two-pronged attack: one group headed for Hill 362B, the other deployed around the airfield. The land around the hill was flat and offered little cover and was targeted by enemy artillery. Shermans were brought forward and under their cover an advance of 500yd was achieved, bringing the troops to the base of the hill.

On the right the Marines moved towards the east of the airfield and came across the remains of Baron Nishi's tank regiment (now deployed as infantry). Heavy fighting ensued and no further progress was made. Nishi Ridge lay 300yd from Hill 362A on the 5th Division front. 'God, not another ridge', complained one marine. Col Chandler Johnson's 28th Regiment advanced along the left side of Hill 362A and encountered heavy fire, but tanks and bulldozers moved forward. An anti-tank ditch had been dug north of the ridge and the Marines were determined to fill it. Under constant mortar fire the ditch was eventually filled, and the troops had a firm foothold between the hill and Nishi Ridge from which to blast both positions. Both the 26th and 28th Regiments were called in and by early afternoon they were at the foot of the ridge. Chandler Johnson walked towards a shell crater expecting to see Marines sheltering inside; all he saw were dead Japanese. As he turned to leave, a shell exploded within feet of him and he was blown to pieces.

HILL 362B AND NISHI RIDGE – D+12

By 3 March, the Americans controlled two-thirds of the island. But the battle was dragging on way beyond the most pessimistic forecasts and the casualties were reaching epidemic proportions. The Marines' figures stood at 16,000, of whom more than 3,000 were dead; the Japanese numbers were staggering: of the 21,000 troops in Lt-Gen Kuribayashi's command at the start of the battle, only 7,000 remained.

D+12 was a day of incredible heroism. Five Medals of Honor were awarded for valour in the field, and one of the fiercest battles of the campaign was fought around Hill 362B, a day-long struggle that cost the Marines 500 casualties. But the best news of the day came with the capture of Nishi Ridge by the 28th Regiment, an achievement that particularly pleased Maj-Gen Rockey, who had envisaged a long struggle. The 3rd Division pitted themselves against the 'Meatgrinder' once more – Col Jordan's 24th against Hill 382 and Col Walter W. Wensinger's 23rd against 'Turkey Knob'. The increasingly rocky terrain was making tank support a rare luxury as the tank dozers fought a losing battle to get the armour to the front line.

Back at Airfield No. 1, the first American aircraft to land on Iwo Jima were beginning to arrive. Medical supplies (especially whole blood donated only days earlier in America) were a priority, but the Japanese were determined to cause the maximum amount of disruption by laying on a fierce mortar barrage that sent the aircraft scurrying to the southern end of the runway. The Marines began to notice the Japanese becoming more selective in their use of ammunition. Supplies were obviously running down and food was becoming desperately short: night-time prowlers would emerge to steal food and water from the US lines, less concerned with getting shot than the need to have a square meal.

FATIGUE AND RAIN – D+13

For the past few days the Marines had enjoyed reasonable weather – the days had been dry and the nights cool – but on Sunday the elements were against them. Dawn brought lowering clouds and constant cold drizzle. Air strikes were abandoned and even the customary naval bombardment that now heralded the daily attack was cancelled because of poor visibility. Once more the 'Meatgrinder' was the focus of the 4th Division. Wherever it was possible for them to operate, the Shermans and rocket-launching trucks blasted the enemy, but the deeply entrenched Japanese simply dug in. The 5th Division in the north relied on 'Zippo' flame-thrower tanks to clear the more exposed enemy positions, while the Marines slogged it out at close quarters with grenades and flame-throwers for every yard of ground. In the centre the 3rd Division had taken nine days to advance 3,000yd, and D+13 saw the front line much the same as it had been on the previous day. An overall weariness was permeating the entire front. Two weeks of the bloodiest fighting that the Marine Corps had ever experienced was taking its toll, a fact that had not escaped the divisional commanders: 'There will be no general attack tomorrow, except for limited adjustments of positions. Each division will utilize the day for rest, refitting and reorganization in preparation for resumption of action on 6th March' – so read the communiqué from the command posts of Generals Rockey, Cates and Erskine.

Lt-Gen Kuribayashi realised that the battle was swinging irrevocably in the Americans' favour: 'Our strongpoints may be able to fight delaying actions for several more days . . . I comfort myself a little seeing my officers and men die without

The flame-thrower was an awesome and horrific weapon. Here two Marines demonstrate its dramatic effect. (National Archives)

regret after struggling in this inch by inch battle against an overwhelming enemy', he radioed Tokyo.

The highlight of the day was the arrival of *Dinah Might*, the first B29 'Superfortress' bomber to land on Iwo Jima. Heading for Saipan after a bombing mission south-west of Tokyo, her bomb-bay doors had jammed in the open position and there was a malfunction in the reserve fuel tank. Without enough fuel for the 1,400-mile trip back to base, the pilot had opted for a touchdown on Iwo Jima. After circling the island twice, Lt Malo brought the huge bomber down at the northern end of the runway. But the landing had not escaped the notice of the Japanese, who greeted it with a hail of artillery fire. The pilot quickly swung the plane around and headed for the Mt Suribachi end of the island, where she attracted a large crowd of curious viewers. The repairs were soon carried out, and within thirty minutes she was thundering along the runway and lifting off into a weak barrage of anti-aircraft fire. This was to be the first of thousands of US aircraft to find refuge on Iwo Jima. The bloody sacrifices of the Marine Corps in securing the island were beginning to pay dividends in the lives of what were to be thousands of Air Force crews.

LIMITED ADJUSTMENTS – D+14

Although it was meant to be a day of 'consolidation and adjustment', no one had told the Japanese, who continued to shell the US lines all day. The Japanese were drastically reduced in numbers and were becoming desperately short of ammunition, food and particularly water; but they had one huge advantage: the further north the battle progressed and the worse the terrain became, the easier it was to defend. The Motoyama Plateau on which the Airfield No. 3 was being constructed, gave way on all sides to a maze of valleys, ravines, cliffs and caves, in which tanks were unable to move without the aid of bulldozers and progress of a few yards became a major achievement. Each enemy soldier had to be winkled out by grenade, demolition charge or flame-thrower; when a Marine squad advanced they never knew from which direction the next bullet would come. The Americans regrouped and replacements were brought forward; tank crews serviced their machines; and food, water and ammunition arrived from the rear. There were new arrivals. The Army, who were to garrison the island after the battle, sent in their first units. And on Airfield No. 1, twenty-eight P51 'Mustang' fighters and twelve P61 'Black Widow' night-fighters, all under the command of Brig-Gen Ernest C. Moore, took up their positions on the airfield hardstanding. There were also two controversial decisions made on D+14: Adm Spruance, along with Secretary of the Navy James Forrestal, left for

Two Marines use a captured Nambo machine-gun. Despite the resemblance they are not Clark Gable and Errol Flynn!
(National Archives)

Guam in the *Indianapolis*; and the 3rd Regiment of the 3rd Division, Marines that Maj-Gen Schmidt would have preferred as front-line replacements instead of the green kids from boot camp, sailed for the Marianas having never set foot on Iwo Jima.

IMPASSE – D+15

On Tuesday morning the battle was renewed with one of the heaviest bombardments to date: 132 artillery pieces fired 22,500 rounds within 67 minutes; offshore battleships, a cruiser and three destroyers poured in 450 rounds of 14in and 8in shells; and 'Dauntless' and 'Corsair' aircraft strafed, bombed and dropped napalm canisters. The attacks were staggered. In the west the 5th Division moved out at 8.00 a.m. and in the east the 4th waited until 9.00 a.m., but the huge barrages seemed to have had little effect on the Japanese, who mounted a fanatical defence. In the centre the 3rd made marginal progress. One element of the 21st Regiment under Lt William Mulvey battled their way to the top of what seemed an endless row of hills and saw the prize that had so long evaded them – the sea. He estimated it to be less than a quarter of a mile away and asked for reinforcements. Twelve men were sent forward, but before they could reach him six were killed and two wounded and Mulvey had to retire under a hail of enemy fire. To add to their woes the Marines of the 5th Division had been under fire from enemy installations sited on Kangoku and Kama Rocks, two groups of small islands off the north-west coast. Three batteries of the Army's 506th Anti-Aircraft Gun Battalion, given the task of silencing them, blasted the islands all day – the results were not impressive, and the Navy complained that they were still being fired on whenever they approached the islands. The Army were given clearance to resume firing when the Japanese showed any sign of renewed activity. Dale Worley made another entry in his diary that day: 'They have almost blown Hill 362 off the map. There are bodies everywhere and the ground is spotted with blood. The smell is sickening.'

BANZAI – D+16

A casualty count had been taken on D+15, 6 March: the Marines had lost 2,777 dead and 8,051 were wounded, with a further 1,102 men out of action with battle fatigue. Maj-Gen Schmidt was a worried man. The battle was not progressing as he and most of the planners had anticipated and the divisional commanders were scouring the rear echelons for anyone who could be thrown into the front line: cooks, mechanics, clerks, drivers and storemen found themselves donning combat gear and moving north.

At a meeting with Schmidt, Maj-Gen Erskine suggested that his Marines make a night attack. The Japanese were aware that the Americans usually confined their fighting to daylight hours and he thought that such an attack might catch the enemy napping. His plan was to infiltrate the enemy lines and capture Hill 362C, the last major obstacle between the 3rd Division and the sea. At 5.00 a.m., the 3rd Battalion of the 9th Regiment under Lt-Col Harold C. Boehm moved forward, and for 30 minutes

their luck held until a Japanese machine-gunner opened up on their left. Their cover blown, Boehm and his men stormed forward to the top of the hill and radioed to Erskine that they had achieved their goal. Erskine was delighted and said, 'we caught the bastards asleep just as we thought we would'. However, the euphoria was short-lived, as Boehm soon realised that he was on Hill 331 and not Hill 362C – in the dark and the rain one hill looked much the same as another. Undismayed Boehm and his men pushed on despite heavy opposition, and by 2.00 p.m. had reached their objective.

On their flanks the advancing 1st and 2nd Battalions soon came upon the remains of Baron Nishi's tank regiment and the 2nd Battalion under Lt-Col Robert E. Cushman Jr found themselves surrounded; it was not until the following day that they could extricate themselves. Heavy fighting was to continue in this area for the next six days in what was to become known as 'Cushman's Pocket'.

In the west the 5th Division's 26th Regiment were approaching yet another ridge just north of the ruins of Nishi village and were amazed to find the enemy opposition virtually non-existent. They proceeded to the summit expecting to come under a fusillade of fire from the far side, but instead the whole ridge disappeared in a massive explosion that was heard for miles around. The Japanese had mined their command post before leaving and it was left to the Marines to recover the bodies of forty-three of their comrades.

In the 4th Division sector a clever manoeuvre by the 23rd and 24th Regiments edged the enemy towards the 25th Regiment, and 1,500 men of Navy Captain Samaji Inouye's command were trapped. Inouye, something of a hothead, elected for a 'banzai' attack and radioed Lt-Gen Kuribayashi for his approval, but the General was furious and refused; Inouye decided to ignore the General and go ahead anyway. As evening fell a bizarre band of Japanese troops began to infiltrate the Marine lines: the sword-wielding officers led the way with men armed with machine-guns, rifles, grenades and even wooden spears bringing up the rear. In the chaos that followed, the Marines fired flares and star shells to illuminate the sky as they slaughtered the onrushing enemy with mortars and machine-gun fire. Daylight revealed the extent of the carnage: over 800 Japanese dead, the largest number of enemy casualties for a single day. From information supplied by the few enemy prisoners, it appeared that Inouye had some fantastic plan to break through to the south, destroy American aircraft on Airfield No. 1, recapture Mt Suribachi and replace the Stars and Stripes with the Rising Sun. His bullet-ridden body, sword in hand, was later discovered among the piles of dead.

FOR CONSPICUOUS GALLANTRY – D+17

The date of 9 March saw steady if unspectacular progress. There was heavy fighting around 'Cushman's Pocket', which still barred the progress of the 3rd Division in its

Opposite: The Bar Man, Charles Waterhouse's fine painting of action on Iwo Jima. Waterhouse served with the Marines during the battle and was wounded in action. (Charles Waterhouse)

bid to reach the north coast, and also in the 'Meatgrinder' around 'Turkey Knob', the main objective for the 4th. Attacking at 7.50 a.m., the 27th Regiment soon ground to a halt and had to await the arrival of Shermans before resuming the battle around 9.00 a.m. With the additional aid of a 75mm howitzer which had to be manhandled through the rocks, an advance of 150yd was achieved by noon. With the loss of so many men in the mad 'banzai' charge, there was little hope for the defenders of the 'Meatgrinder'. Constant pounding by Sherman tanks and 'Zippo' flame-throwers, massive artillery barrages and determined attacks by Marines proved to be too much for the diminishing survivors, who were gradually blasted out of their strongpoints as first 'Turkey Knob' and then the 'Amphitheater' succumbed to the overwhelming firepower of the American artillery and armour. Only in 'Cushman's Pocket' were the Japanese able to maintain a tenuous foothold.

The day is best remembered for two outstanding feats of bravery in which two Marines won the Medal of Honor. Pfc James D. La Belle, a 19-year-old, was sharing a shell hole with two other Marines, waiting for enemy fire to slacken before attempting to move forward, when a Japanese soldier threw a hand grenade which landed a few feet from the group. Without hesitation La Belle threw himself on top of

Men of G Company, 24th Marine Regiment take a break while they wait for the tanks to move forward against pillboxes between Airfields 1 and 2. (USMC)

A Navy doctor tends to a wounded Marine in a former Japanese installation, somewhere in 4th Marine Division's zone. (National Archives)

it and was killed instantly, saving the lives of his comrades. Near Kitano Point, the 2nd Battalion of the 27th Regiment were engaged in a push. Lt Jack Lummus, a 29-year-old former professional football player, ran out in front of his men and was floored by the blast from a hand grenade. Jumping up, he ran to an enemy gun emplacement and silenced it. Another grenade wounded him in the shoulder, but again he got to his feet and attacked the emplacement, killing all its occupants. He turned and shouted to his men to move forward, but had stepped on a mine. Both his legs were blown off. To his men he looked as though he was in a hole, but as the dust cleared they were amazed to see him standing on his bloody stumps urging them forward. Lummus died later that afternoon in the 5th Division Field Hospital from shock and loss of blood.

THE BREAKTHROUGH – D+18

The long-awaited breakthrough to the sea was achieved when a twenty-eight-man patrol reached the north coast in the 3rd Division sector. At last the Japanese force was split in two. The patrol leader, Lt Paul Connally, perhaps sensing the significance of the occasion, filled his water bottle with seawater, and when the patrol returned his CO sent it to Maj-Gen Erskine with the message, 'for examination, not consumption'. Erskine was delighted. But the cost so far in their quest to reach the coast had been appalling: of the troops of the 3rd Division who had landed on Iwo Jima thus far, 3,563 had been killed, wounded or were missing.

That night, as the troops bedded down in whatever shelter they could find among the moonscape that was now their home, they heard the drone of hundreds of aircraft as they skirted the east of the island: 334 'Superfortresses' were heading for Tokyo for the first of Maj-Gen Curtis E. LeMay's 'fire-raising' raids. In a spectacular attack which destroyed almost a quarter of the city and killed more than eighty thousand people, LeMay spelled out his intentions for the future. And the 20th Air Force's assault on the Japanese mainland was a campaign in which Iwo Jima was to play a vital role.

THE FINAL BATTLES – D+19

Maj-Gen Schmidt and Lt-Gen Kuribayashi both realised that the battle was reaching its final stages. Split down the middle and with no overall command, the Japanese continued to mount bitter and bloody resistance. Kuribayashi moved his command to the north-west corner of the island to a well-prepared area 500yd south of Kitano Point. It was a defenders' paradise, a maze of ravines, caves and gullies that harboured the General's remaining 1,500 defenders. In a message to Tokyo he said, 'the enemy's bombardments are very severe, so fierce that I cannot express or write it here. The troops are still fighting bravely and holding their positions thoroughly.' When the US War Department released the casualty figures for Iwo Jima there was consternation in America, with people questioning the cost of this 'useless piece of real estate'. To placate the public, Iwo Jima was declared 'secure' on 14 March and a ceremony was conducted 200yd north of Mt Suribachi. The words of Maj-Gen Schmidt's personnel officer were lost as an artillery barrage blasted Japanese positions around 'Cushman's Pocket'. The irony of the situation was apparent to all. Holland Smith was there and turned to Maj-Gen Erskine with tears in his eyes, saying, 'this was the worst yet, Bobby'.

'GOODBYE FROM IWO' – D+20–D+36

With the battle apparently in its final stages, the Navy withdrew to Guam, leaving only a few destroyers behind. Air support was now the responsibility of the P51 'Mustangs' operating from Airfield No. 1. With the enemy now confined to two distinct areas – 'Cushman's Pocket' and Lt-Gen Kuribayashi's stronghold in the north-west (soon dubbed the 'Gorge' by the Marines) – conventional battle was abandoned as the infantry slugged it out in a labyrinth of caves and rocks. Tanks could only operate if a bulldozer could clear a path for them, and artillery was dramatically reduced as the front lines merged. The 3rd Division fought a bloody battle for 'Cushman's Pocket' and came upon Baron Nishi, now partially blinded, and a few of his men, who put up

US Command and Staff List

Expeditionary Troops (TF 56)
Commanding General	Lt-Gen Holland M. Smith

V. Amphibian Corps (VACLF)
Commanding General	Maj-Gen Harry Schmidt

3rd Marine Division
Commanding General	Maj-Gen Graves B. Erskine
3rd Regiment (not active)	Col James A. Stuart
9th Regiment	Col Howard N. Kenyon
21st Regiment	Col Hartnoll J. Withers

4th Marine Division
Commanding General	Maj-Gen Clifton B. Cates
23rd Regiment	Col Walter W. Wensinger
24th Regiment	Col Walter I. Jordan
25th Regiment	Col John R. Lannigan

5th Marine Division
Commanding General	Maj-Gen Keller E. Rockey
26th Regiment	Col Chester B. Graham
27th Regiment	Col Thomas A. Wornham
28th Regiment	Col Harry B. Liversedge

US Task Force Organisation
Overall Command of Iwo Jima Operation	Adm Raymond A. Spruance
Task Force 51 (Joint Expeditionary Force)	Vice-Adm Richmond K. Turner
Task Force 52 (Amphibian Support Force)	Rear-Adm William H.P. Blandy
Task Force 53 (Attack Force)	Rear-Adm Harry W. Hill
Task Force 54 (Gunfire and Covering Force)	Rear-Adm Bertram J. Rogers
Task Force 56 (Expeditionary Troops)	Lt-Gen Holland M. Smith
Task Force 56–1 (Landing Force)	Maj-Gen Harry Schmidt
Task Force 58 (Fast Carrier Force 5th Fleet)	Vice-Adm Marc A. Mitscher
Task Force 93 (Strategic Air Force Pacific Area)	Lt-Gen Hillard F. Harmon
Task Force 94 (Forward Area Central Pacific)	Vice-Adm John H. Hoover

JAPANESE COMMAND AND STAFF LIST

Commander in Chief	Lt-Gen Tadamichi Kuribayashi
Chief of Staff	Col Tadashi Takaishi

Army Units
109th Division	Lt-Gen Tadamichi Kuribayashi
145th Infantry Regiment	Col Masuo Ikeda
17th Mixed Infantry Regiment	Maj Tamachi Fijiwara
26th Tank Battalion	Lt-Col (Baron) Takeichi Nishi
2nd Mixed Brigade	Maj-Gen Sadasue Senda
Brigade Artillery	Col Chosaku Kaido
Army Rocket Unit	Capt Yoshio Yokoyama

Navy Units
Commanding Officer	Rear-Adm Toshinosuke Ichimaru
Naval Guard Force	Capt Samaji Inouye
125th Naval Anti-Aircraft Defence Unit	Lt Tamura
132nd Naval Anti-Aircraft Defence Unit	Ens Okumara
141st Naval Anti-Aircraft Defence Unit	Lt Doi
149th Naval Anti-Aircraft Defence Unit	Not known
Operations	Cdr Takeji Mase
Communications	Lt-Cdr Shigeru Arioka
Engineering	Lt-Cdr Narimasa Okada
Supply	Lt-Cdr Okazaki
Mt Suribachi Commander	Capt Kanehiko Atsuchi

Japanese prisoners were very rare on Iwo Jima. Here a group of curious Marines gathers to see one of the few that were taken. (National Archives)

a stubborn resistance until 16 March, when the 'Pocket' finally fell silent. The Baron is thought to have killed himself, but none of his staff lived to verify the story.

In a battle famous for its ferocity, the final phase reached heights of savagery that are difficult to imagine. The 'Gorge' was about 700yd long and 300–500yd wide, with a series of canyons leading off on both sides; it was here that Lt-Gen Kuribayashi planned his last stand. The 28th Regiment moved up the west coast and took up their positions overlooking the 'Gorge', while the rest of the division attacked from the centre and the east. In a week of frantic fighting the Japanese were gradually squeezed further back into the ever-shrinking enclave. So badly mauled were the 2nd Battalion that they had to be withdrawn. The 1st Battalion was down to its third commander in nine days: one had been decapitated, the second maimed by a landmine, and now the third had lost his left arm. By 24 March the Japanese were pinned down in an area only 50yd square, and the last hours were approaching. Lt-Gen Kuribayashi made his final transmission to Chichi Jima: 'All officers and men, goodbye from Iwo.'

THE LAST ACT

'Among the Marines who fought on Iwo Jima, uncommon
valor was a common virtue.'
                                              (Admiral Chester Nimitz)

In the pre-dawn darkness of 26 March the final act of the tragedy was played out.
A group of Kuribayashi's men joined up with other survivors from scattered positions
on the west coast and crept silently through the ravines of the 5th Division sector.
They headed for the tented area, between Airfield No. 2 and the west coast, which was
occupied by a mixture of Seabees, Air Force personnel, shore parties and AA gunners,
most of them sleeping. In a three-pronged attack, they slashed tents and stabbed
sleeping men, threw grenades and fired pistols at the hapless sleepers. The noise soon
attracted nearby Marines, soldiers and shore parties, who joined the battle in a frenzy
of hand-to-hand fighting. Dawn revealed that 44 Airmen and 9 Marines had been
killed, with a further 19 wounded; of the attackers, 262 were killed and 18 captured.
Lt Harry L. Martin of the 5th Pioneers had organised a defence line and single-
handedly killed four of the enemy machine-gunners before being killed himself; he was
to be Iwo Jima's final Medal of Honor recipient.

With Mt Suribachi in the background, the 5th Marine Division cemetery is flanked by 3rd Division on the left and 4th Division on
the right. (USMC)

The entrance of Kuribayashi's cave today. (Taro Kuribayashi)

The circumstances of Lt-Gen Kuribayashi's death are uncertain. It has been suggested that he died fighting in the 'Gorge' or that he killed himself; but in correspondence with the author, his son, Taro, says that he was killed by gunfire and buried at the foot of a tree. Sgt Oyama, who was with the General at the time, was later taken prisoner after being seriously wounded and returned to tell the story after he was released by the Americans.

With the battle over, the dirty, weary and emaciated Marines trudged back to the eastern beaches to be shipped out to the waiting transports. Many were too weak to haul themselves up the netting which had been lowered down the sides of the ships and sailors had to drag them aboard. What had been envisaged as a short, sharp battle had developed into the grimmest, most costly, battle in Marine Corps history. In all, the Marines lost 5,885 dead and 17,272 wounded. The Navy had 881 killed, with a further 1,917 wounded. Grim as these figures are, the Japanese casualties were staggering. The figures are impossible to calculate accurately, but it is known that the garrison stood at 21,060 shortly before the battle and that 867 Army and 216 Navy personnel were taken prisoner, few of them voluntarily, so the death toll can be assumed at 19,977.

Iwo Jima was captured to facilitate the 20th Air Force bombing campaign against Japan. Gen Paul W. Tibbets, the pilot of the B29 bomber *Enola Gay* that dropped the atom bomb on Hiroshima, told the author in an interview, 'From 4th March 1945, when the first B29 in distress landed on Iwo Jima, until the end of the war, more than 2,200 aircraft made emergency landings on Iwo, many with wounded crewmen on board who would not have made the return trip to their home bases. Had it not been for the heroic valour of the Marines in securing the island and the Navy Seabees who built the runways, more than 22,000 pilots and crewmen would have perished in crash landings in the sea.'

The capture of the Philippines and the invasion of Okinawa in April 1945 accelerated the pace of the war; the 20th Air Force fire-raising raids and the dropping of the atom bomb ended it; and the island of Iwo Jima, secured at a terrible cost in Marine Corps lives, played a vital role in these events. The United States' highest decoration, the Medal of Honor, was awarded to twenty-seven combatants at Iwo Jima, a figure that

Left: The scars of the battle still remain, as these photographs taken in 2000 testify. (Taro Kuribayashi) *Right*: A section of the underground network today. (Taro Kuribayashi)

represents a third of the total number of awards to members of the USMC during the whole of the war. Adm Chester Nimitz's famous words, 'Among the Marines who fought on Iwo Jima, uncommon valor was a common virtue', could not have been more appropriate. Lt-Gen Kuribayashi conducted a brilliant defence of the island, inflicting massive casualties on his enemy. He proved without doubt to be Japan's greatest wartime general, and was, in 'Howlin' Mad' Smith's opinion, 'our most redoubtable adversary'.

FLAGS ON MT SURIBACHI

Associated Press photographer Joe Rosenthal's picture of Marines raising the flag on Mt Suribachi was to become the most famous photograph of the war. Because of its superb composition and patriotic connotations, there have always been accusations that it was posed for the occasion. In correspondence with the author, Joe Rosenthal explained the circumstances surrounding the event. On 23 February, Joe went to the 28th Regiment command post and learned that there was a forty-man detachment on its way up the volcano, following two patrols that had already reached the summit. With Joe was Bob Campbell, a combat photographer, and Sgt Bill Genaust USMC, a cine photographer who was killed nine days later at Hill 362. They started the ascent with a group of Marines. About halfway up they met Lou Lowery, a photographer for *Leatherneck*, the Marine Corps magazine, who told them that a flag had been raised and that he had photographed the event. Joe and his companions continued to the top, where they saw the flag flying and also saw a group of men dragging a long iron pipe and holding another flag. He learned that they were going to take down the first flag and replace it with a bigger one. He toyed with the idea of a shot showing one flag coming down and the other going up, but left that to Campbell, while he and Genaust concentrated on the new flag-raising.

With Genaust on his right he took his picture and later took another shot of Marines waving and cheering under the new flag – the posed picture that caused all the confusion. The charge of 'posed' picture levelled at his famous image is easily discounted by a frame-by-frame examination of the cine film taken by Genaust at the same time – one frame is identical to Rosenthal's picture. The 'posed' myth still persists to this day and has been a sore point with Joe since the end of the war: 'I can best sum up what I feel by saying that of all the elements that went into the making of that picture, the part I played was the least important. To get that flag up there, America's fighting men had to die on that island and on other islands. What difference does it make who took the picture? I took it, but the Marines took Iwo Jima,' he says. The six flag-raisers, all now deceased, were, from left to right, Pfc Ira H. Hayes, Pfc Franklin R. Sousley, Sgt Michael Strank, PhM 2c John H. Bradley, Pfc Rene A. Gagnon and Cpl Harlon H. Block. Sousley, Strank and Block were all killed on Iwo Jima. Both flags now hang in the Marine Corps Historical Center in Washington, DC.

6

OKINAWA

THE FINAL BATTLE

By the end of 1944, the Japanese were faced with defeat on all fronts. The war was lost, but the mindset of the High Command was such that they preferred to sacrifice the remainder of their military and naval resources than accept a surrender. The two giant pincers that had gripped the central Pacific – MacArthur's south-west thrust, which had driven through the Solomons and the Dutch East Indies, and Nimitz's 'island hopping' drive through the Gilberts, Marshalls and Marianas – had now converged at Leyte and Mindoro in the Philippines, leaving the Japanese forces in bypassed islands and atolls, isolated and with no hope of reinforcement or supply.

Again the question of how to proceed with the final invasion of Japan came to the fore. MacArthur favoured a landing on the Chinese mainland after bypassing Formosa. Adm King, Chief of Naval Operations, considered the capture of Formosa an essential prerequisite to any attack on the Japanese mainland, but his preference for Formosa was undermined when the Japanese launched a major offensive south of the Yangtze river in May 1944. The success of this offensive and the failure of the devious Chiang Kai-shek, Commander of the Chinese Nationalist Army, to offer any serious resistance forced the Joint Chiefs of Staff in Washington to reconsider their options.

The answer to the problem came from Adm Spruance, who suggested an invasion of Okinawa in the Ryukyus chain of islands 350 miles south-west of the Japanese mainland. The island already had well-established airfields, and there were excellent harbours from which an invasion could be mounted. Nimitz was in general agreement and at a meeting with Spruance and King in San Francisco in September 1944 confirmed that he had sufficient Army and Marine troops under his command to implement the operation. The recommendation was formally accepted by the Joint Chiefs who issued a directive on 3 October for the occupation of Okinawa under the code-name 'Operation Iceberg'.

A number of serious problems presented themselves early in the planning stage: the distance from existing bases in the Marianas meant that the US Navy would have to bear the brunt of the initial support for the landings; carrier planes would have to supply coverage for the invasion, thus exposing the task forces to the kamikaze attacks which were becoming an increasing feature of the latter stages of the war – and with

G Company, 129th Infantry Regiment, 37th Infantry Division, open up on a Japanese position with a 37mm gun. This action, typical of the street fighting in the campaign to take back the Philippines, took place near Manila, January 1945. (National Archives)

an estimated 3,000–4,000 enemy aircraft still operational on the Japanese mainland the risk would be huge. Spruance mapped out a broad operational plan and passed it to Adm Kelly Turner; he in turn produced a detailed scenario within five weeks, which was accepted by the Joint Chiefs on 1 February 1945. The operation was to be in three stages: small adjacent islands in the south were to be captured first to provide advanced base facilities, followed by the occupation of southern Okinawa; next came the seizure of the remainder of the island plus Ie Shima, an island off the north-west coast and the site of a major airfield; and finally the mopping-up of the Nansei Shoto, the remaining islands of the Ryukyus group. The opening day of the operation was set, rather incongruously, for 1 April, April Fool's Day. Okinawa is some sixty-four miles long, and its width varies from eighteen miles at the Motobu Peninsula to a mere two miles at the Ishikama Isthmus, where the island is virtually divided into two sections. The sparsely populated north is covered in masses of high hills and dense forest, while the more heavily populated south is characterised by a gentler terrain with open plains just south of the Ishikama Isthmus, and contains the two major towns of Naha and Shuri.

THE ATTACKING FORCE

There were two main groups for 'Operation Iceberg': the Joint Expeditionary Force and the Covering Force. The Covering Force was subdivided into two fast-carrier groups. Task Force 58 under Vice-Adm Marc Mitscher (succeeded on 28 May by Vice-Adm John S. McCain), consisted of four fast-carrier groups (58–1 to 58–4) accompanied by battleships, cruisers and destroyers. TF58 could muster nearly a thousand aircraft, and its principal responsibility was to contain Japanese air power during the landings. The other carrier group was Task Force 57 under Vice-Adm Bernard Rawlings, a Royal Navy force from the British Pacific Fleet made up of four carriers, two battleships and an escort screen of cruisers and destroyers. They were

6th Marine Division badge.

given the task of protecting the left flank of the operation by attacking enemy airfields in the southern Sakishima Gunto islands of Miyako, Ishigaki and Iromote. The Joint Expeditionary Force (TF56) consisted of the 10th Army under the command of Lt-Gen Simon Bolivar Buckner, the son of a Civil War general, and was a new formation made up of the XXIV Corps of the US Army (7th and 96th Infantry Divisions), under Maj-Gen John R. Hodge, and the III Amphibian Corps (1st and 6th Divisions USMC), under Maj-Gen Roy Geiger USMC. Also attached were the

77th and 27th Infantry Divisions and the 2nd Division USMC. Instead of the usual designation of 'D-Day' for the 1 April landings, the prefix 'L-Day' was substituted; this was because the Iwo Jima and Okinawa operations were planned simultaneously and Iwo Jima had been given the 'D-Day' title first. The landing force was split into two sections: the Northern Landing Force (TG56–2), made up of III Amphibian Corps (1st and 6th Marine Divisions), and the Southern Landing Force (TG56–3) of the XXIV Army Corps (7th and 96th Infantry Divisions). The selected area was on the west coast of the northern half of Okinawa between Nagahama and Chatan, which contained the two major airfields of Yontan and Kadena (see map on p. 203).

Lt-Gen Simon B. Buckner (left), Commander of 10th US Army, with Maj-Gen Roy Geiger USMC, Commander of III Amphibian Corps. (USMC University Archives)

THE DEFENDING FORCE

'One plane for one warship, one boat for one ship, one
man for ten enemy, one man for one tank.'
(Battle slogan of the Japanese 32nd Army)

Exactly one year before the American invasion, Lt-Gen Masao Watanabe activated
the 32nd Army for duty on Okinawa and over the next year a constant stream of
reinforcements were to bolster his force. In July 1944, Watanabe was replaced by
Lt-Gen Mitsuru Ushijima, who based his HQ at Shuri, Okinawa's second largest town
and ancient royal capital. Two miles inland from Naha on the west coast and in an
elevated position, Shuri became the centre of what was to become the Shuri Defence
Line, a complex network of pillboxes, caves, fortified burial tombs and tunnels constructed to supplement the natural defensive terrain. Throughout the summer and
autumn of 1944 further reinforcements arrived, including the 24th Division with
three infantry regiments, the 62nd Division, a light division of two brigades, and the
44th Independent Mixed Brigade and 27th Tank Regiment – all of which brought the
strength to over 77,000, a considerably higher figure than the American estimate of
60,000–70,000. Additional forces such as naval personnel, engineers and conscripted
Okinawan Home Guards brought the final total to well over 100,000 men. The
US forces were to face a higher concentration of artillery than they had on any other
of the Pacific campaigns. The artillery commander, Lt-Gen Kosuke Wada, had at his
disposal more than 250 pieces of 70mm and 320mm spigot mortars and a profusion of
heavy machine-guns and other automatic weapons. As with the Japanese commanders
on Peleliu and Iwo Jima, Ushijima's intention was to inflict the maximum number of
casualties on the enemy and prolong each action to the utmost.

PRE-INVASION OPERATIONS

Preparations for the invasion had begun as early as September 1944 when the first
aerial reconnaissance flights were made. B29 bombers of 21st Bomber Command
photographed the island and later the task was taken up by carrier planes from
USS *Bunker Hill* and USS *Hornet*, who produced a staggering 28,000 vertical and
oblique pictures. Later the fast carriers of TF58 launched a series of strikes over Japan
with the sole purpose of destroying as many Japanese aircraft as possible, in the air or
on the ground. Mitscher was determined that as few enemy aircraft as possible would
be available to attack the landing force. It was during this operation that the carriers
USS *Wasp* and USS *Franklin* were seriously damaged by Japanese bombers. The *Wasp*
was out of action for several days and suffered the loss of 101 of her crew. The
Franklin sustained the heaviest damage ever inflicted on a US carrier, and only heroic
fire-control measures by the crew saved her from floundering; altogether 724 officers
and men were killed with a further 265 wounded. The carrier limped to Pearl Harbor

and after basic repairs made the 12,000-mile voyage to the Brooklyn yard in New York under her own power.

In late March 1945, the old battleships of the bombardment group began operations which continued right up to L-Day. The USS *Tennessee, Texas, Maryland, Arkansas, New Mexico, New York, Colorado, Nevada, West Virginia* and *Idaho* pounded the enemy beaches and inland installations, expending 5,162 tons of ammunition in preparation for the April landings. The final element of the pre-invasion operation was the seizure of the island group of Kerama Retto some 15 miles south-west of Okinawa. At dawn on 26 March, five battalions of the 77th Infantry Division went ashore and for the next three days swept through the islands; by the 29th all eight were secure.

It was Vice-Adm Turner who had suggested that the Kerama Retto would be a useful base for fuel and ammunition; his decision was to be fully justified when four floating docks were sited there later in the campaign to repair the large numbers of ships damaged during the heavy kamikaze attacks. An unexpected bonus was the discovery of over 350 plywood suicide boats (*Renraku tei*), which were fitted with two 264lb depth charges. These were designed to run alongside American ships, trip the depth charges, causing them to roll from their racks and sink the ships – the boat's pilot had five seconds to make his getaway before the explosion!

A shot of the USS *Franklin* off the coast of Okinawa after a kamikaze attack. (IWM NYP80747)

The final phase of the operation was the capture of Keise Shima, a group of tiny islands some eight miles west of the town of Naha. On 31 March, just a day before the assault on Okinawa, two battalions of the 420th Artillery Group equipped with 155mm guns were landed against minimal opposition, and by L-Day the guns were in position and zeroed in; they could reach the area around Naha, Okinawa's largest town, and provide support as the troops advanced.

L-DAY – THE MAIN LANDINGS

Before daybreak the troops began loading their Amtracs and landing craft as a final pre-invasion barrage plastered the landing beaches either side of the village of Hagushi. The two main objectives for L-Day were the airfields of Yontan, a mile and a half to the north, and Kadena, the same distance to the south, and the GIs and Marines were told to expect heavy opposition. As the now familiar order, 'Land the landing force', was issued by Vice-Adm Turner, dozens of LCI(G) gunboats moved close offshore and blasted the beaches with their 3in and 40mm guns, and minutes later an eight-mile-long line of Amtracs began its 4,000yd dash to the beaches.

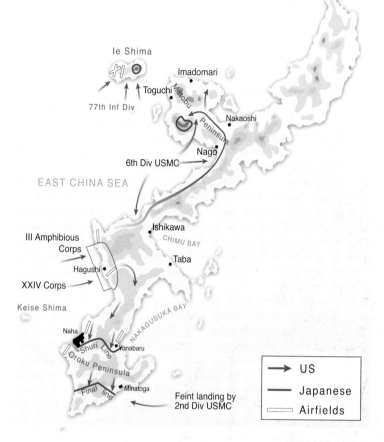

Left: The USS *Idaho* fires a salvo from her 14in guns at Okinawa on 1 April 1945. The picture was taken from USS *West Virginia*. (National Archives)

Ie Shima

Imadomari

Toguchi

Nakaoshi

Motobu Peninsula

Nago

6th Div USMC

EAST CHINA SEA

77th Inf Div

Ishikawa

CHIMU BAY

III Amphibious Corps

Taba

Hagushi

XXIV Corps

Keise Shima

NAKAGUSUKA BAY

Naha

Shuri Line

Yonabaru

Oroku Peninsula

Final line

Minatoga

Feint landing by 2nd Div USMC

→ US
— Japanese
▭ Airfields

The invasion fleet off the coast of Okinawa on L-Day. (National Archives)

The beaches north of Hagushi were the target of the III Amphibian Corps' 1st and 6th Marine Divisions, while the Army's 7th and 96th Divisions of the XXIV Corps headed for the area south of the village. At the same time a feint attack was carried out by the 2nd Marine Division off the south coast of Okinawa near the town of Minatoga (see map on p. 203). Ironically, it was this similar diversionary force that suffered the heaviest casualties of the day. Enemy aircraft mounted an attack and a kamikaze slammed into LST-884, which was carrying 300 Marines. The ship burst into flames and ammunition began to explode. Twenty sailors and Marines were killed and another twenty-one were wounded; another plane hit the transport *Hinsdale*, causing a complete loss of power and killing sixteen of the crew.

As the troops came ashore on the Hagushi beaches they came under light artillery and mortar fire, but resistance ashore was virtually nil; the untrained service troops of

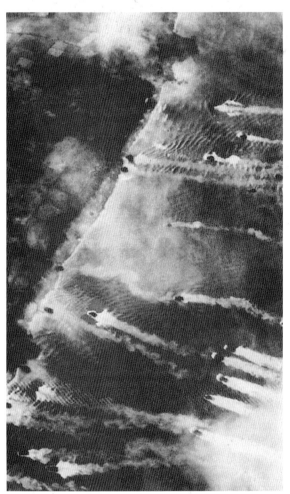

the 1st Specially Established Regiment fled, and the Marines and GIs moved rapidly inland. By noon the Marines were at the edge of Yontan airfield and the Army at Kadena airfield – neither were expected to be taken until L+3. The veteran newspaper columnist Ernie Pyle remarked, 'Never before have I seen an invasion beach like Okinawa – there isn't a dead or wounded man in our whole sector of it.' So quiet was it that a Japanese 'Zero' landed on Yontan airfield; the pilot got out of his plane and was walking towards the hangar before he realised his mistake.

All day the advance continued eastward. There was some slight opposition on the Army front but to the north the Marines faced negligible resistance and before dark there were some 50,000 troops ashore on a beachhead which was between 4,000 and 5,000yd in depth. Casualties for the L-Day landings were reported as 28 dead and 104 wounded, an amazing contrast to the first days on Tarawa and Iwo Jima.

LVTs make the final run-in to the Hagushi beaches on L-Day. (National Archives)

As a Seabee bulldozer levels nearby ground, a 'Corsair' fighter comes in to land on Kadena airfield. (USMC University Archives)

L+1 – 'WHERE IS THE ENEMY?'

Lt-Gen Buckner and Maj-Gen Geiger could hardly believe their luck. Already the troops were taking positions that they had figured would take three or four days to reach. The only problem they were having was in getting supplies ashore fast enough to keep up with the advance. The plan was for the two corps to drive across the island to the east coast and split the enemy in two. The two Marine Divisions had little trouble in accomplishing their task: the 6th Division under Maj-Gen Lemuel Shepherd reached the foothills of Mt Yontan by nightfall and by L+2 were almost at the Nakadomari–Ishikama line, the narrowest part of Okinawa, some twelve days ahead of schedule; two days later the 1st Division had reached the east coast at Chimu Bay. In a mere four days the troops had achieved what the planners had estimated would take three weeks. Lt-Gen Buckner aboard the command ship *Eldorado* was forced to make some drastic alterations to his battle plans: the III Amphibian Corps, spearheaded by the 6th Division, were now to move to the north, to the upper two-thirds of the island, while the XXIV Corps directed their forces to the south. As at Peleliu and Iwo Jima, Lt-Gen Ushijima knew that he was fighting a lost cause, but he was also determined to exact a massive toll on enemy troops in the process. He was better equipped to wage his war of attrition than had been Kuribayashi or Nakagawa, and he had a larger defence force and much more artillery at his disposal. His defences were cleverly placed, minefields and tanks guarded the approaches to his strongpoints, and his men were secure in well-prepared positions.

SECURING THE NORTH

The Marines of the 6th Division wasted no time in their drive north. So fast did they move that their artillery had difficulty in keeping pace. By 7 April, the town of Nago had been taken, and its port was soon open for the delivery of vital supplies. To the north-west of Nago lay the Motobu Peninsula; it was here that the first serious opposition was encountered. Col Takesiko Udo, with his 2,000-strong 44th Independent Mixed Brigade, consisting of two rifle battalions, an anti-tank company and a regimental gun company, had decided that here would be the location for their stand. The Colonel's shrewdest move was his choice of defensive position. The highest peak

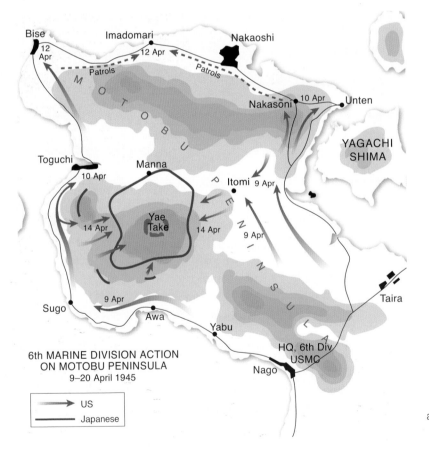

6th MARINE DIVISION ACTION
ON MOTOBU PENINSULA
9–20 April 1945

Opposite: An F6F 'Hellcat'
approaching USS *Randolph*.
(National Archives)

in the peninsula was the 1,200ft-high Yae-Take, a mass of ridges and ravines to which he added a series of underground cave networks in which he established his HQ.

For several days the 6th Marine Division attempted to locate Udo's position as they scoured the peninsula. They struck lucky on 12 April, when friendly Okinawans informed them that the Japanese were concentrating south of the Mann river. The attack on Udo's stronghold began on the morning of the 14th, the 4th Regiment advancing from the west and the 29th from the east with massive support from Marine artillery, Navy carrier planes and naval gunfire from the USS *Colorado*, which was stationed to the west of the peninsula. By 15 April, the noose around Yae-Take had tightened considerably: the 29th Regiment were in control of high ground to the rear of the peak, and the 4th held a key hill to the south-west. Udo was now surrounded and by the next day the Marines were working their way up the rocky slopes to the summit of Yae-Take. A massive barrage of mortar fire brought them to a temporary halt as they neared the top, but troops advancing from the opposite side of the hill swept over the ridges and cleared the summit after fierce hand-to-hand fighting.

The battle was not quite over. The Japanese regrouped in the woods at the base of the hill and mounted a desperate 'banzai' charge, but as was always the case it ended in mass slaughter. With the hill secure the Marines spent the next few days mopping up the rest of the area. Col Udo's command post was located with his radio equipment, but the elusive Colonel was long gone; he was never found by the Americans.

With the capture of the Motobu Peninsula, operations in the northern half of Okinawa were all but over. More than 2,500 enemy troops had been killed and only 46 taken prisoner. It was obvious to Lt-Gen Buckner that the majority of the defenders were in the south of the island. The III Corps had lost 246 killed and 1,000 wounded in their northern operation, and the 6th Marine Division had successfully survived its baptism of fire.

THE TAKING OF IE SHIMA

Three and a half miles to the west of the Motobu Peninsula lay the island of Ie Shima, the site of a major airfield, defended by over 3,000 troops augmented by 1,500 armed civilians. The kidney-shaped island is five and a half miles long and three miles wide and is surrounded by a coral reef. The town of Ie lay to the southeast of the island, the main topographical feature of which was a 600ft-high conical limestone peak called Iegusugu Pinnacle (see map on p. 210).

A supporting gunfire unit was formed (TU.52.21.1) under Rear-Adm B.J. Rogers, consisting of the battleship *Texas* and the cruisers *Birmingham* and *Mobile*, which began its preliminary bombardment on 13 April. The troops for 'Operation Indispensable' as it was code-named, came from the Army's 77th 'Statue of Liberty' Division. They landed on 16 April with two regimental combat teams (RCTs), under heavy covering fire from the gunfire unit. Initial resistance was light as the 306th Infantry

Famed war correspondent Ernie Pyle shares a cigarette with a Marine patrol. Pyle was later killed by machine-gun fire on Ie Shima, a nearby island fortress. (USMC)

landed on 'Green beach T–1' and the 305th hit 'Red T–1' and 'Red T–2'; but it stiffened as they advanced inland. The troops were met with fanatical resistance around the airfield complex, not only from Japanese troops, but also civilian fighters, including women armed with wooden spears. But by evening the airfield was in US hands and the troops were moving east towards Ie town and the Iegusugu Pinnacle. By the next day the GIs were at the approaches to Ie and the 307th Infantry, accompanied by elements of the 706th Tank Battalion, were landing on 'Red T–3' beach in the south, the town having been surrounded. On 18 April the fighting was concentrated around the town centre and an administrative building called Government House Hill. Most of Ie town had been cleared by the 20th, but the Pinnacle was not taken until the following day, when Ie Shima was officially declared secure. Even so, mopping-up operations continued until the 26th.

One of the casualties on Ie Shima was the popular war correspondent Ernie Pyle, a veteran of the war in Europe, who was killed by machine-gun fire on 18 April. The Japanese had lost 4,700 killed, including many armed civilians, with 409 taken prisoner; US losses were 218 dead and 900 wounded. The 77th Infantry Division were immediately moved back to the mainland, soon to be in combat again, and the entire civilian population of Ie Shima was removed from the island and not returned until after the war. The Ie Shima operation was described as 'a masterpiece of planning and execution'. By many GIs it was remembered as 'the place where we lost Ernie Pyle'.

Above: US Marine Corps Shermans on Okinawa, 6 May 1945. (National Archives)

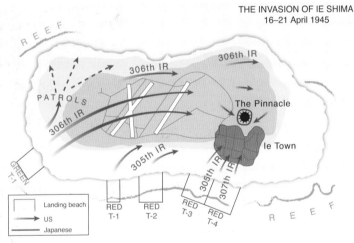

THE PUSH TO THE SOUTH

As the Marines were clearing the north of the island, the Army's XXIV Corps had moved south and by 4 April Maj-Gen Hodge had the 7th Infantry Division on the east flank and the 96th on the west. The first major obstacle was the Pinnacle, a 30ft-high outcrop on a ridge just east of the town of Arakuchi, which was defended by the 14th Independent Infantry Battalion under 1/Lt Tamagawa. It took a series of concentrated attacks by the 184th Infantry Regiment before Tamagawa was outflanked. A similar obstacle was 'Cactus Ridge', in terrain that was too rough for armour to be used. The position was only taken after a bayonet charge by men of the 383rd Infantry on 6 April; and the positions known as 'Red Hill', 'Tombstone Ridge' and 'Triangulation Hill' on the 7th Division's front were also all captured by unsupported

Above: Men of 7th Marines wait until phosphorus shells take effect. (USMC)

Right: A Marine shaves, knee-deep in water in the middle of a bivouac area. (USMC)

infantry assaults. By 8 April, the XXIV Corps had cleared these and many similar strongpoints, but had suffered over 1,000 casualties while killing or capturing 4,500 of the enemy.

Lt-Gen Buckner was aware that the Japanese had established a line across the full width of the island roughly four miles north of the capital, Naha. The Japanese called it the Machinato Line, and behind it lay their main inner defence ring around the ancient capital of Okinawa, Shuri. Lt-Gen Buckner had moved his HQ from the *Eldorado* to shore on 14 April and was impatient at the lack of progress in the south. For over a week the 7th and 96th Divisions had been stalled at the eastern and western ends of the line, so he decided to bring in another division, the 27th, who had previously seen action on Saipan. Buckner assigned the 27th the western end of the line and moved the 96th to the centre, with the 7th on the east.

In an attempt to break the deadlock, Buckner planned a massive attack all along the line for 19 April. It was preceded by the most concentrated artillery barrage yet mounted: 27 artillery battalions (18 Army and 9 Marine) took part, raking the Japanese lines from east to west with 324 artillery pieces and firing over 19,000 shells. When the barrage had subsided, the Navy took over with a bombardment by

A kamikaze makes a wave-top approach at the port side of the USS *Missouri* (BB-63), 11 April 1945. (USMC)

The moment of impact. Kamikaze attacks continued unabated throughout April and May, resulting in the loss of 26 US ships sunk and 225 damaged and the highest US Navy casualty rate of the war (BB-63), 11 April 1945. (USMC)

6 battleships, 6 cruisers and 6 destroyers, followed by Navy and Marine aircraft with bombs, rockets, napalm and machine-gun fire. The 7th Infantry Division attacked 'Skyline Ridge', the main strongpoint at the eastern end of the enemy line, but were repulsed by shredding enemy fire. In the centre the 96th were faced with the heavily defended Nishibaru Ridge, and few gains were made; while the 27th in the west made a limited advance on the Urasoe–Mura Escarpment, but lost twenty-two tanks when the 193rd Tank Battalion crossed between Kakazu and Nishibaru Ridges, the greatest loss incurred by US armour for any day on Okinawa.

On 23 April, Adm Nimitz flew in to Yontan airfield to discuss the situation with Buckner. He was concerned about the number of kamikaze attacks that his fleet were suffering and wanted the land operation speeding up so that they could end their protracted stay. In one of the few instances when he lost his temper, he made it clear that unless Buckner got his ground operations moving within five days he would get someone in who would. With Nimitz was Lt-Gen Alexander Vandegrift, the conqueror of Guadalcanal and now Commandant of the US Marine Corps. He suggested that an amphibious landing behind the enemy lines in southern Okinawa could relieve the pressure on Buckner's men, and, moreover, he had men available, the 2nd Marine Division. Buckner opposed the idea, saying that such an operation would complicate his supply problems, and made it clear that he considered the best solution would be to bolster his manpower for his frontal attacks on the Japanese defences. By implication he was stating that tactics on Okinawa were the business of the Army. Nimitz was prepared to allow Buckner a free hand, but only if he produced results.

One of Buckner's first decisions was to relieve Maj-Gen George W. Griner of his command of the 27th Division and to assemble a task force consisting of four battalions from the 7th and 96th Divisions together with the 102nd Engineer Battalion from the 27th to attack the stronghold of Kakazu Ridge. The attack was mounted on 24 April, but the force were amazed to find that the Japanese had made a skilful withdrawal; the enemy had decided that their first line of defence was no longer tenable and had moved back to the Urasoe–Mura Escarpment.

Marine personnel load projectiles into a mobile rocket-launcher during 10th Army's drive to the south of Okinawa. (USMC)

In the final week of April, the XXIV Corps laboured to secure the installations between the abandoned line and the Urasoe–Mura, and the 7th Division captured the important prominences of 'Conical Hill' and Kochi Ridge; in the west the 27th mopped up 'Item Pocket', and in the centre the 96th advanced against Maeda Escarpment. The north face was so steep that the 307th Infantry had to employ 50ft ladders to reach the top and then lower cargo netting borrowed from the Navy, draping it down the cliff for the following troops to climb. As the final days of April ebbed away, Buckner took steps to bolster his force: the 1st and 6th Marine Divisions were brought down from the north and the 77th Division left Ie Shima to relieve the battered 96th. The moves were very timely because the Japanese had a surprise up their sleeve.

THE JAPANESE COUNTER-OFFENSIVE

In Lt-Gen Ushijima's HQ in Shuri Castle a stormy argument was in progress. Lt-Gen Isamu Cho, Ushijima's Chief of Staff, was pressing for a counter-offensive against the Americans to stall their advance. Ushijima was not in favour and Col Hiromichi Yahara, 32nd Army Operations Officer, was vehemently against such a move. Cho was something of a hothead. He was one of the conspirators in the Cherry

An Okinawan civilian emerges, after US forces threw a smoke grenade into the cave in which he had been hiding. After the battle it was estimated that over 122,000 Okinawans had died as a result of Japanese or American combat action or suicide – a figure larger than the combined death toll at Hiroshima and Nagasaki. (USMC)

Opposite: A Japanese ammunition dump explodes after flame-throwers detonated it, June 1945. (National Archives)

Society plot of 1931 which had attempted to overthrow the government and replace it with a military dictatorship. He was also the instigator of the order to kill all prisoners during the occupation of Nanking in 1937. He argued that a counter-offensive could push the Americans back for at least two miles and boost the morale of the troops, but Yahara insisted that 'the Army must continue current operations, calmly recognising its final destiny – annihilation is inevitable no matter what is done'. He argued that the preliminary bombardment for such an operation would reveal the location of the Japanese artillery and invite a massive US retaliation. Yahara's argument fell on deaf ears. Fuelled by large quantities of sake the other staff officers all agreed with Cho, and so eventually did Ushijima, declaring, 'each soldier will kill at least one American devil'. The offensive was set for 4 May, with the 24th Infantry Division designated to spearhead the attack.

During the night of 3/4 May, the Japanese began a huge artillery barrage, the largest encountered by US forces in the whole of the Pacific War, with over 5,000 rounds falling on the forward elements of the 77th Division. Simultaneously, several hundred troops in landing craft and barges headed for the east coast in an attempt to slip behind US lines. The amphibious operation was a total failure: US Navy vessels located the enemy almost at once and blew the flimsy craft out of the water; the few Japanese who reached the shore were finished off by troops of the 7th Division. On the west coast

another landing ended in disaster when a navigational error put the Japanese ashore in the 1st Marine Division zone and the invaders were all slaughtered on the offshore reef.

The main land attack was directed against the Urasoe–Mura Escarpment and timed for 5 a.m. on 4 May. Again the operation ended disastrously: two battalions of the 24th Division failed to get in position and were caught in the open by American artillery and mortars, with devastating results. In the centre the attack lacked any cohesion or momentum and was repulsed with horrendous casualties. A belated attempt to reach the Tanaburu Escarpment after dark ended with one battalion retreating after losing 248 men and another being surrounded by 7th Division troops and having to make a fighting retreat in which 370 men were killed. By the evening of 5 May, Ushijima was forced to admit that the counter-offensive had been a total disaster – he had called it off at 6.00 p.m. With tears in his eyes he apologised to Col Yahara and began counting the cost: in addition to 7,000 dead and the loss of large amounts of equipment, US forces had also been able to locate 20 of Ushijima's artillery positions and destroy them. The American units had suffered fewer than 700 casualties and continued their steady advance to the south.

THE ADVANCE ON SHURI

Capitalising on the failure of the Japanese, Lt-Gen Buckner reorganised his front in preparation for his own attack to the south. The 6th Marine Division was brought south and placed on the right of XXIV Corps, doubling the forces so that he now had a front comprised of four divisions; from east to west they were the 1st and 6th Marine Divisions of III Corps and the 77th and 96th of XXIV Corps, with the 7th Division in temporary reserve. The plan was to surround Shuri: the XXIV Corps were to advance from the east and the III Amphibian Corps from the west, while the centre was to be contained by the 77th Infantry. The attack got under way on 11 May, but despite coordinated action along the entire front it soon disintegrated into a series of intense battles for individual positions. It took ten days of ferocious fighting before the Japanese line broke.

Some of the heaviest fighting took place just north of the town of Asato at 'Sugar Loaf Hill'. The hill was one of three mutually supporting strongpoints, the others being 'Half Moon Hill' and 'Horseshoe Hill', which were part of a complex defended by the 15th Independent Mixed Regiment under Col Seiko Mita. 'Sugar Loaf' proved to be one of the hardest battles of the whole campaign. Honeycombed with underground tunnels, and with pillboxes and mortar positions on both slopes, its approach could be blanketed by artillery fire from 'Shuri Heights' only hundreds of yards to the east. Tanks were brought forward in support but were soon knocked out by 47mm anti-tank guns. The battle continued for four days until tanks worked their way around either side of the hill and broke the Japanese defences. The 6th Division losses were heavy: in the ten days since the advance had got under way they had lost 2,662 men killed or wounded.

In the south of Okinawa, Marines man a .30 Browning machine-gun. (USMC)

'Sugar Loaf' was to be only one of a series of formidable defence positions that had to be taken: the 1st Marine Division slogged their way across Wana Ridge and Dakeshi; the 77th Division assaulted the 'Chocolate Drop', 'Wart Hill' and 'Flattop Hill'; and the 96th were confronted with 'Dick', 'Oboe' and 'Conical' Hills, all strength-sapping battles that had to be fought before the main Japanese defence line around Shuri could be approached.

ON TO THE SHURI LINE

With Nimitz's instructions for a speedy advance ringing in his ears, Buckner ordered his commanders to prepare for another offensive. The enemy still offered strong resistance in the centre, but the breakthrough came on the left in the area occupied by the 96th Division at 'Conical Hill'. To Buckner's delight the 383rd Infantry Regiment seized the eastern slopes and allowed the 7th Division to pour down a narrow corridor in the centre to occupy the town of Yonabaru. What looked like a promising advance was soon stalled, however, when the weather deteriorated, turning the roads into quagmires and bogging down the tanks and self-propelled artillery. In the west the 6th Marine Division made a crossing at the Asato river on 23/24 May and entered the town of Naha, the capital. There was little resistance, and the Marines moved further eastward through the Kokubu Hills in the hope of trapping the main Japanese defending force at Shuri.

The foul weather not only hampered Buckner's troop movements, it also curtailed aerial operations. The reconnaissance planes that so far had been Buckner's eyes were grounded at Kadena and Yontan airfields, leaving the General to guess what Ushijima was up to. He told his staff, 'I think all Jap front-line troops are in the Shuri position. They don't appear to be falling back.' Lt-Gen Buckner could not have got it more wrong. At a sombre meeting in the caves below Shuri Castle on 21 May, Ushijima called together all his commanders for an urgent meeting to plan the next move. The Japanese had suffered massive losses, some 64,000 in the Shuri area alone. The issue was straightforward: should they make their final stand at Shuri or should they escape to the south of the island in the hope of prolonging the battle and inflicting even more casualties on the enemy? It was Col Yahara who swayed the argument this time: 'It was recognised that to stay would result in a quicker defeat', he said later, and plans were laid for evacuation to the south.

Ushijima did not abandon the Shuri Line immediately; he left some 5,000 men around Shuri Castle, who offered such stiff resistance against advancing American forces that US Intelligence officers were convinced that the enemy still held the line in strength. Meanwhile, the retreat to the south continued. Aided by the miserable weather the 32nd Army gradually moved men and equipment along the churned-up roads in a brilliantly executed withdrawal that kept the Americans guessing for days and allowed the bulk of the Army to escape.

The ruins of Shuri Castle, with the town of Shuri in the background. (USMC University Archives)

On 26 May, the weather improved sufficiently for carrier planes to overfly the area south of Shuri, where they reported the movement of large numbers of people and equipment. A heavy barrage was laid on by the 8in guns of the cruiser USS *New Orleans*, with tragic results. As Lt-Gen Ushijima's withdrawal got under way, he ordered all Okinawans to move to the Chinen Peninsula; most disobeyed the order, thinking that they would be safer staying with the Japanese troops. Although the 32nd Army suffered many casualties during the retreat, the civilians suffered many more, and by the time the withdrawal ended an estimated 15,000 had been killed.

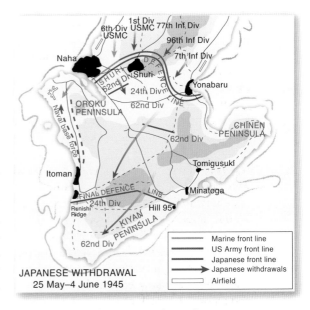

JAPANESE WITHDRAWAL
25 May–4 June 1945

On 29 May, elements of the 1st Marine Division entered Shuri Castle. A flag-raising ceremony was arranged to celebrate the fall of this important stronghold, but the only one that could be found was a Confederate banner; so the Stars and Bars flew over Shuri until a Stars and Stripes flag that had been raised at Peleliu replaced it.

Meanwhile, Ushijima was consolidating his new defence line across the Kiyamu Peninsula. With Lt-Gen Cho and Col Yahara he set up his HQ in a cave inside Hill 89 some ten miles south of Shuri. The four-mile line started at Hill 95 on the east coast and ended at Kunishi Ridge on the west. In between rose two forbidding escarpments named Yoza Dake and Yaeju-Dake. There were no more hills to the rear; this was where Ushijima would make his final stand. 'The present position will be defended to the death, even to the last man,' he ordered.

USHIJIMA'S LAST STAND

Realising that the main body of Ushijima's army had escaped, Lt-Gen Buckner revised his plans. The 96th Division in the centre, the 7th Division on the east coast and the 1st Marine Division on the west coast would pursue the retreating Japanese, leaving the 77th Division to mop up around Shuri. But once again the weather intervened, the inadequate roads could not cope with the masses of tracked vehicles, and the move to the south was painfully slow. The 6th Marine Division, who had just taken Naha, speeded things up by mounting an amphibious crossing of the Kokuba Estuary and moving into the Oroku Peninsula, which was defended by a 5,000-man naval-base force under Rear-Adm Minoru Ota. Most of Ota's force had previously withdrawn from the Shuri Defence Line, along with the 32nd Army; but they now preferred to

A wounded Marine, his clothing blown from his back, is evacuated to the rear. (USMC)

return to their former positions rather than fight alongside the Army. Without consulting Ushijima, Ota moved his force north and bitter fighting developed.

By 9 June, the Marines had forced the enemy into a small pocket, where they resisted until the 12th, when the area was secured. Over 4,000 men of the naval-base force were killed, and Ota and his staff committed suicide. The American casualties were particularly heavy, over 1,608 – more than those suffered in the capture of Shuri. The Marine crossing of the Kokuba Estuary was to be the last opposed amphibious assault of the whole war.

In the centre of the island, Ushijima had deployed the remains of his army, now down to 8,000 men in the 24th Division, 3,000 in the 32nd, with a few reserves in the 44th Independent Mixed Brigade. They would fight and die where they stood, holding a line stretching from the town of Itoman on the west coast to Yaeju-Dake in the east. The weather came to the aid of the American forces on 5 June: the rains came to a sudden end and the flooded roads began to dry out, allowing the Army and Marine units to move south. By the 8th, they were in position for a general attack.

At the eastern limit of Ushijima's line was Hill 95, just south of Minatoga. The 7th Division had no alternative but to launch a frontal assault, as its seaward side was a cliff that dropped for 300ft into the sea and its western side was a steep valley within range of the Japanese guns on the Yaeju-Dake Escarpment only two miles to the west. It took two days of close-quarter fighting to capture the hill, but its elimination allowed the 7th Division to move westwards towards the 1,200yd-long Yaeju-Dake stronghold. Maj-Gen Archibald V. Arnold, the 7th Division Commander, approved a plan for a night-time attack and, at 3.30 a.m. on 12 June, the GIs advanced through a thick fog that reduced visibility to around 10ft. Within two hours they were at the summit and were amazed to find it undefended; the Japanese had evacuated the ridge for the night to avoid the American artillery fire which was raining down on them. At daybreak, as the Japanese returned to their positions, they were mown down by riflemen of the 17th Regiment; in an action lasting only a week, the eastern flank of Ushijima's line had collapsed.

Heavily laden troops of H Company, 382nd Infantry Regiment, climb a hillside in southern Okinawa. (US Army)

To the right, the 1st Marine Division were beginning the assault on Kunishi Ridge to the east of Itoman, the western anchor of Ushijima's line. To reach the ridge the Marines had to cross an exposed valley that left both men and tanks dangerously open to enemy mortar, machine-gun and anti-tank fire. Again the US forces opted for a night attack, and by dawn on 12 June two companies had reached the crest of the 2,000yd-long barrier. Charles Owen of the 1st Battalion 7th Marine Regiment recalled:

'We had to advance across a flat field of rice paddies for 800yd, exposed to enemy fire from Kunishi. The ridge was honeycombed with 47mm anti-tank guns and automatic-weapon emplacements, minefields, caves, pillboxes and slope defences. We were supported by M4 tanks from the 1st Tank Battalion. The casualties were so high that Col Snedeker [Col Edward W. Snedeker] decided to send two companies to the top by night. We thought that this was a crazy idea, but they made it to the top. Casualties began to mount as we tried to cross the 800yd three times, and the CO of C Company Tanks had the idea of using tanks to ferry the infantry up the ridge. With only two men from the crew in the tank, six Marines could be carried. This was the first time the Marine Corps used tanks to carry reinforcing infantry. I remember one of the tank crew kidding us about how bad we smelled. I told him that the only time we got our ass washed was when it rained. We were supposed to leave the tank through the top hatch, but the first person to try it got killed. We had to leave by the escape hatch in the bottom and when you did this you were in hell. The Japs were in front, and to the rear, and on both flanks.'

Men of 17th Infantry Regiment, 7th Infantry Division, use a 37mm anti-tank gun against the caves in the Yaeju-Dake on Okinawa. (US Army)

Pte Charles H. Owen, aged 14 in 1942, just after boot camp. By the time he landed on Okinawa 'Chuck' Owen was already a 16 year old "veteran" having previously fought at Peleliu. He went on to serve in Korea and Vietnam before retiring from the Corps in 1962. (Charles H. Owen)

By 17 June the ridge was in American hands and the whole of Ushijima's line was crumbling as more and more tanks and armour were able to move south on the rapidly improving roads. Realising that the end was near, Ushijima ordered his remaining troops to disperse and form guerilla units in the Kiyan Peninsula. On 22 June, Lt-Gens Ushijima and Cho prepared to commit suicide. A witness described the scene: 'Each man bared his stomach for disembowelment by a ceremonial knife, at the same time bowing his head for decapitation by the Adjutant's drawn sword. A simultaneous shout and a flash of a sword and both Generals had nobly accomplished their last duty to the Emperor.'

They were not the only senior officers to die in the final days of the battle. On 18 June, Lt-Gen Buckner went to a forward observation post to watch Marines advance along a valley. He was standing next to a rocky outcrop when an enemy shell exploded nearby, driving a coral splinter into the General's chest. He died ten minutes later, one of the most senior officers to be killed in action during the Second World War. Maj-Gen Roy Geiger assumed command, becoming the only Marine to command a field army. The appointment was only temporary; the Army's Lt-Gen Joseph 'Vinegar Joe' Stillwell was rushed to Okinawa, but by the time he arrived the battle was over.

A Marine flame-thrower opens up on Japanese who refuse to surrender. (USMC)

III AMPHIBIAN CORPS – MARINE DIVISIONS

	1st Division	2nd Division	6th Division
Assault Strength	26,274	22,195	24,356
Regiments	1st/5th/7th	2nd/6th/8th	4th/22nd/29th
Artillery Regiments	11th	10th	15th
Tank Battalions	1st	2nd	6th
Engineer Battalions	1st	2nd	6th
Motor Transport Battalions	1st	2nd	6th
Medical Battalions	1st	2nd	6th
Armoured Amphibian Tractor Battalions	3rd	–	1st
Naval Construction Battalions (Seabees)	145th	130th	58th
Marine Amphibian Truck Companies	3rd	2nd	6th
Provisional Rocket Detachments	4th	–	5th

The Marine Corps started the operation with 88,500 men, of whom 66,636 participated in the battle.

XXIV CORPS – INFANTRY DIVISIONS

	7th Division	27th Division	77th Division	26th Division
Assault Strength	21,929	16,143	20,981	22,330
Infantry Regiments	17th/32nd/184th	105th/106th/165th	305th/306th/307th	381st/382nd/383rd
Division Artillery Battalions	48th/49th/57th/31st	104th/105th/249th/106th	304th/305th/902nd/306th	361st/362nd/921st/3rd
Engineer Combat Battalions	13th	102nd	302nd	321st
Medical Battalions	7th	102nd	302nd	321st
Tank Battalions	711th	193rd	706th	763rd
Amphibian Tank Battalions	776th	–	708th	780th
Amphibian Tractor Battalions	536th	–	715th	728th
Anti-Aircraft Battalions	502nd	–	93rd	504th
Medical Field Hospital	69th	68th	36th	31st
Medical Portable Surgical Unit	52nd/66th	96th/98th	68th/95th	51st/67th

The Army started the operation with 102,250 men, a figure which rose to 190,301 by the end.

ARMY AND MARINE CORPS CASUALTIES

Marines	Killed in action	Wounded in action	Missing in action	Total
1st Division USMC	1,067	6,418	40	7,525
2nd Division USMC	56	364	9	429
6th Division USMC	1,622	6,689	15	8,326
Army				
7th Infantry Division	1,122	4,943	3	6,068
27th Infantry Division	711	2,520	24	3,255
77th Infantry Division	1,018	3,968	40	5,026
96th Infantry Division	1,506	5,912	12	7,430
III Amphibian Corps	35	149	4	188
XXIV Corps	55	346	2	403
				38,650

Mopping up continued for many weeks. Scores of enemy stragglers were holed up in caves and tunnels and had to be winkled out in a series of minor operations that not only resulted in the final suppression of Japanese resistance but also in the death of many US troops. With the war in Europe over, the war in the Pacific assumed a prominent role in the American news media and the huge casualty figures raised cries of outrage from the public. The influential journalists William Randolph Hearst and Robert McCormick, both cronies of Gen Douglas MacArthur, launched a bitter attack against the 'island hopping' campaign in general and Nimitz and his Marines in particular; it was a controversy to which MacArthur, his eyes on the American Presidency, added his voice, remarking that the campaigns 'sacrificed thousands of American soldiers because they insisted in driving the Japanese off the islands'.

THE SEA WAR

The land battle for Okinawa stands alongside Tarawa, Peleliu and Iwo Jima in its savagery, while the casualties incurred surpassed those of any previous battle. But what made it unique were the equally fierce battles fought by the Navy off the island's coast. As early as January 1945, plans were being laid by the Japanese to counter a possible invasion of the island by authorising the assembly of a fleet of over 4,500 Army and Navy aircraft for an operation named 'Ten-Go' (meaning 'Heavenly Operation'), which would consist of a series of mass-formation suicide attacks called Kikusui (or 'Floating Chrysanthemums'). In addition, a small number of piloted flying bombs known as *Ohkas* ('Cherry Blossoms') would be carried into the attacks

A Japanese plane explodes in mid-air over USS *Hornet* (CV-12), 14 May 1945. (USMC)

strapped to the underside of twin-engined bombers. The pilots of these aircraft were all young volunteers imbued with the code of bushido and with a fanatical devotion to the Emperor. To the Westerner they would be better known as kamikaze. The 'Ten-Go' operation would be executed by the 5th Air Fleet under Vice-Adm Matome Ugaki, who frantically assembled his fleet of aircraft. Anything that could fly was pressed into service: obsolete fighters, seaplanes, reconnaissance planes, twin-engined bombers – all were collected and sent to bases in Formosa, the Sakishima Gunto and the home island of Kyushu. The pilots were given only a basic training, but this still took time, and this delay, allied to the chronic shortage of aviation fuel, prevented Ugaki from launching any attacks on 1 April, L-Day.

THE DEATH OF THE YAMATO

As a supplement to the 'Ten-Go' operations the Imperial Japanese Navy were preparing to send the battleship *Yamato* and the light cruiser *Yahagi* to sea in an attempt to lure Task Force 58 away from Okinawa. The plan indicated the desperation within the top ranks of the Navy, that they were prepared to sacrifice one of the largest battleships ever built in what would obviously be a suicide mission. Built in the late 1930s the IJN *Yamato* was a beautiful vessel, displacing nearly 70,000 tons, with 18.1in guns and an armoured belt 16in thick and 9in thick armoured decks. Her turbines could bring her up to a top speed of 27.5 knots. She was originally designed as one of three, but her sister ship the *Musashi* had been sunk off Leyte Gulf in October 1944, and the third vessel was converted into an aircraft carrier, the *Shinano*, which was sunk by the US Navy submarine *Archerfish* while on its way to be fitted out. At 10.00 a.m. on 7 April, aircraft from the carriers of TF58–1 were alerted to take off and headed north to intercept a ten-ship enemy force that had been sighted by a US submarine. Flying through a driving rainstorm and heavy cloud the pilots spotted the unmistakable shape of the *Yamoto* at 12.32 p.m. and were subjected to a heavy barrage of anti-aircraft gun-fire.

The attacking force from TF58–1 consisted of over 380 aircraft from the carriers *Bennington*, *Hornet*, *San Jacinto* and *Belleau Wood* under the command of Cdr Edward G. Konrad, flying from the *Hornet*. The aircraft were a mixture of bomb-carrying F4U 'Corsairs', SB2C-1 'Helldivers', F4F 'Wildcat' fighters, F6F 'Hellcat' fighters and TBM 'Avenger' torpedo bombers. The initial attack came from the 'Helldivers', which succeeded in dropping two bombs on the stern of the *Yamato*, while others sank the *Asashimo* and damaged the *Kasumi*. The next wave of fighter-bombers went for the battleship and scored four hits, two on the superstructure, one on the flight deck and one near the bow; elsewhere, three hits were registered on the *Yahagi*. The final attack from TF58–1 resulted in three torpedo hits by 'Avengers' from the *Belleau Wood* and four bomb hits all around one of the 18.1in turrets. The attacks had lasted for only twenty minutes, but now Konrad handed over to Cdr Harmon G. Utter from the *Essex* to lead the second attack by TF58–3 from the carriers *Bunker Hill*, *Cabot*, *Bataan* and *Hancock*.

Rain and heavy cloud continued to hamper the operation, and the aircraft from the *Hancock* failed to locate the target. The first wave of 'Avengers' made their approach just as the *Yamato* swung to starboard, presenting the full length of her port side to the torpedo bombers and, together with a second wave, they claimed six torpedo hits. The *Yamato* was now listing and her speed had dropped to 18 knots. But her agony was not yet over, as aircraft from TF58–4, which included the carriers *Yorktown*, *Intrepid* and *Langley*, were now arriving and circling like so many vultures eager to attack their prey. Cdr W.E. Rawdie, the next strike controller, found it difficult to coordinate the attack in the foul weather; it became something of a free-for-all, in which the crippled *Yahagi* was finally sunk.

Conditions aboard the *Yamato* were now chaotic. Although the gunners continued to put up a withering anti-aircraft barrage, her list to port had become more pronounced, and the 'Avengers' concentrated on the exposed starboard side, scoring at least two hits. The engine rooms began to flood, the *Yamato* began steaming in a wide circle and shortly after 2.00 p.m. she lost all power. The devastation on board the ship was appalling. The whole of the upper deck was a mass of twisted metal, and below it was even worse: bodies and parts of bodies were everywhere and compartments were rapidly flooding. At 2.20 p.m., the order to abandon ship was given as the *Yamato* began to sink by the head with a list of 90 degrees. When it reached 120 degrees a massive explosion ripped her apart, sending a huge column of smoke into the air to a height of 6,000ft. The number of officers and men who died in the inferno was colossal – 3,063 – leaving only 269 survivors to be picked up by the few destroyers that had come through the attacks unscathed.

At 1.40 p.m., when it was obvious that the *Yamato* was doomed, Mitscher had ordered an end to the sorties. American losses were light: nine aircraft had been shot down and one of the pilots had been rescued by flying boat. The Japanese did exact some revenge later in the day when a heavy air raid was mounted on TF58 by a large number of bombers; eighteen were shot down, but one penetrated the defences and bombed the carrier *Hancock*, blowing a large hole in the flight deck and dislodging the forward lift. Twenty-eight men were killed and fifty-two others wounded. The *Hancock* remained in action for a considerable time before she was detached to Ulithi for repairs.

THE KAMIKAZES

'These unreasonable measures were all that was left to us.'

(Emperor Hirohito)

With the build-up of aircraft complete – the Army's 8th Air Division and the Navy's 1st Air Fleet in Formosa and the Sakishima Gunto and the 5th Air Fleet in Kyushu on the Japanese mainland – the kamikaze force was in a position to begin operations.

As was common with Japanese forces, there appeared to be little coordination between the Army and the Navy; the man responsible for directing most of the attacks from Japan was Rear-Adm Toshiyuki Yokoi, who had the backing of the Combined Fleet HQ.

The first major attack developed on 6 April over two of the task groups of TF58 north-east of Okinawa. Yokoi dispatched 120 aircraft, but around half failed to locate their target and flew on to Okinawa. One aircraft homed in on the carrier USS *Bennington* and crashed into the sea only yards from her stern, damaging the rudder; the *Belleau Wood* narrowly evaded another. Day after day and week after week the kamikaze attacks continued. The principal targets were the destroyers and other vessels on picket duty, and most attacks were timed for dawn or twilight when the attackers were difficult to identify. The effect on the sailors of the 5th Fleet was dramatic. The constant alerts and lack of sleep took their toll. In one case a sailor suddenly announced to a shipmate, 'It's too hot today', as he jumped overboard never to be seen again; and the constant anticipation of a fiery death was the cause of many breakdowns.

The Navy responded to the onslaught with a series of heavy raids on the kamikaze bases, but eventually it was only the loss of scores of planes in the attacks that finally ended the campaign, and by the end of Japanese resistance on Okinawa there were fewer than fifty planes available. In all fifty-seven Allied warships were sunk by kamikazes, some off the Philippines, but most in the waters around Okinawa. More than 1,900 suicide planes had been involved, and the US Navy lost almost 5,000 sailors killed and an equal number wounded, the heaviest loss of life in any naval engagement during the war.

The last surviving pre-war US carrier, USS *Enterprise* (far right) with newer ships of the Pacific Fleet. (IWM NYF22732)

USS *Bunker Hill* on fire after a kamikaze attack off Okinawa. The attack ruptured fuel lines that fed a conflagration in the hangar and on the flight deck. This caused severe damage, killing 400 of the crew and injuring 264. (US Navy)

A typical example of a kamikaze attack can be illustrated by the events of 11 May, when the fleet carrier USS *Bunker Hill* (CV17), part of Task Force 58 and the flagship of Vice-Adm Marc Mitscher, was hit while mounting air attacks on Okinawa from a position 76 miles to the east of the island. At 10.00 a.m., the carrier was preparing to launch her aircraft. Thirty planes were on the flight deck and a further forty-eight were below in the hangar deck being fuelled and armed. The *Bunker Hill* had been resupplied at sea only the day before and had taken aboard 1,873,000 gallons of fuel oil and a full supply of aviation gasoline. A 'Zero' fighter emerged from heavy cloud on the starboard side and crashed among the planes on the flight deck, causing a series of intense fires as their fuel tanks exploded. Seconds later another kamikaze broke through the clouds in a near-vertical dive and hit at the base of the island. Within minutes the ship was a raging inferno from amidships to the fantail. Damage-control parties immediately set to work, turning on sprinkler systems, breaking out hoses, closing hatches and throwing ammunition overboard, while neighbouring ships rushed to her aid. The cruiser *Wilkes-Barre* and three destroyers came alongside and directed their hoses at the fires, and Mitscher reluctantly transferred his flag to the carrier USS *Enterprise*. While the attendant ships were trying to fight the fires and rescue the wounded, *Bunker Hill*'s Commanding Officer, Capt George A. Seitz, swung the carrier to her broadside so that the flames and smoke would not be blown the length of the ship; and later, when gasoline from ruptured pipes was accumulating in the hangar deck, he ordered a sharp 70-degree turn so that the fuel could be washed overboard through openings at the side of the deck. These manoeuvres and an heroic

USS *New York* (BB-34) on Nimitz Day, 19 October 1945, (National Archives)

The USS *Enterprise* (CV-6) in October 1941. Damaged near Guadalcanal in August 1942 and in the Battle of Santa Cruz in October 1943, she was finally put out of action by kamikaze attacks in 1945. (National Archives)

fire-control effort by the crew finally brought the blaze under control, but 404 officers and men had perished, most of them asphyxiated by the thick smoke which was spread throughout the lower decks by the ship's ventilation system. The carrier was critically damaged but managed to limp to the Brooklyn Shipyard in New York, where repairs kept her out of the remainder of the war.

TASK FORCE 57

All through 'Operation Iceberg' the left flank of the Joint Expeditionary Force was covered by Task Force 57, the British Pacific Fleet, whose operations centred on the Sakishima Gunto, a group of islands between Okinawa and Formosa where a number of kamikaze airfields were located. The presence of the fleet was politically motivated. Churchill had pressed Roosevelt to accept a British naval force, a move that was bitterly opposed by Chief of Naval Operations Adm King, a confirmed anglophobe. However, Nimitz and Spruance were more accommodating and welcomed the Royal Navy force as a valuable addition to their command. The task force was centred around the carriers HMS *Indomitable*, *Victorious*, *Indefatigable* and *Illustrious*, escorted by the battleships *Howe* and *King George V* and the cruisers *Swiftsure*, *Black Prince*, *Argonaut*, *Euryalus*, and the New Zealand cruiser *Gambia* plus eleven destroyers.

The British Pacific Fleet was nominally commanded by Adm Bruce Fraser but as he outranked both Spruance and Halsey he did not fly his flag at sea, remaining instead at the task force base in Sydney, Australia. At sea the commander would be Sir Bernard Rawlings, a happy choice as he got on well with his American colleagues, something that could not be said for the commander of the four carriers, Rear-Adm Philip Vian, who was described by one member of the senior staff as 'an awkward bastard'.

British carriers were generally smaller than the US Navy's 'Essex' class fleet carriers, and embarked fewer aircraft; but they did enjoy one huge advantage over their American counterparts in having 3in-thick steel flight decks compared to the US Navy's wooden decks. As a US liaison officer aboard HMS *Indefatigable* put it, 'When a kamikaze hits a US carrier, its six months repair at Pearl – when one hits a Limey carrier, it's a case of "Sweepers, man your brooms".' Task Force 57 was also deficient in modern aircraft and relied heavily on American models. Of the 218 planes embarked at Sydney only 51 were of British manufacture, a sad reflection on the state of pre-war Fleet Air Arm aircraft construction (throughout the war the standard carrier torpedo bomber was the 'Swordfish', a biplane with a top speed of under 100mph in which the crew sat in open cockpits. It looked like something left over from the First World War). One of the biggest disappointments was the 'Seafire', a naval adaptation of the famous 'Spitfire'. It inherited the 'Spitfire's' short range and had a weak undercarriage which could not cope with the robust landings inherent in carrier operations. As a result, the bulk of TF57's operations were mounted by US 'Hellcat', 'Avenger' and 'Corsair' aircraft.

The task force's main role was to attack the airfields in the Sakishima Gunto, particularly the islands of Ishigaki and Miyako, which housed three airfields apiece, to make sure that the airfields remained out of action. The first attacks lasted for 26 days: 28 enemy aircraft were destroyed in the air and a further 34 on the ground. The enemy soon retaliated and one kamikaze hit the *Indefatigable*'s flight deck, causing a number of casualties. Further strikes on Ishigaki and Miyako were carried out in April in which the airfield runways were cratered. The task force was next deployed against targets in Formosa at the request of Adm Nimitz, after which the force withdrew to refuel. It was at this time that the carrier *Formidable* replaced the damaged *Illustrious*.

By 4 May, TF57 was back at the Sakishima Gunto, where the battleships and cruisers were detached to bombard Miyako, leaving the carriers dangerously exposed. The Japanese took advantage of the situation and launched another kamikaze attack in which the *Formidable* suffered a hit on the flight deck, denting it for 2ft, killing eight crew and wounding forty-seven. Minutes later a 'Zero' hit the *Indomitable*, though it simply bounced over the side and into the sea. During operations in May the *Victorious* was hit twice, the subsequent fires soon being brought under control, and the *Formidable* was hit again by a low-flying aircraft which ploughed through planes ranged across the flight deck. After a final round of strikes in late May the task force retired to Manus for repairs and replenishment in preparation for the invasion of the Japanese mainland, a task that never materialised.

During the whole of its time at sea Task Force 57 carried out 4,691 sorties, dropped 927 tons of bombs and fired 950 rockets. It destroyed over 100 enemy aircraft and lost 26 in combat, with a further 134 lost to kamikaze attacks, hangar fires or landing accidents. Some 41 pilots were lost and 44 ships' crew killed, with a further 83 wounded. TF57 denied the Japanese the use of many of the facilities in the Sakishima Gunto and drastically reduced the kamikaze operations from Ishigaki and Miyako – a fact that is usually overlooked in accounts of 'Operation Iceberg' – earning high praise from Adm 'Bull' Halsey.

'THESE PROCEEDINGS ARE CLOSED'

'The strength and willpower, devotion and technical resources applied by the United States to this task, joined with the death struggle of the enemy place this battle among the most intense and famous in military history. We make our salute to all your troops and their commanders engaged.'

(Winston Churchill on Okinawa)

'Operation Iceberg' was over, but the cost had been high. US forces had lost over 7,000 troops killed with a further 31,000 wounded, with the Navy losing 4,900 officers and men killed and nearly 5,000 wounded; plus 22 ships had sunk and 254 were damaged. Although Okinawa was to be the last of the 'island hopping' campaigns, the invasion of the Japanese mainland was still the next item on the agenda, and the generals and admirals viewed the prospect with trepidation. From their experiences at Peleliu, Iwo Jima and now Okinawa, they knew that the assault on Japan would be little short of a bloodbath. Every beach, town, village and field would be defended to the death by both the Army and the civilian population, and casualties on both sides would be horrendous. Estimates were for the war to continue into 1946 or even 1947.

Plans for the invasion of Japan had begun in December 1944 with 'Operation Olympic', the code-word for the assault on Kyushu, the most southerly of the mainland islands. This would be followed by 'Operation Coronet', the invasion of the main island of Honshu. 'Olympic' would be spearheaded by 500,000 men of the 6th Army under Gen Walter Kreuger, supported by the US 3rd and 5th Fleets supplemented by the British Pacific Fleet. The main invasion of Honshu would entail a landing 50 miles east of Tokyo by the US 1st and 8th Armies and three divisions of British and Commonwealth troops, with massive naval and aerial support from the US and British Navies and heavy bomber support from the Marianas in the shape of the 20th Air Force and the RAF.

Above: Nagasaki, totally destroyed on 9 August 1945. (US Army)

Left: Japanese officials arrive on USS *Missouri* to sign the articles of surrender, 2 September 1945. Minister Mamoru Shigemitsu, his deputies Ketsuo Okayoki and Toshikaya Kose, and Gen Yoshijiro Umezu, are among them. (National Archives)

In the meanwhile, the bombing campaign by the 20th Air Force B29s continued as town after town disappeared under a firestorm of incendiary bombs, civilian morale plummeted and Japan's economy was virtually ruined. Civilian casualties soon exceeded 200,000 and food prices rocketed but the government was still unwilling to bring the war to an end. Like Hitler, they blamed the people for not living up to their expectations. Within weeks of the fall of Okinawa the Japanese government underwent a change. Gen Tojo had resigned as prime minister after the loss of Saipan and was replaced by Gen Kuniaki Koiso; but he too found his position untenable and also resigned in favour of the 78-year-old Adm Kantaro Suzuki, a known moderate. The move was generally regarded as the first step towards bringing the war to an end.

President Roosevelt died on 12 April 1945 and was succeeded by Harry S. Truman. The new president knew nothing of the Manhattan Project, America's hugely expensive and highly secret programme to develop a nuclear bomb, until he was informed by Henry Stimson,

Right: Gen Douglas MacArthur signs the Japanese surrender documents, with Lt-Gen Jonathan Wainwright and Lt-Gen Arthur Percival behind him. (National Archives)

the Secretary of War. At the Potsdam Conference he was informed of the success of 'Operation Trinity', the detonation of the first atom bomb in the desert at Alamogordo in New Mexico. The consequences of exploding a nuclear device were still unknown; the New Mexico bomb had worked, but there were still scientists who believed in the possibility of an unstoppable chain reaction in the atmosphere, and the dangers of the after-effects of radiation were still a mystery. Truman was faced with a decision that would alter not only the future of the war but possibly the whole future of warfare. Should he drop the bomb, knowing that the casualties among the Japanese civilian population would be huge, or continue with plans for the invasion of the Japanese mainland and risk the loss of possibly a million or more Allied servicemen? At the Potsdam Conference Truman asked Russia to honour its promise to declare war on Japan within three months of the defeat of Germany. Stalin agreed, but Truman decided that the bomb should be dropped before the Russians intervened. He had a deep mistrust of Stalin, who was making unrealistic demands in return for his cooperation.

At 2.45 a.m. on Monday 6 August 1945, Col Paul Tibbets lifted the B29 'Super-fortress' bomber *Enola Gay* off the runway at the huge airfield on Tinian; in the

Hiroshima after the bomb. (IWM MH29427)

The aftermath of the atomic explosion at Hiroshima, 6 August 1945. (IWM SC278262)

JAPANESE CASUALTIES

The total number of Japanese and Okinawan troops killed in action is difficult to assess. The Americans' estimate was somewhere in excess of 142,000 casualties, but a more realistic figure is 66,000 killed and half of the survivors wounded. There were 7,400 prisoners, and more than 10,000 Imperial Japanese Army and Imperial Japanese Navy and 8,000 Okinawan conscripts survived the battle. More than 4,600 kamikaze crewmen died and more than 3,650 sailors on the *Yamato* were killed.

JAPANESE COMMAND STRUCTURE
HQ – 32nd Army

24th Division	Independent Machine Gun Battalions
62nd Division	66th Independent Engineer Battalion
44th Independent Mixed Brigade	Shipping Engineer Regiments
Independent Battalions, Naval Infantry	Shipping HQ
3rd and 4th Commando Units	36th Signal Regiment
27th Tank Regiment	32nd Army Field Ordnance Depot
5th Artillery Battalion	72nd Land Duty Command
100th Heavy Artillery Battalion	Field Hospital
1st Artillery Mortar Regiment	Air Force Units
Independent AA Artillery Battalions	Naval Personnel
21st AA Headquarters	Okinawan Home Guard (*Boeitai*)
MG Cannon Battalions	Volunteer Youth Groups (*Tekketsu*)

Occupation troops debark from transport ship *Bruleson*, 4 August 1945. (National Archives)

bomb bay was a 10ft-long cylinder code-named 'Little Boy'. The B29 was joined over Iwo Jima by two more 'Superfortresses' carrying photographers and observers. At 8.15 a.m. they were over the city of Hiroshima. It took 43 seconds for the bomb to fall the 31,000ft into the centre of the city. The blast, which was equivalent to 12,500 tons of TNT vaporised everything for miles around and killed 78,000 people instantly. Thousands more were to die later from their wounds or from the after-effects of radiation. A second atomic bomb, 'Fat Boy', was dropped by the B29 *Bockscar* into the centre of Nagasaki on 9 August, killing a further 24,000 people. Prime Minister Susuki advised the Emperor that the war must be brought to an end. 'The time has come to endure the unendurable', Hirohito told his war minister.

The final act of the war was played out on the decks of the battleship USS *Missouri* in Tokyo Bay. Japan's foreign minister led a nine-man delegation to stand before a mass of Allied officers headed by Gen Douglas MacArthur to sign the instruments of surrender. After the long process of signing a multitude of documents was over, MacArthur stepped to the microphone and said, 'Let us pray that peace be now restored to the world and that God will preserve it always. These proceedings are now closed.'

SELECT BIBLIOGRAPHY

Belote, James and William, *Typhoon of Steel*, Harper & Row, New York, 1970

Boyne, Walter J., *Clash of Titans: World War II at Sea*, Simon & Schuster, New York, 1995

Dunnigan, James, *Victory at Sea*, William Morrow, New York, 1995

Feifer, George, *The Battle of Okinawa*, Lyons Press, Connecticut, 2001

Foster, Simon, *Okinawa, 1945: The Final Assault on the Empire*, Arms & Armour Press, London, 1994

Hallas, James H., *The Devil's Anvil: The Assault on Peleliu*, Praeger, London, 1994

Hunt, George P., *Coral Comes High,* Harper & Brothers, 1946

Kerr, E. Bartlett, *Flames Over Tokyo*, Donald I. Fine, New York, 1991

Lane, John E., *This Here is G Company*, Brightlights Publications, 1997

Manchester, William, *Goodbye Darkness*, Little Brown, 1980

Moran, Jim, *Peleliu 1944*, Osprey, Oxford, 2002

Ross, Bill D., *Iwo Jima: Legacy of Valor*, Random House, New York, 1986

——, *Peleliu: Tragic Triumph*, Random House, New York, 1991

Rottman, Gordon, *Okinawa: The Last Battle*, Osprey, Oxford, 2002

Sledge, Eugene, *With the Old Breed at Peleliu and Okinawa*, Presidio Press, 2007

Vat, Dan van der, *The Pacific Campaign*, Simon & Schuster, New York, 1991

Waterhouse, Charles, *Marines and Others*, Sea Bag Productions, Edison, New York, 1994

Wheeler, Richard, *Iwo*, Lippincott & Cromwell, New York, 1980

Wright, Derrick, *Tarawa: A Hell of a Way to Die*, Crowood Press, Marlborough, 2002

——, *To the Far Side of Hell: The Battle for Peleliu*, Crowood Press, Marlborough, 2002

——, *The Battle for Iwo Jima*, Sutton Publishing, Stroud, 2003

INDEX